ZAHA HADID

Edited by Yoshio Futagawa
Photographed by GA photographers
Designed by GA design center

Copyright ©2014 A.D.A. EDITA Tokyo Co., Ltd.
3-12-14 Sendagaya, Shibuya-ku, Tokyo 151-0051, Japan
All rights reserved. No part of this publication may be reproduced,
stored in a retrieval system, or transmitted,
in any form or by any means, electronic, mechanical,
photocopying, recording, or otherwise,
without permission in writing from the publisher.

Copyright of photographs
©2014 GA photographers
Copyright of drawings, renderings
©2014 Zaha Hadid Architects

Printed and bound in Japan

ISBN 978-4-87140-688-8 C1052

ZAHA HADID

ザハ・ハディド

Concept of the exhibition "ZAHA HADID" (Tokyo Opera City Art Gallery, 2014)
展覧会「ザハ・ハデイド」(東京オペラシティ アートギャラリー, 2014)の会場構成コンセプト

Zaha Hadid's relationship with Japan began early in her career. The country holds an unparalleled reputation for its innovative and forward-thinking approach to technology, engineering and design, yet maintains and respects deep tradition and craftsmanship within today's society. With such duality comfortably entrenched in the national character, it is thus no surprise that Japan was among the earliest to adopt Zaha Hadid's work—an architecture that embraces the future with confidence; exploring new concepts and materiality in buildings that engage, integrate and adapt to the complexities of contemporary life patterns.

In the early 1980's Hadid designed the Tomigaya and Azabu Jyuban buildings in Tokyo and then built the Moon Soon interior in Sapporo at the end of that decade, and it is a revisiting of these projects with which the exhibition begins. Original drawings, paintings and models are accompanied by meticulously recreated furniture designed for the Moon Soon.

Alongside these formative Japanese projects, rarely exhibited early paintings by Hadid, as well as a selection of vintage models, are displayed within The Field of Towers. The forty-six small towers each represent an iteration of her practice's investigations into parametric tower design. The close proximity of works from Hadid's early years to its current research focus creates a rich visual and conceptual dialogue, inviting the viewer to grasp the contextual threads that connect more than thirty years of her projects.

Entering Gallery 2, the viewer is met with a 28-metre projection, continuing the journey through the firm's archive—a journey that has been consciously mapped via an exhibition design that is itself based on the structure of an urban master plan. Highlights of this journey are showcased within the space, comprised of a carefully curated selection of Hadid's projects both conceptual and built, and examples of her innovative furniture and design collaborations. Each architectural project exhibited displays the formal and geometric complexity with structural audacity and material authenticity engrained within its DNA.

Throughout the exhibition we also find examples of Hadid's explorations into contemporary use of the most traditional of materials such as wood and stone: including the curvilinear theatre of the Heydar Aliyev Centre hand-crafted in oak; the undulating roof of the London Aquatics Centre in ash, and the organic forms of the Mercuric Tables carved in Carrara marble.

An interactive virtual reality installation is presented in the far corner of the gallery, inviting the viewer to wear 3D glasses and experience the Galaxy Soho project in Beijing as well as the New National Stadium, Tokyo. Transitioned by this virtual flight from archive, to present, to future, the exhibition culminates in a display devoted to the forthcoming New National Stadium of Japan.

Hadid has said architecture is ultimately about well-being: every design revolves around how people will use and enjoy space. Throughout her repertoire we sense the evolution of each project as the very specific result of context, local culture, programmatic requirements and innovative engineering coming together - allowing architecture, city and landscape to seamlessly combine in both formal strategy and spatial experience. These projects define inspirational public spaces where Hadid's concepts of seamless spatial flow are made real – creating a whole new kind of civic space for the city.

These principles are strikingly evident in the design for the New National Stadium.

The exhibition outlines how the stadium's design offers maximum accessibility to sport and culture for everyone in Tokyo. Community facilities and public walkways are integrated within the design, with the civic realm of the surrounding environment extending into the building. Through models, drawings and imagery, we learn how this user-focused, highly adaptable stadium will ensure the greatest use by Japan's sporting, cultural, civic and community organizations for many generations to come.

Zaha Hadid Architects

ザハ・ハディドと日本との関係は，彼女のキャリアの初期に始まった。この国は，テクノロジー，エンジニアリング，そしてデザインに対する革新的で先進的な取り組みに関して比類のない評価を確立している一方で，今日の社会に深く根ざした伝統や職人技術を維持し，尊重している。国民性に十分に定着したこの二重性のもとに，日本がいち早くザハ・ハディドの作品を取り入れたことは驚くには当たらない。その建築は，自信を持って未来を受け入れ，複雑な現代の生活様式に関わり，融合し，適応する新しいコンセプトとマテリアルを探求するものである。

　1980年代初頭，ハディドは東京の富ヶ谷と麻布十番にビルを設計し，80年代の終わりには札幌で「ムーンスーン」の内装を手がけた。この展覧会は，これらのプロジェクトへの再訪から始まる。オリジナルの図面，ペインティング，模型とともに，「ムーンスーン」のためにデザインされた家具が細部まで正確に再現され，展示される。

　これらキャリア当初の日本でのプロジェクトに加え，これまでほとんど展示されたことのないハディドによる初期のペインティングや選りすぐりの模型がフィールド・オブ・タワーズに展示される。この46個の小さいタワーは，それぞれパラメトリックなタワー・デザインについて繰り返し行われた探求の試みを表している。ハディドの初期の作品と現在の探求の焦点とが近接していることにより，豊かな視覚的および概念的対話が生まれ，30年以上にわたって生み出されたプロジェクトを繋ぐ文脈を理解することができる。

　ギャラリー2では，鑑賞者は28メートルに及ぶプロジェクションに迎えられ，アーカイブを辿る旅を続けることになる。それは，都市計画の構造に基づいた展示デザインを通して，意識的にマッピングされた旅である。この旅のハイライトは，入念に選ばれたビルト/アンビルトのプロジェクトと，画期的な家具やデザインのコラボレーション作品の実例の展示である。展示されたそれぞれの建築プロジェクトは，構造の大胆さとマテリアルの信頼性がそのDNAに組み込まれた，形態及びジオメトリの複雑性を示している。

　展示全体を通して，木や石といった最も伝統的なマテリアルを現代的に利用した試みを見ることができる。「ヘイダル・アリエフ・センター」のハンドメイドのオーク材でつくられた曲線なシアター，アッシュ材が用いられた「ロンドン・アクアティクス・センター」の波打つ屋根，カラーラ大理石を彫ってつくられた「マーキュリック・テーブル」の有機的な形態などである。

　ギャラリーの隅にはヴァーチャル・リアリティのインスタレーションがあり，3Dグラスを着けて北京の「ギャラクシーSOHO」や東京の「新国立競技場」をインタラクティブに体験することができる。アーカイブから現在，未来へとヴァーチャルに移行するこの展覧会は，「新国立競技場」の展示でクライマックスに達する。

　ハディドは，建築は結局のところは人間の幸福を目的としており，それぞれのデザインは，人々がいかに空間を使い楽しむかを中心に考えられていると述べている。彼女の作品群の全体を通して，それぞれのプロジェクトが，コンテクスト，ローカルな文化，プログラムの要件，革新的な技術が一体となった固有の結果として生まれたことを理解することができる。これにより，建築，都市，ランドスケープが，形態と空間体験の両面において連続的に結びつくことが可能になる。これらのプロジェクトでは，シームレスで流動的な空間というハディドのコンセプトが具現化した創造的なパブリック・スペースが現れ，都市の人々のための全く新しい空間を生み出している。

　これらの哲学は，「新国立競技場」のデザインに顕著に現れている。

　展覧会では，この競技場のデザインがあらゆる人々にいかにスポーツと文化への最大限のアクセスを提供するかが示される。公共設備と歩道がデザインに組み込まれ，周辺の公共空間が建物の中に引き込まれる。模型，図面，映像を通して，ユーザーに焦点を合わせ，高度に柔軟性のあるこの競技場が，確実に，日本のスポーツ，文化，市民，コミュニティの各種団体によって，今後何世代にもわたり，最大限に活用されるものであることがわかるだろう。

ザハ・ハディド・アーキテクツ

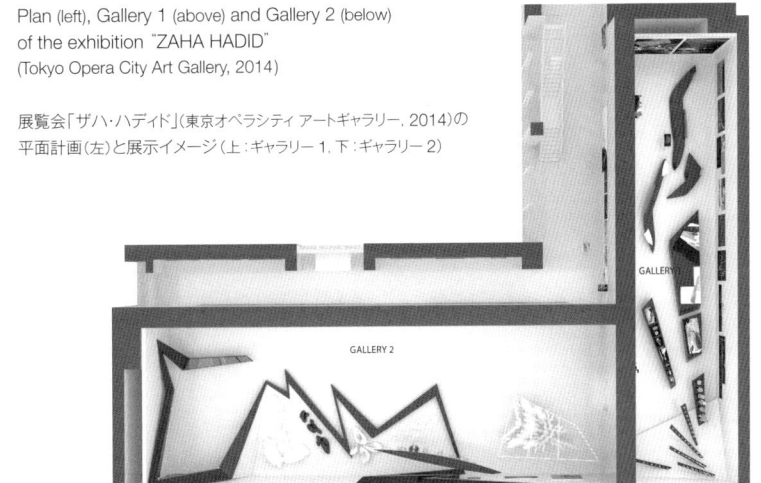

Plan (left), Gallery 1 (above) and Gallery 2 (below) of the exhibition "ZAHA HADID" (Tokyo Opera City Art Gallery, 2014)

展覧会「ザハ・ハディド」(東京オペラシティ アートギャラリー，2014)の平面計画(左)と展示イメージ(上：ギャラリー1，下：ギャラリー2)

photo by Brigitte Lacombe

ZAHA HADID

Born in Baghdad, Iraq in 1950.
She attended American University of Beirut (Bachelor of Mathematics) in 1971 and studied architecture at Architectural Association (AA) School, London from 1972 to 1977. She was awarded Diploma Prize in 1977.
She became a partner of OMA/Office for Metropolitan Architecture in 1977 and taught at AA with OMA collaborators Rem Koolhaas and Elia Zenghelis, and later led her own studio at AA until 1987.
She has held Kenzo Tange Chair at Graduate School of Design, Harvard University; Sullivan Chair at University of Illinois, School of Architecture, Chicago; and guest professorships at Hochschule für Bildende Künste in Hamburg and Masters Studio at Columbia University, New York. She was also Eero Saarinen Visiting Professor of Architectural Design at Yale University, New Haven, Connecticut. Currently she is Professor at University of Applied Arts in Vienna, Austria.
She established private practice in London in 1979. She received Pritzker Architecture Prize in 2004, Praemium Imperiale from the Japan Art Association in 2009. She was made a Dame Commander of the Order of the British Empire by Queen Elizabeth in 2012.
She is currently principal of Zaha Hadid Architects, London.

ザハ・ハディド

1950年、イラク・バグダッド生まれ。
1971年、ベイルート・アメリカン大学で数学学士取得後、1972年から77年まで、英国建築協会附属建築学校(AAスクール)で建築を学び、主席で卒業。
卒業後、建築設計事務所OMAの所員として、レム・コールハースとエリア・ゼンゲリスと共にAAスクールで教鞭を取り、その後1987年まで自身のスタジオを持つ。ハーバード大学デザイン大学院(丹下健三記念講座)、イリノイ大学シカゴ建築学校(サリバン記念講座)では教授を、ハンブルク造形美術大学、コロンビア大学大学院(ニューヨーク)、イェール大学(コネチカット州ニューヘイブン)ではエーロ・サーリネン客員教授を務めた。現在、ウィーン応用芸術大学(オーストリア)教授。
1979年、ロンドンにて設計事務所を設立。2004年にプリツカー建築賞、2009年に高松宮殿下世界文化賞をそれぞれ女性として初めて受賞。2012年にはエリザベスⅡ世より、大英帝国勲章のデイム・コマンダーの称号を授与。現在、ザハ・ハディド・アーキテクツ(ロンドン)所長。

012 **INTERVIEW 1995**
1995 | Zaha Hadid
インタヴュー 1995　ザハ・ハディド

133 **INTERVIEW 2007**
2007 | Zaha Hadid
インタヴュー 2007　ザハ・ハディド

220 **THE INSTRUMENTALITY OF APPEARANCES IN THE PURSUIT OF A LEGIBLE URBAN ORDER**
2014 | Patrik Schumacher
判読可能な都市秩序の追求手段としての外観　パトリック・シューマッハ

234 **PROJECT DATA**
作品データ

022 **THE PEAK**
1982-83 | Hong Kong, China | Proposal for leisure club
ザ・ピーク　中国, 香港

034 **THE WORLD (89 DEGREES)**
1983 | Painting
ザ・ワールド (89°)

036 **GRAND BUILDINGS, TRAFALGAR SQUARE**
1985 | London, U.K. | Mixed-use development
トラファルガー広場計画　イギリス, ロンドン

040 **TOMIGAYA BUILDING**
1986 | Tokyo, Japan | Office building
富ヶ谷のビル　東京

044 **AZABU JYUBAN BUILDING**
1987 | Tokyo, Japan | Mixed-use office building
麻布十番のビル　東京

048 **BERLIN 2000**
1988 | Berlin, Germany | Painting
ベルリン 2000　ドイツ, ベルリン

050 **VICTORIA CITY AERIAL**
1988 | Berlin, Germany | Mixed-use development
ヴィクトリア・シティ・エアリアル　ドイツ, ベルリン

052 **HAFENSTRASSE OFFICE & RESIDENTIAL DEVELOPMENT**
1989 | Hamburg, Germany | Mixed-use development
ハーフェン通りのオフィス&住宅開発計画　ドイツ, ハンブルク

054 **KMR, ART AND MEDIA PARK**
1989-93 | Dusseldorf, Germany | Site development
KMR アート&メディア・パーク　ドイツ, デュッセルドルフ

058 **MOON SOON**
1989-90 | Sapporo, Japan | Restaurant and bar interior design
ムーンスーン　北海道札幌市

068 **VITRA FIRE STATION**
1991-93 | Weil am Rhein, Germany | Private firestation
ヴィトラ社消防所　ドイツ, ヴァイル・アム・ライン

078 **CARDIFF BAY OPERA HOUSE**
1994-96 | Cardiff, Wales, U.K. | Proposal for opera house
カーディフベイ・オペラハウス　イギリス, ウェールズ, カーディフ

082	**ROSENTHAL CENTER FOR CONTEMPORARY ART** *1997-2003	Cincinnati, Ohio, U.S.A.	Museum* ローゼンタール現代美術センター　アメリカ, オハイオ州, シンシナティ	194	**CREVASSE VASE & NICHE** *2005/2011, 2010	Alessi	Vase, centrepiece* クレヴァス・ベース&ニッチ
094	**MAXXI: NATIONAL MUSEUM OF XXI CENTURY ARTS** *1998-2009	Rome, Italy	Museum* MAXXI 国立21世紀美術館　イタリア, ローマ	196	**WMF CUTLERY** *2007	WMF	Cutlery* WMFカトラリー
110	**PHAENO SCIENCE CENTER** *2000-05	Wolfsburg, Germany	Mixed-use center for science* フェーノ科学センター　ドイツ, ヴォルフスブルク	198	**MELISSA SHOES** *2008	Melissa	Shoes* メリッサ・シューズ
122	**LONDON AQUATICS CENTRE** *2005-11/2014	London, U.K.	Aquatics centre* ロンドン・アクアティクス・センター　イギリス, ロンドン	200	**ORCHIS** *2008	Seating sculpture* オルキス
142	**HEYDAR ALIYEV CENTER** *2007-12	Baku, Azerbaijan	Mixed-use cultural center* ヘイダル・アリエフ・センター　アゼルバイジャン, バクー	202	**GLACE COLLECTION** *2009	Atelier Swarovski	Jewellery* グレース・コレクション
150	**MOBILE ART - CHANEL CONTEMPORARY ART CONTAINER** *2007-14	Hong Kong, China / Tokyo, Japan / New York, U.S.A. / Paris, France* *Traveling exhibition pavilion designed for CHANEL* モバイル・アート – シャネル・コンテンポラリーアート・コンテナ 中国, 香港/東京/アメリカ, ニューヨーク/フランス, パリ	204	**LACOSTE SHOES** *2009	Lacoste, Pentland	Shoes* ラコステ・シューズ
158	**DONGDAEMUN DESIGN PARK** *2007-14	Seoul, Korea	Mixed-use design centre* 東大門デザイン・パーク　韓国, ソウル	206	**LIQUID GLACIAL** *2012	David Gill Galleries	Dining & coffee table* リキッド・グレイシャル
168	**JOCKEY CLUB INNOVATION TOWER, HONG KONG POLYTECHNIC UNIVERSITY** *2007-13	Hong Kong, China	School of design development* 香港工科大学ジョッキー・クラブ・イノヴェーション・タワー　中国, 香港	208	**ARIA & AVIA LAMPS** *2013	Slamp	Lighting* アリア&アヴィア・ランプ
174	**THE SERPENTINE SACKLER GALLERY** *2009-13	West Carriage Drive, Kensington Gardens, London, U.K.	Art gallery and restaurant* サーペンタイン・サックラー・ギャラリー　イギリス, ロンドン, ケンジントン・ガーデンズ	210	**ZEPHYR SOFA** *2013	Seating* ゼファ・ソファ
178	**BEIJING CBD CORE AREA** *2010-	Beijing, China	Masterplan and tower design* 北京中央商業地区コア・エリア　中国, 北京	212	**MERCURIC TABLE COLLECTION** *2013	Citco	Set of tables* マーキュリック・テーブル・コレクション
184	**NEW NATIONAL STADIUM OF JAPAN** *2012-19	Tokyo, Japan	Athletics stadium* 新国立競技場　東京	214	**SKEIN COLLECTION** *2013	Caspita	Jewellery* スケイン・コレクション
		216	**NOVA SHOES** *2013	United Nude	Shoes* ノヴァ・シューズ
		218	**DESIGN COLLECTION** *2014	Zaha Hadid Design	Homewares* デザイン・コレクション

INTERVIEW 1995
ZAHA HADID

インタヴュー1995
ザハ・ハディド

Yoshio Futagawa First, tell me about your childhood.
Zaha Hadid I was born and brought up in Baghdad. Mine was a very interesting family: very liberal, very open minded. I was very independent at a very young age and my parents always encouraged me to do and pursue whatever I wanted. Never was there in my upbringing a feeling that women are different than men. My family was always interested in education. There was a lot of pressure on me and my two brothers to excel. My two brothers also went to school in England. Education was seen as a passport to a different way of life. There was a belief that education and knowledge could enable you to do things, and without it you are imprisoned and part of the underclass.

Futagawa What did your parents do?
Hadid My father was an economist but he was also very involved in politics. He was involved with the Iraqi Democratic Party and he was, before the revolution, part of the opposition because they wanted to make sure that Iraq became independent. He was also heavily involved in industry because he felt that the only way a country could become totally independent was to become industrialized. He was involved with many companies that were partly shared by the government in Iraq. He was an important writer for politics and a well known politician. He was very involved with OPEC and oil issues and nationalization of oil and becoming independent as an oil manufacturing country. He was very independent in his achievements and life. My father was educated in England, he went to the London School of Economics and he came back with a very optimistic view of how to change the situation in Iraq, to make it more productive, to change the fugitive laws, and agriculture laws and everything.

Futagawa Could we say that your family was very westernized for a family in Iraq?
Hadid Yes, westernized but it also really believed in Iraq. My father really was instrumental in changing views and becoming independent, and he fought for that all his life. I came from that kind of background, a background that believes in internationalism and an open view of the world——countries communicating with other countries——but also believing in Iraq's independence and that it should not become part of the colonial powers. The root of that independence would be free thinking and also independence in the industries so you don't have to import everything. Therefore there was a plan to start industries which were not heavy industries but lighter industries which were to do with the extraction of oil or hygienic things. He was also involved in housing projects. I think he was a very interesting person. So I come from a tradition of modernism, a tradition of looking forward and trying to do things in a very progressive way.

Futagawa You mentioned the importance of education in your family. Please elaborate on what your early education was like?
Hadid I went to a nun's school but it was also very progressive. It had very good teachers. We had a fantastic head mistress who was a nun but very rambunctious and wanted the girls to do well in school. She would get very good professors in the sciences and the arts. It coincided well with my parent's idea of education. It was a reli-

二川由夫　どのような子供時代を送られたのですか。
ザハ・ハディド　バグダッドで生まれ，育ちました。とても楽しい一家で，非常にリベラルで，心の広い人たちでした。私は小さいころから独立心が強く，両親は，自分のやりたいと思うことは何であろうと追求していくように，常に励ましてくれました。女性は男性と違っているといった雰囲気はまったくありませんでしたし，非常に教育熱心で，私と二人の兄弟には人より抜きんでなければならないという大きなプレッシャーがありました。二人とも私同様，イギリスの学校に進んだのです。教育は，よりよい生活へのパスポートであり，教育と知識無しには，何事も為せず，狭い世界に閉じこめられ下層階級に属してしまうというのが信念になっていました。
二川　ご両親は何をされていたのですか。
ハディド　父はエコノミストでしたが，政治にも深く関わっていました。イラク民主党と関係があり，革命の前には革命に反対していました。というのはイラクの独立を確実なものにしたかったからです。また父は，一国が真に独立した存在となる唯一の方法は工業化にあると考えていたため，産業界にも深く関わっていました。半官半民の多くの会社に関係し，政治に関する重要なライターであり有名な政治家でした。OPECや石油問題，石油の国有化，石油産出国として独立するといったことにも深く関わっていたのです。彼は仕事においても家庭においても非常に自由な独立人でした。父は英国で教育を受け，ロンドン大学経済学部で学び，イラクの将来についてとても楽観的なヴィジョンを抱いて帰国しました。生産性を高め，亡命法，農業法など，すべてを変革するのだという。
二川　イラクでは非常に西欧的なご家庭だったのですね。
ハディド　ええ，西欧的でしたが，イラクを深く信じてもいました。父はこの国のものの見方を変え，その独立に役立とうとしていました。一生がそのための戦いでした。私はこうした背景のなかで育ったのです。インターナショナリズムを信じ，他の国々と世界的に交流する開かれた視野をもつ一方で，植民地勢力の一部に入るべきではないという，イラクの自主独立に対する信念も併せもつ。そうした独立の根は自由な考え方をもつことと共に，産業においても独立性をもつことにあります。そうすればすべてを輸入する必要はないわけですから。このために，重工業ではなく石油からの抽出物や衛生品などに関わる軽工業をスタートさせるという計画もその一部に入っていましたし，集合住宅をつくる計画にも関係していました。彼は非常に興味深い人間だったと思います。つまり私は，モダニズムの，先を見つめ，非常に進歩的な方法で物事をやりとげようとする伝統を引き継いでいるのです。
二川　ご家庭で受けた教育が重要だったわけですね。小さい頃受けた教育がどんなものであったか，もう少し詳しく聞かせて下さい。
ハディド　私が行ったのは修道院附属の学校で，非常に進歩的でもありました。先生たちが素晴らしかった。校長は修道尼だったのですが，ファンタスティックで勇ましい人で，女生徒たちが良い成績をとることを望んでいました。特に科学と芸術は非常に優秀な先生を集めていました。それは両親の教育に対する考え方と一致していました。キリスト教の学校でしたが，私はクリスチャンではありません。イスラム教徒ですからキリスト教的な科目は受けませんでした。私はそれには距離をおいていました。
　学校には，ユダヤ，イスラム，キリスト教の少女たちがいましたから，なかなか面白かったです。イスラム教徒としての伝統的な教育を受けなかったのはこのためです。アラブ世界ではイスラム文化とアラブ文化は同じものです。それは文化的状況であって宗教的状況ではないので

Zaha Hadid (interview for GA Architect 5 in 1985)
ザハ・ハディド(『GA Architect 5』の取材当時,1985年)

gious school but I was not a Christian; I am a Muslim so the whole Christianity issue didn't apply to me. I was at a distance from it.

The school was interesting because it had Jewish girls, Muslim girls and also Christian girls. That's the reason I never had a traditional education as a Muslim. In the Arab world, Islamic culture and Arab culture are the same. It's a cultural situation, not a religious situation. Many people there believe in the code of Islam which is the same code as the Arab world in a way. They are very much related, but not in a myopic way.

Futagawa Why did you study mathematics?

Hadid Well, I always wanted to become an architect, since I was eleven years old. My parents were involved with an architect who was a friend of the family and, doing a house for my aunt and he always came with a model of the house.

My father and mother also took me to exhibitions of architecture and my parents were both interested in design and architecture. So I remember wanting to become an architect from a very young age but I was also very good at maths and was always intrigued by the field of modern mathematics and the connection between philosophy, maths and physics. This became a short diversion for me.

Futagawa How about art?

Hadid That always went with it. Art and maths. But I didn't really formally do art. I was always leaning more towards the sciences than the arts.

Futagawa Did you have a particular specialty in mathematics?

Hadid No, not really. Applied maths, physics and logic. I was going to go to University in Switzerland but I changed my mind. I realized I must go on to architecture because that's what I really wanted to do and I came to London and the AA School.

Futagawa Why did you choose the AA? And how was the AA at the time?

Hadid When I first came here I went to another school of design and there I met a professor who was teaching in the Centre Polytechnic and he asked me what I wanted to do and I said architecture. He said that, if that was the case, I should apply quite soon and the best school to do that is the AA. I had heard of the AA from before, and so I went.

す。そこに住む多くの人は,ある意味でアラブ世界の慣例と同じイスラムの慣例を信じています。それらは非常に深く関わっていますが,近視眼的なものではありません。

二川 後年,何故,数学を専攻されたのですか。

ハディド 本当は,11歳のころから,ずっと建築家になりたいと思っていたのです。家族ぐるみで親しく付き合っていた建築家がいて,彼は叔母の家を設計していたのですが,その家の模型をもってよく家に来ていました。

父も母も建築の展覧会へよく私を連れていきましたし,二人ともデザインや建築が好きだったのです。それで,とても小さいころから建築家になりたいと思っていたのは覚えています。しかし,数学もよくできたので,近代数学の分野,そして,哲学,数学,物理学との関連性に常に心を惹かれていました。これは,私にとって短い寄り道だったのです。

二川 芸術についてはどうですか。

ハディド アートと数学は常に身近なものとしてありました。でも,アートを正式に学んだことはありません。常に芸術よりも科学の方に傾いていました。

二川 数学の分野で特別に専門の領域をお持ちでしたか。

ハディド いいえ。応用数学,物理学,論理学を勉強していました。そしてスイスの大学に進もうとしていたのですが,気持ちを変えたのです。建築に進むべきだと気づいたわけです。それが本当にやりたいことだったからですが。そうしてロンドンのAAスクールへ入りました。

二川 なぜAAを選ばれたのですか? そして当時のAAはどんな様子だったのでしょう。

ハディド 最初,ロンドンに来たときは別のデザイン学校に通っていたのですが,そこでポリテクニックの教授をしていた先生に会いました。何をやりたいのかと聞かれて,建築だと答えたのです。彼は,すぐに願書を出すべきで,一番良い学校はAAだと言いました。前からAAのことは聞いていましたし,それでAAへ行くことになったのです。

私が入ったとき,AAはとても混沌としていました。70年代のデザインから社会学や他の方向へとシフトしている時期でした。AAの面白いところは,混沌のなかにあっても,常に方向づけてくれる人がいるのだけれど,そういう人を自分で見つけなければならないし,どのようにやっていくか自己教育しなければならないという点です。それはとてもよい経験でした。キャリアのごく始めの時期から焦点をきちんと定めなければならなかったわけですから。そして焦点が定まらなければ,何がやりたいのかも判らないでしょう。とても面白い時期でした。ちょうどアルヴィン・ボヤルスキーが1年前に就任したところで,教育システムは実に新鮮で,ほとんどがぶっつけ本番の実験といってもいいものでした。この学校の歴史のなかでも非常にエキサイティングな時代です。そんな時期に居合わせて幸運だったと思います。

学校でのこのような変化はとても重要です。というのは,状況が新鮮であるという単なる事実が,そうでなければしなかったようなことを人にさせるからです。また,人々が政治的な自説を固持するという時代でもありましたので,活発な論争が行われていました。とても素晴らしい人たちがいました。時に迷ったとしても,それさえもよいことでした。真剣に集中しなければならないと気づかせてくれますし,自分の道を選択する時間を与えてくれますから。自身の運命に対し指揮をとらねばならないのです。

二川 自分の道をどのように選択したのでしょうか。

ハディド 私は,様々に個性の際立った人たちの中にいました。3年の

When I joined the AA it was very chaotic. It was a period when there was a shift from the design of the seventies to sociology and other things. What was interesting about the AA was that amongst the chaos there were always people who could direct you but you had to find these people and you had to teach yourself how to do things. That was a very good experience because very early on in your career you had to be quite focused because if you weren't focused you would not know what you wanted. It was a very interesting period because Alvin Boyarsky had just joined the AA a year before and the system of education was quite fresh, almost a first hand experiment. It was a very exciting moment in the school's life. I feel very lucky that I was there at that time.

I think change in a school is very important, because by the mere fact that conditions are fresh it makes people do things they otherwise wouldn't do. It was also a time when people were very politically opinionated and there were lots of conversations. There were very good people. You might get lost at times but even that was good because you'd realize that you really had to concentrate and give yourself time to choose your path. You had to be in command of your own destiny.

Futagawa How did you choose your path?

Hadid I was with many different people. In my third year I was with Léon Krier who I still like a lot but who I disagree with completely. In my fourth year, by elimination, I met Elia Zenghelis and I thought he was one of the very few people on my juries who understood what I was trying to do. In my fourth year I tried his studio, and a few months after the year started there was a tremendous affinity between Rem Koolhaas, Elia and myself. I was there with them for two years.

Futagawa Did your designs begin to change?

Hadid No. But I had sometimes been unhappy with what the school was able to offer me. I thought there must be another way of doing things, and it was possible to do something different with Elia and Rem, because they were not dogmatic and they wanted people to test ideas without knowing where those ideas might lead. Well, they might have known but they did not tell us. That was very important; it was a journey of discovery for all of us. That's what made the bond between the students and them very strong.

When I finished I went on to work with Elia and Rem for about three years and then went on my own for about seven years.

Futagawa Tell me more about your involvement with OMA.

Hadid Well, in my fourth year I did not know whether or not anything I was doing was in any way good. At the end of my fourth year they told me they thought I was among the very few students who understood what they were trying to do. That established a very strong link between me and them. When I finished I became a partner but for only one year. Not because I didn't get along with them, but because I felt that I had to be independent. In the beginning I thought I would only be independent for a short period of time because we thought we would always work together but it didn't work out.

Futagawa It was only three of you at the time?

ときは，レオン・クリエのスタジオにいました。彼のことは今でもとても尊敬していますが，完全に意見が合うわけではありません。4年では，エリア・ゼンゲリスに出会いました。彼は，ジュリーのなかで，私がやろうとしていることが何であるか理解してくれた数少ない一人だと思います。4年になると彼のスタジオに入りました。その学年が始まった数カ月後には，レム・コールハースとエリアと私の間にはびっくりするほどの親近感が生まれていました。私はそのスタジオに2年間いることになります。

二川 あなたのデザインは変わり始めましたか？

ハディド いいえ。学校が私に与えてくれるものにいつも満足していたわけではなかったのです。別のやり方があるはずだと考えていました。そして，エリアとレムと一緒なら何か違うことをやれそうでした。彼らは教条的ではなかったし，どこに導いていくのかを知ることなしに，そのアイディアを試すことを人に望んでいたからです。知っていたのかもしれませんが，私たちには言いませんでした。それはとても重要なことでした。つまり私たち皆にとって，発見の旅だったからです。それこそが私たち学生と彼らを非常に強くつなぐものでした。

学校を卒業した後，私はエリアとレムと一緒に3年ほど仕事をしました。それから，自分で仕事を始めて7年ほどになります。

二川 OMAでの仕事についてもう少し詳しく聞かせて下さい。

ハディド 4年になって，自分のしていることが良いのかどうか判らなくなりました。学年末に，彼らは，私が，彼らのやろうとしていることを理解しているひと握りの生徒の一人だと言いました。それは私と彼らに非常に強い繋がりをつくりました。卒業すると，彼らのパートナーとなりましたが，1年だけでした。彼らとうまくいかなかったからではなく，私は独立すべきだと感じたからです。初めは，短い時間だけ自由であればよいと考えていました。というのは私たちはいつも一緒に仕事するものと考えていましたから。しかしそれはうまくいきませんでした。

二川 当時は3人だけだったのですか。

ハディド そうです。何故なら，私は彼らと比べて経験の差がありすぎたのです。私には自分自身を見つける方法が必要でした。彼らは今でも非常に親しい友達です。私にとってそれはとても大切な協力関係であり友情でした。結局，私たちが一緒にやったのはハーグの「オランダ国会議事堂計画」(1979年)だけでした。

二川 では，OMA以外，どの事務所でも仕事されていないわけですね。

ハディド していません。学生のとき夏休みに働いたことはありますが，それ以来ありません。振り返ってみると，これが良かったのか悪かったのか確信がもてませんが，良いことといえば，他の人と仕事をすると，自分の見方に焦点があてられることです。一方，自分だけでいるということは，自由にしてくれますし，物事を違った風に追求していくようにさせてくれます。それはオフィスで働いているときには得られないことです。

二川 そうした経験をしそこなったと感じませんでしたか。

ハディド いいえ。私には合っていなかった方法だと思っていますから。でも他の人にとっては正しい方法かもしれませんね。

二川 香港「ザ・ピーク」(1983年，p.022〜)のコンペ前のことについてお聞きしたいのですが。

ハディド 当時，私はオフィスをもっていませんでした。私は教職に就いていて，傍らでコンペの準備をしていました。自分の家で，学生に手伝ってもらいながら仕事をしていました。「ピーク」の前には私の兄弟の住宅を設計していました。実施図面も何もかもすべて私たちで描いたの

Hadid Yes. It didn't work out because I felt I was at a different point than they were in our careers and I needed a way of finding myself. For me, it was a very important collaboration and friendship, and we remain very close friends, but we had to go on in different ways. So we only did the Dutch Parliament building in the Hague (1979) together.

Futagawa Is OMA the only partnership you've been involved with?

Hadid I worked for people in the summers when I was a student, but not after that. Looking back I'm not sure if it was a good thing or a bad thing. It's good in that sometimes when you work with people it focuses your view. On the other hand, being on your own frees you and lets you pursue things differently. The trade off is that you don't get the experience of working in an office.

Futagawa Didn't you feel that you missed that experience?

Hadid No. For me I think it would have been the wrong thing to do. But for other people it might be the right thing to do.

Futagawa Tell me about yourself before the Hong Kong Peak (1983, p.022-) competition.

Hadid I didn't have an office. I was teaching and doing competitions, working out of my house with students helping me. I was doing a house for my brother before the Peak and that was interesting because we had to do all the working drawings and everything.

Futagawa Does it still exist?

Hadid No. Actually he never did it. It came close but he got cold feet. I'm sure he regrets it now. But I learned the lesson that you never do things for family.

Then we did the Peak and it was only after the Peak that I opened my own office. Before that I always worked out of my house, which was fine. An office is a tremendous burden. The minute you open an office your life changes; it's a completely different ball game.

My office is really more of a studio which I think is important. I have always thought the problem with most practices is that there is almost no connection between practice and ideas like there is in school, and I really wanted a studio where you could test ideas. That's what my office is about. Of course, to strike the right balance between experimentation and practice is always very difficult. You need funding for it and most clients don't want to pay for that sort of thing although they might benefit from it. For me it's an important and instrumental part of architecture.

It's been very interesting but very difficult. We decided to do everything differently. We decided to draw the projects differently, to explain them differently.

Futagawa Do you feel that somehow people misunderstood your intentions?

Hadid I think people can't deal with things which they are not used to, and it takes a long time for people to understand. I had an interesting experience the other day, at a lecture in Dresden. A lot of people were there who had seen me lecture three years ago and they said my work had become clearer or that they understood better. When I first showed my work they couldn't understand it, because first of all they could understand that my drawings are not

で，とても面白かったです。

二川　それはまだあるのですか。

ハディド　いいえ。実際には彼は建てなかったんです。建てる寸前まではいったのですが，彼はこわくなったんでしょうね。今は残念がっているでしょうけれど。でも，家族のために何かをしては決してならないという教訓を得ました。

それから，「ピーク」の設計をして，事務所を開いたのはその後です。それまでは，いつも自宅で仕事をしていたけれど，不都合はありませんでした。オフィスというのは驚くほどの重荷です。オフィスを開いた途端に，生活は変わります。それはまったく違うゲームです。

私のオフィスはスタジオのようなものです。そのことが重要だと思っていましたから。多くの事務所の問題は，学校で体験したような，実務とアイディアの間の繋がりがほとんど無いということだといつも考えていました。アイディアをテストできるスタジオが本当に欲しかったのです。それが私の今のオフィスです。もちろん，実験と実務とのバランスをとることは常に困難なことです。実験には資金が必要ですし，大半のクライアントは，その恩恵を受けることになるかもしれないのに，そうしたことには支払いたがりません。私にとって実験は大切で，建築の手段となる部分なのです。

とても面白くとても難しいものです。私たちはデザインをすべて変えると決めていました。プロジェクトの一つひとつに違う図面を描き，すべて異なる表現をとろうと決めたのです。

二川　人があなたの意図を何か誤解していると感じることがありますか。

ハディド　人は慣れていないことはどうしていいか判らないものです。それを理解するまでには長い時間がかかります。ドレスデンで講義をしたとき面白いことがありました。そこにいた多くの人がその3年前の私の講義に来ていたのですが，彼らは，私の作品が前より明解になった，前より理解できたと言うのです。最初に私の作品を見せたとき，彼らは理解できませんでした。というのは，何よりもまず，私のドローイングはイラストレーションではないことが理解できなかったからです。私のドローイングは建物ではありません。建物についてのドローイングなのです。最終的に生まれてくるものについてのイラストではないのです。テキストのようにそれを見る必要があります。ドローイングというものは，アイディアを探索するための道具であることを誤解し，単なるイラストレーションだと考えたのだと思います。私にとっては，それは大切な道具です。何が正しいか誤りか見ることのできる唯一の方法なのです。

二川　現在，設計中のものや着工を待っているものなど，たくさんのプロジェクトをお持ちですね。最近は，いわゆる普通のドローイングも描かねばならなくなっていると思います。例えば「ヴィトラ社消防所」(1993年，p.068〜)ですが，ぼくにはとても印象的でした。というのは，あなたの建物は，ドローイングの質を維持しながら，非常に現実的な局面も備えています。香港「ピーク」の時は，あなたがこうした解決をなさるとは考えてもいませんでした。

ハディド　そうですね，自分では解決していましたが，人々はそれを理解しなかったと思います。第一に，モダニズムの伝統のなかではまったく抽象的な建物を建てることができるということを，人々は理解しなかったのだと思います。そのドローイングを理解できなかったし，そのプロジェクトも理解できなかったのです。「ヴィトラ」のパースを見ると，写真とそっくりですが，人々が，このパースが実現されたことを理解したのはすべてが

Office of Zaha Hadid Architects (in 1995)　ザハ・ハディド事務所（1995年当時）

illustrations. My drawings are not the building. They are drawings about the building. They are not illustrations of a final product. You have to look at it like a text. I think they misunderstood that the drawing was really a tool to explore ideas and not simply an illustration. For me they are important tools because they are the only way I can see whether something is right or wrong.

Futagawa　Now you have many projects that have been or will be constructed and you have to have more conventional drawings as well. Take Vitra Fire Station (1993, p.068-) for example. I was impressed because the building maintains the quality of the conceptual drawings but it also has a very practical aspect. At the time of the Hong Kong Peak I don't think you had resolved such solutions.

Hadid　Well, I had but I think people didn't understand it. I think that first, people didn't understand that in the tradition of modernity one could build a building that was quite abstract. People couldn't understand the drawings, and they couldn't understand the project. If you look at the perspective drawings of Vitra, they are very similar to the photographs but it was only afterwards that people could see that this could be achieved. When we talked about movement and energy and all of that, people wondered how that would translate into a building because obviously a building isn't going to actually move. With Vitra it was possible to achieve this quality of lightness and the building almost seems to float. It isn't heavy and there is also the contrast of solid and light.

People also didn't understand my use of color; they thought that the colors in the paintings would be the colors of the building. Sometimes it is, sometimes it isn't. The paintings show that depending on the time of day there could be red, but the building isn't necessarily painted red. So, although there was a very strong link with the renderings, it was misunderstood.

There is also this whole idea of projection. The projection of the drawing became very important; it became the basis of the whole project. The project became a projected space.

Then, at one point in time, there was an interest in shifting from planes to the idea of volumes and what this meant to the quality of the space. It doesn't have to be a big space, it's just the quality of a space that matters.

終わった後でした。動きとエネルギーをめぐって私たちが話していたとき，彼らはそれらをどのように建物へと翻訳していくのか不思議がっていました。実際には動かないのがあたりまえですから。「ヴィトラ」では，この軽さを実現でき，建物はほとんど浮かんでいるように見えます。重くなく，ソリッドな部分と軽い部分とのコントラストがあります。

私の色彩の使い方についても誤解がありました。ペインティングに使った色彩がすなわち建物の色だと思われたのです。時にそうであり，時にそうではありません。ペインティングは，一日のある時には，赤くなるはずだということを示していて，建物を必ずしも赤く塗ることではありません。つまり，レンダリングと強い繋がりがあるのです。

それから，投影という考え方があります。ドローイングの投影は非常に重要なものです。それはプロジェクト全体の基盤を構成しています。プロジェクトは投影された空間になるのです。

次に，ある時点で，平面からヴォリュームのアイディアへとシフトすることへの関心が浮かび上がります。それが意味するのは空間の質です。空間の大きさではなく，その質が問題です。

二川　初期のころのスキームは，もっぱら平面的なものでした。最近の建築はずっとヴォリューム感のあるものになっています。水平方向に重なる層の代わりに垂直の面を挿入し，アイディアを安定させています。「ヴィトラ」はこの意味での最初の作品ですね。

ハディド　1988年あるいは89年から，今までの時期は非常に重要です。初期のプロジェクトはまだ非常にフラットなものですが，ヴォリュームについても考え始めています——平面の位置やそれらをどのようにヴォリュームのなかへと投影させるかとか。「ヴィトラ」や「KMRアート＆メディア・パーク」(1993年，p.054~)につながる，この時期の私の作品を全部見れば，平面のレイヤーとは反対にヴォリュームのレイヤーへと進んでいることが判るはずです。これは重要な変貌だと思います。なぜなら，それはより空間に関わっており，どのように空間を重ねていくかということだからです。私にとっても，非常にエキサイティングな仕事の時期でした。

二川　そうですね。初期の作品では，各平面のグラフィックなアーティキュレーションは，必ずしもヴォリューム感があるものではないですね。しかし，「ヴィトラ」ではすべてのヴォリュームが素晴らしく美しい空間性を備えています。

ハディド　「ヴィトラ」では，細かく気を配りました。シンプルなものになるはずでしたから，非常に注意を払ったのです——それは驚くほどの正確さを要求しました。日本でのプロジェクト，「麻布十番のビル」(1987年，p.044~)と「富ヶ谷のビル」(1986年，p.040~)の計画を進めていたとき，敷地が非常に狭かったので，その数インチといえ無駄にできませんでした。正確であることに対するよい訓練でした。

「ヴィトラ」もまた，時計のように非常に精密なものでした。完璧に近づけねばなりませんでした。たくさんのものが削除され，4枚の壁は3枚になり，さらに2枚になりました。

二川　「富ヶ谷」では，プログラム上の面積についての要求はあったのですか。

ハディド　敷地とすべての要求項目を提示されました。建物はその枠組みに適合させなければなりませんでした。面白かったですね。要求項目を非常に注意深く解釈していく必要がありましたから，手袋をデザインしているみたいでした。すべての敷地境界線，すべての建築制限に，どのように完璧にフィットさせていくか。それは要求事項を入念に

Interview 1995

Futagawa Your early schemes were more about planes, and now your architecture has become more volumetric. Instead of layers placed horizontally, you've inserted planes vertically and stabilized your ideas. Vitra is a first in this sense.

Hadid The period of time from 1988 or 1989 up until now is very important. My earlier projects were still very planar but my work began to be about volumes——the position of planes and how they could project into volumes. I think if you look at all the work of this period, which lead to Vitra and KMR, Art and Media Park (1993, p.054-), you can see that it became much more about layers of volumes as opposed to layers of planes. I think this was a very important transformation because it dealt more with space and how spaces are layered. For me it was a very exciting period of work.

Futagawa Yes, in your early work, I found graphic articulations on each plane which were not necessarily volumetric. But at Vitra all the volumes have very beautiful spatial qualities.

Hadid At Vitra we used a lot of scrutiny. It was supposed to be simple and so we looked very carefully at it——it required tremendous precision. When we worked on the Japanese projects, Azabujuban Building (1987, p.044-) and Tomigaya Building (1986, p.040-), the sites were so small we needed every inch of them. It was good training in precision.

Vitra was also very precise, like a clock. It had to be close to perfect. It underwent a lot of elimination. Four walls would become three, and then two.

Futagawa At Tomigaya were you given square-footage requirements for specific parts of the program?

Hadid The building had to be fit into the frame of the site and all its requirements. It was interesting because we had to be very careful in interpreting the requirements, it was like designing a glove. How do you fit a building in perfectly with all the site lines and all the regulations. It was an outcome of an elaborate diagram of requirements and because it was so tight it taught us to be very precise.

Futagawa Also, at the Moon Soon (1990, p.058-) in Sapporo you used a very powerful color scheme, but at Vitra you suddenly revert to only bare concrete.

Hadid Well at Vitra, it was more about spaces. I decided to use concrete because to me concrete is the most plastic material. It is the material most suitable for this kind of work. Tomigaya was also concrete but I think it was more suitable in the particular case of Vitra.

Originally the idea was to use no color on the outside and color inside. But then I decided to make it very monotone because I felt it required that sense of purity. We wanted to use only light. I discovered that the minute you color the planes you lose the quality of the volumes; it becomes again a planar thing and I wanted the volumes to read.

Futagawa I notice that the same changes have occurred in your drawings.

Hadid Well, we still use color. Earlier, color was not just about the color of the building, but the building with light. I'm sure there is the possibility of the use of color if the conditions allow for it. Color

Interior of office (in 1995)　事務所内部（1995年当時）

検討したダイアグラムの産物です。非常に制約が厳しかったので，私たちに，厳密に正確であれと教えてくれました。

二川　札幌の「ムーンスーン」(1990年，p.058〜)では，非常に強い色彩を使っていましたが，「ヴィトラ」では突然，素のままのコンクリートへと急旋回しましたね。

ハディド　ええ。「ヴィトラ」は，空間の問題だったんです。ここではコンクリートを使うと決めました。私にとって，それは最も可塑的な材料だからです。こうした類の建物には最適の材料です。「富ヶ谷」もコンクリートですが，「ヴィトラ」は，さらにそれが相応しい特別のケースです。

最初は外側には色を使わず，内部に使うつもりでした。結局，非常にモノトーンなものとすることに決めました。そうした純粋な感覚を必要としたからです。光だけを使いたいと思いました。平面に色彩を使った途端に，それはヴォリューム感を失うことに気がつきました。色をつけると平面的なものに戻ってしまいます。私はヴォリュームが読めるものにしたかったのです。

二川　同じ変化がドローイングにも起こっていますね。

ハディド　そうですね。でも，まだ色彩を使っています。最初は，色彩は単なる建物の色ではなく，光と建物に関わるものでした。もし状況が許せば，色彩をそのように使う可能性があると確信しています。70年代に人々がフェイクな材料を使うようになって，色彩がこの構想のなかに入ってきたのです。私の答えは，フェイクな材料の代わりに色彩を使うこと，そして色彩を構想全体と切り放せないものとして使うことでした。次に，透明性とソリッドなもの，そしてこの二つを互いに衝突させるというアイディアへと転換しました。

二川　今，あなたは，透明性の方に関心が傾いていると言ってよいのでしょうか。

ハディド　ものによります。両方を使うことができるのですから。「カーディフベイ・オペラハウス」(1996年，p.078〜)では，ロビーは外部より心が躍るようなものにすべきでした。ですから状況によります。

二川　「カーディフ」についてお聞かせ下さい。

ハディド　「カーディフ」もまた緻密なスタディによって生み出されたものです——平面の扱い，空間構成から非常に単純な動きを編成することによ

came into the story because in the seventies people would use fake materials. My response was to use color instead——to make color an integral part of the story. Then I also shifted from color to the idea of transparency and solids and how these two things could impact each other.

Futagawa Is it fair to say that now you're more interested in transparency?

Hadid It depends. You can use both. In Cardiff the lobby should be more vibrant than the outside, so it depends on the situation.

Futagawa Tell me about the Cardiff Bay Opera House (1996, p.078-).

Hadid Cardiff was also a product of precision——an understanding that you can eliminate wasted space by very simple moves in terms of the planes, in terms of spatial organization. KMR, in terms of experience, had an incredible impact on Cardiff. The KMR material is very elaborate, and although it was much bigger, it also required precision and interpretation.

Over the years I learned many lessons from many different people. Working with Peter Rice was very important, because he was not only a brilliant engineer and friend, but because in working with him I learned that in any project you have to decide what is important and what is not so important. Like writing, you have to be able to edit. You can have hundreds of ideas but you have to decide on what is most important. In KMR it was important to decide on things early. So although the KMR project and Cardiff are not very similar, KMR lead on to Cardiff because we had the confidence to solve all the technical, and economical problems.

Futagawa Peter Rice did the structure for KMR?

Hadid Peter worked on almost all the projects except for Vitra, but we didn't only work with him. We have a very good engineer, Jane Wernick, whom Peter recommended from Arup's, and we always work with a team. Peter was really such a creative engineer, but he also helped us with strategic planning.

Futagawa After confronting structural and systematic problems in your recent projects, have you changed the way you design?

Hadid Not really. And people may not realize this about my work, but when I design I always keep in mind how it would work and that's why it's so reductive. I try never to design structure afterwards. To me structure is very integral to design.

With Cardiff we didn't want to do a traditional opera house: the idea of a colossal mass with no air, no light, hiding all the ancillary spaces. I always thought that these must be unpleasant places to train as a singer. We decided to do it in reverse, a building that allows air and light to come into all the spaces, except for the theater.

Also you have to understand that Americans work in a very different way than the Europeans. Americans design a diagram and this diagram is built. That could be interesting, for example Oscar Niemeyer's designs in which the engineering aspects are very exciting. The design process stops at the building permit. They don't extend the process into production. Obviously there are economic reasons for this but I think many buildings suffer from it

って，無駄な空間を削除できるというある種の理解です。「KMR」は，経験の点で，「カーディフ」に強い影響を与えています。「KMR」での材料の扱いは，非常に精緻なものです。「カーディフ」よりずっと大きな建物ですが，精密さと適切な解釈を必要としました。

長い間，私はたくさんの人から，いろんなことを教わりました。なかでもピーター・ライスと一緒に仕事をしたことはとても重要でした。彼は優れたエンジニアであり友人であったばかりでなく，彼と一緒に仕事をすることによって，どのようなプロジェクトにおいても，何が重要か，何がそれほど重要ではないかを決めなければならないことを学んだからです。著作のように，編集作業が必要なのです。何百ものアイディアが浮かぶでしょうが，何が最も重要であるか決めなければならない。「KMR」では，物事を早く決めることが重要でした。「KMR」と「カーディフ」のプロジェクトはそれほど似てはいなかったのですが，「KMR」は「カーディフ」の役に立ちました。すべての技術的経済的局面を解決する自信をもてたからです。

二川 ピーター・ライスは，「KMR」の構造も担当されたのですか。

ハディド ピーターは，「ヴィトラ」を除くほとんどのプロジェクトを担当してくれました。私たちは彼と仕事をしただけではありません。私の事務所にはジェイン・ワーニックという優秀なエンジニアがいますが，彼女はピーターが，アラップから推薦してくれたのです。しかし，仕事は一つのチームで進めます。ピーターは，衆知のように創造的なエンジニアですが，プランニング上のストラテジーについても助言してくれています。

二川 最近のプロジェクトで構造やシステマティックな問題に直面した後，設計の方法を変えましたか。

ハディド いいえ，あまり。人は気づかないかもしれませんが，設計するときはいつも，現実にそれがどのようになるかを心に留めています。このことが，デザインがとても還元的である理由です。構造を後から設計したいと思ったことはありません。私にとって構造はデザインすることと一体なのです。

「カーディフ」は，伝統的なオペラ・ハウスにしたくありませんでした。巨大なマス，外気も自然光も入らず，補助スペースは全部隠されている，といったもの。こうした建物は歌手がトレーニングする場所として居心地が悪いに違いないといつも思っていましたから，その逆をやろうと決めました。外気や自然光が，舞台・客席を除いてすべてのスペースに入ってくるような建物です。

また，アメリカ人の仕事の進め方はヨーロッパの人とはまったく違うことを理解する必要があります。アメリカ人はダイアグラムを設計し，そのダイアグラムが建設されます。面白いことです。例えば，オスカー・ニーマイヤーのデザインは技術的な部分がとても素晴らしい。デザイン・プロセスは，計画が認可された時点で停止してしまいます。彼らはこのプロセスを建設の過程にまで拡げていきません。これには明らかに経済的理由がありますが，多くの建物がその悪影響を受けていると思います。デザイン・プロセスをあまりに早く停止してしまうわけですから。建設過程での変更を知らされたときに，他の情報を考慮する余裕がありません。私たちはもっと柔軟な状況にいたいのです。やむをえない予測不可能な状況に直面したとき，多くの人は変更が必要なことを理解しないものです。

二川 それは判ります。あなたのオフィスで，サーキュレーション・システムのスタディをたくさん見せてもらいました。同じ建物のためのものですが，それぞれが極端に違っていますね。

because you stop the process too early. You don't allow for other information when it comes to you to inform change. We want situations that are more flexible. A lot of people don't understand that changes are necessary when you face the unforeseen circumstances that always come up.

Futagawa Yes, I saw many studies at your office of, say, circulation systems that were extremely different but in the same building.

Hadid Those studies are very instrumental. For example I wanted a sense of continuous transparency and so it was necessary to change the circulation pattern in certain places. That's an instance where I decided it was more important to have transparency than to place the circulation in the most economical way.

I think the process of design development through the production stage is crucial. That's what is lost in many practices in the States. In England it is much more common, especially by the high-tech architects because the details are elaborated during construction. It's an issue of time, but it's also an issue of people understanding how important it is to do this. It's different if you're just designing a box with layers. You don't need to do this, you just churn it out, but if you work like we do this process has to be continuous. It's like fine tuning.

As you move along you decide what is most important. For example one might think that the shell is important, but I think that it's not that important, we could always reshape it. It is the arrangement of the spaces which is more important, or the idea. The idea has to be very clear. It can't get confused. As long as there is clarity in the idea, you can change other things.

Sometimes you have to compromise. For example, people don't think it's a good idea to compromise on materials but I think materials don't need to be expensive as long as you use them well. You don't have to have marble flooring, you can do things in a much more interesting way. You can do something else with detailing or use lighting. For me, luxury is in the quality of space; it's not about how big it is or how expensive it is but about spatial quality. This is always difficult to quantify in drawings or in models. You only know it when you see it.

For me, the quality of a space has to be very generous and this could be achieved through a variety of ways. Our quantity surveyor for Cardiff also worked with us on KMR knew our approach, but other quantity surveyors could not understand how we could do an opera house without having gold and marble everywhere. It is more important for me to maintain the ideas than to use expensive materials.

Regulations must also always be interpreted the right way. There is never one way of doing something and for that you need the time and flexibility to interpret everything. It's like reading the Bible or any set of religious guides. You have to be able to move around them in an interesting way because all these things are quite fluid and not rigid.

at Zaha Hadid House, London, 1995

ハディド こういったスタディはとても役に立ちます。例えば，私は連続する透明性というものをつくりたかったのですが，このためにいくつかの場所でサーキュレーション・パターンを変える必要がありました。これは，サーキュレーションを最も経済的に設置することより，透明性をつくることの方が重要だと考えたケースです。

建設段階を通しての，デザインの展開プロセスは決定的なものだと思います。この点が，アメリカでは，多くの実施段階において失われています。イギリスでは，これはごく普通のことで，特にハイテクの建築家は，工事の間もディテールを練り上げていきますからね。それは時間の問題ですが，また，それを行うことが大切だと理解しているかどうかの問題でもあります。単に重層する箱型建築をつくるのであるなら話は別で，プロセスは必要ではなく，ただつくればいいのだけれど，私のような建物をつくるのなら，このプロセスを続けなければいけません。微妙なチューニングのようなものです。

プロセスに沿って進んでいきながら，何が最も重要かを決めます。例えば，ある人はシェルが大切だと思うかもしれない。でも私はそれほど大切だと思わないかもしれない。私たちは常にその形をつくり直していくことができます。それは，もっと重要な空間の配置，つまりアイディアなのです。アイディアは明解でなければなりません。混乱したものにすることはできません。アイディアに明晰性があるかぎり，他のものへ変換できるのです。

時には妥協も必要です。例えば，材料について妥協するのはよくないと人は考えますが，私はそれが上手く使われる限り，材料は高価である必要はないと思います。大理石を床に使わなければならないということはありません。代わりに，ディテール処理や照明の使い方など，もっと面白い方法がとれます。私にとっての贅沢さとは空間の質のなかにあるのです。大きさとか，それにかけたお金の額とかではなく，空間のクオリティの問題です。この点については，ドローイングや模型で推し量ることは難しいですね。実際にそれを見たときに初めて判るのですから。

私の考える空間の質というのは非常に豊かなものであるべきで，これはさまざまな方法でつくりあげられます。「KMR」でも一緒だった「カーディフ」での積算担当者は，私たちの仕事のやり方を知っていましたが，他の積算士は，金や大理石などを使わずにオペラ・ハウスがどうしてできるのか理解できませんでした。それとはまったく違うものが必要でした。高価な材料を使うことより，アイディアを保ち続けることの方が，私にはずっと大切です。

建築規制も常に正しい方法で解釈しなければなりません。何かをするのに，一つの方法しかないということは絶対にないのです。そのために，すべてを解釈するのに時間と柔軟性が必要です。聖書や宗教書を読むようなものです。これらの本の周りを楽しく動き回らなければならないのです。そうした本はとても流動的で，硬直したものではないのですから。

（1995年，ロンドン，ザハ・ハディド邸にて）

WORKS 1982-

1982-83
THE PEAK
ザ・ピーク

Hong Kong, China

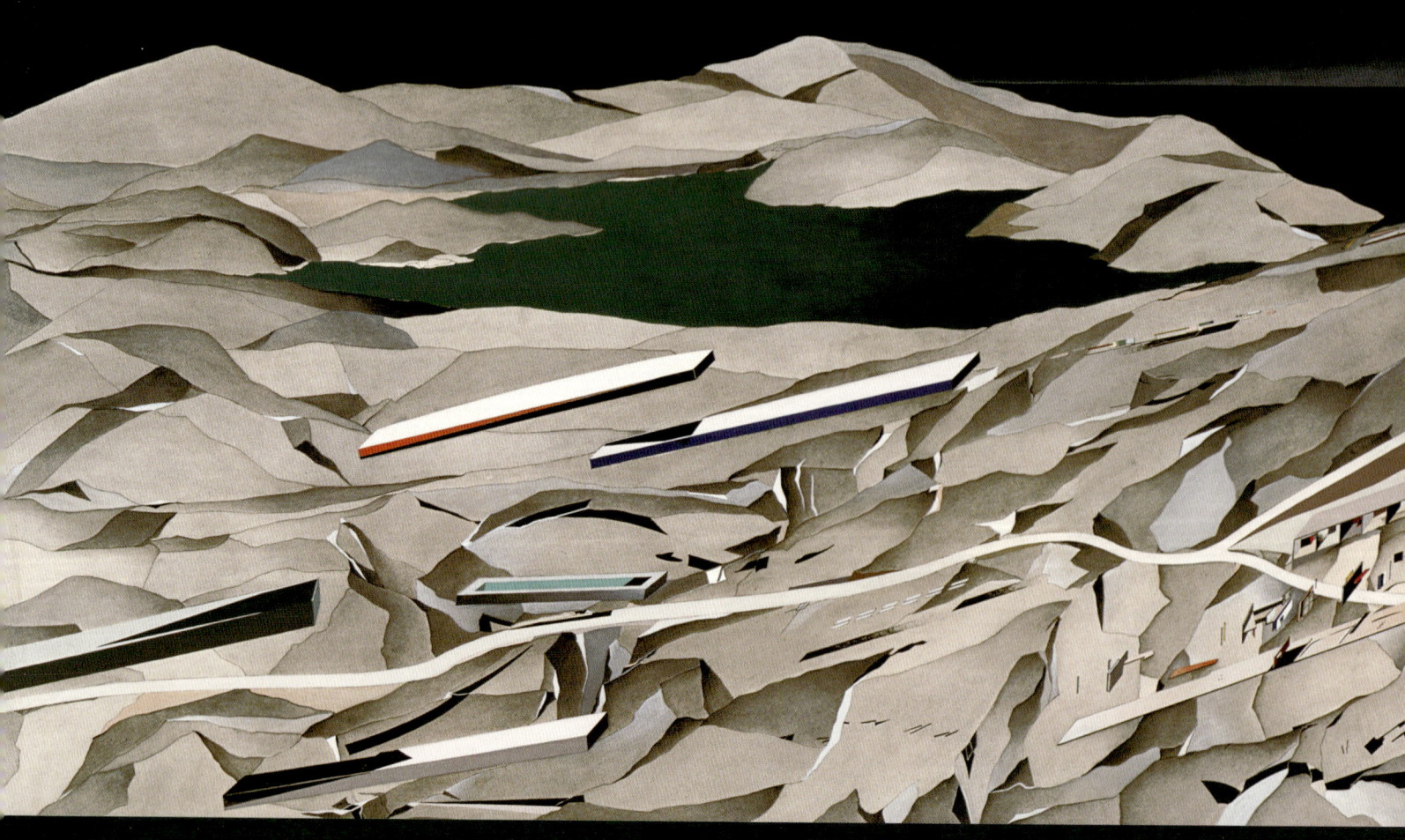

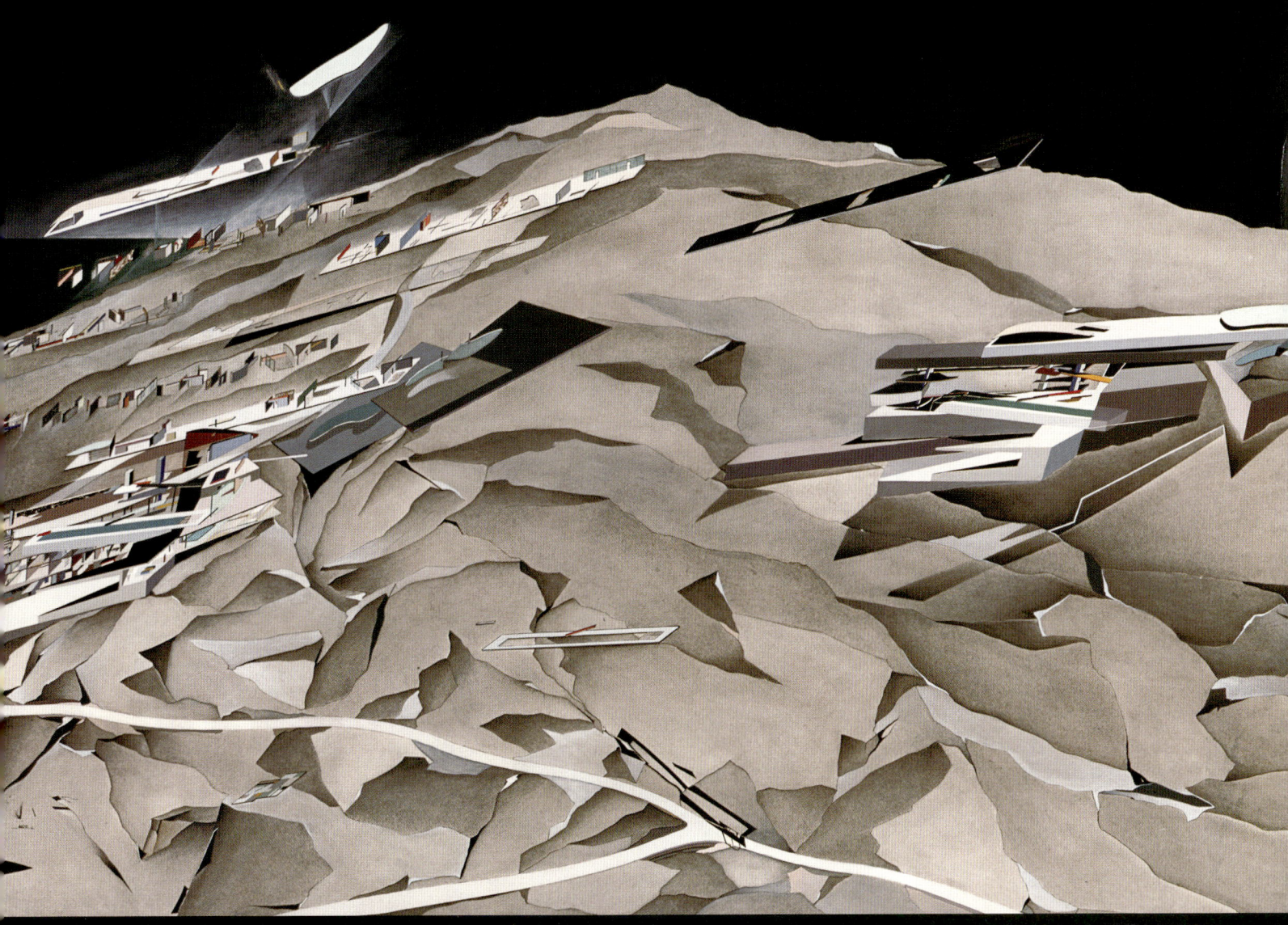

Exploded isometric　分解アイソメトリック

The Peak

Site plan 配置

The design and creation of a building which could be an architectural landmark in a major city such as Hong Kong is not necessarily a difficult formal exercise. Yet it does raise important issues both conceptually and programmatically in relation to the histories of the twentieth century architectural design. The site demands programmatic inventiveness and an overwhelming significance in relation to and as a relief from, the congestion of the city itself.

The prevailing conditions are varied; abetting the spirit of intensity and prosperity in Hong Kong and Kowloon. Literally set over the city, high on a hill, the site rests free from the condensed urban environment yet is still integrated with the land and water below. To accentuate the dramatic visual conditions and natural arterial features, constructive elements of various materials are thrust onto the site, impacting vertically and horizontally a kind of Suprematist geology. The architecture is like a knife cutting through the site. It cuts through traditional principles of organisation and reconstitutes new ones, defies nature and resists destroying it.

The area of the site to the south of the Crown Land is excavated, it's highest point levelled to the lowest point of the site. The excavated rock is then polished and incorporated into various parts of the site, forming a man-made polished granite mountain. These new granite cliffs are erected merging into the top of the site. The excavated segment, extending into the hill, is replaced with the facilities for the club's hedonistic activities.

The building is layered horizontally, with architectural beams superimposed on each other, constituting a series of programmes. The first layer houses fifteen double height studio apartments with glazed fronts. The second layer rests on the first and contains twenty apartments and its roof forms the main podium of the club above.

The club itself is a void thirteen meters high suspended between the roof of the second layer and the underside of the penthouse layer. The club facilities extend both physically and programmatically into the proposed man-made mountain. This void becomes the new architectural landscape within which all of the club elements are suspended at varying heights. Above the club void is the forth layer comprising the four separate penthouse apartments, each with an individuality and integrity of its own.

Resting on the highest point of the site, the top (fifth) layer of penthouses includes the promoter's apartment and private swimming pool at the northern end. The dining room and grand living room are separate elements on the deck for use by the promoter's family only.

Seen from Hong Kong, the mountain cliffs forms a backdrop to both leisure and intellectual activities, which are suspended in the air. The architecture is a condenser of luxurious and 'high' living, intense in its programme. The final result is a composite of all the programmatic beams peering over the mountainside, and these suspended satellites constitute a modern geology. Offering and symbolising the pinnacle of the high life, the Peak's beams and voids are a gentle seismic shift on an immovable mass.

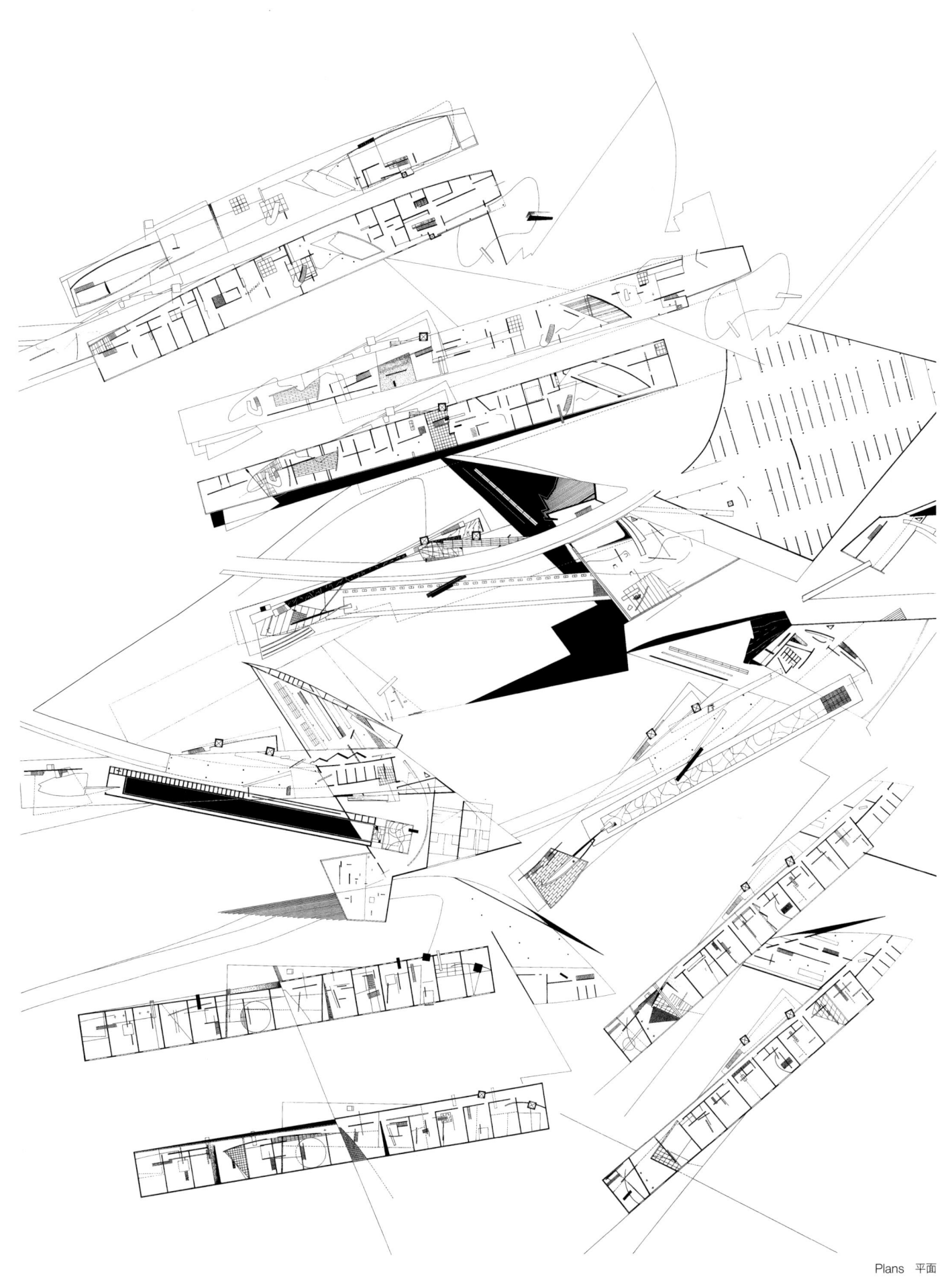

Plans 平面

The Peak

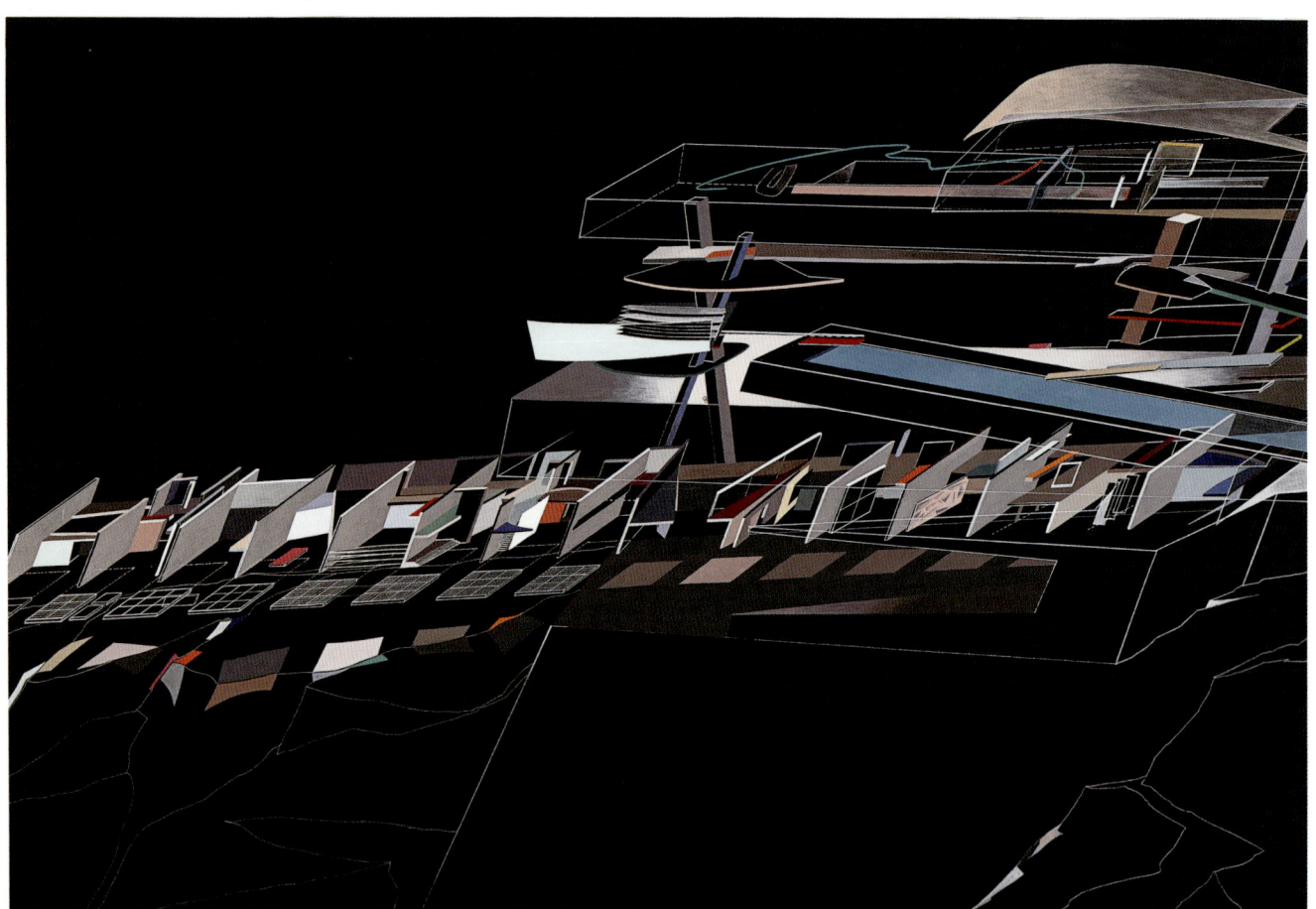

Studio apartments and void (above) スタジオ型アパートとヴォイド（上）
Elements of void (below) ヴォイドの要素（下）

The Blue Slabs　ブルー・スラブ

The Peak

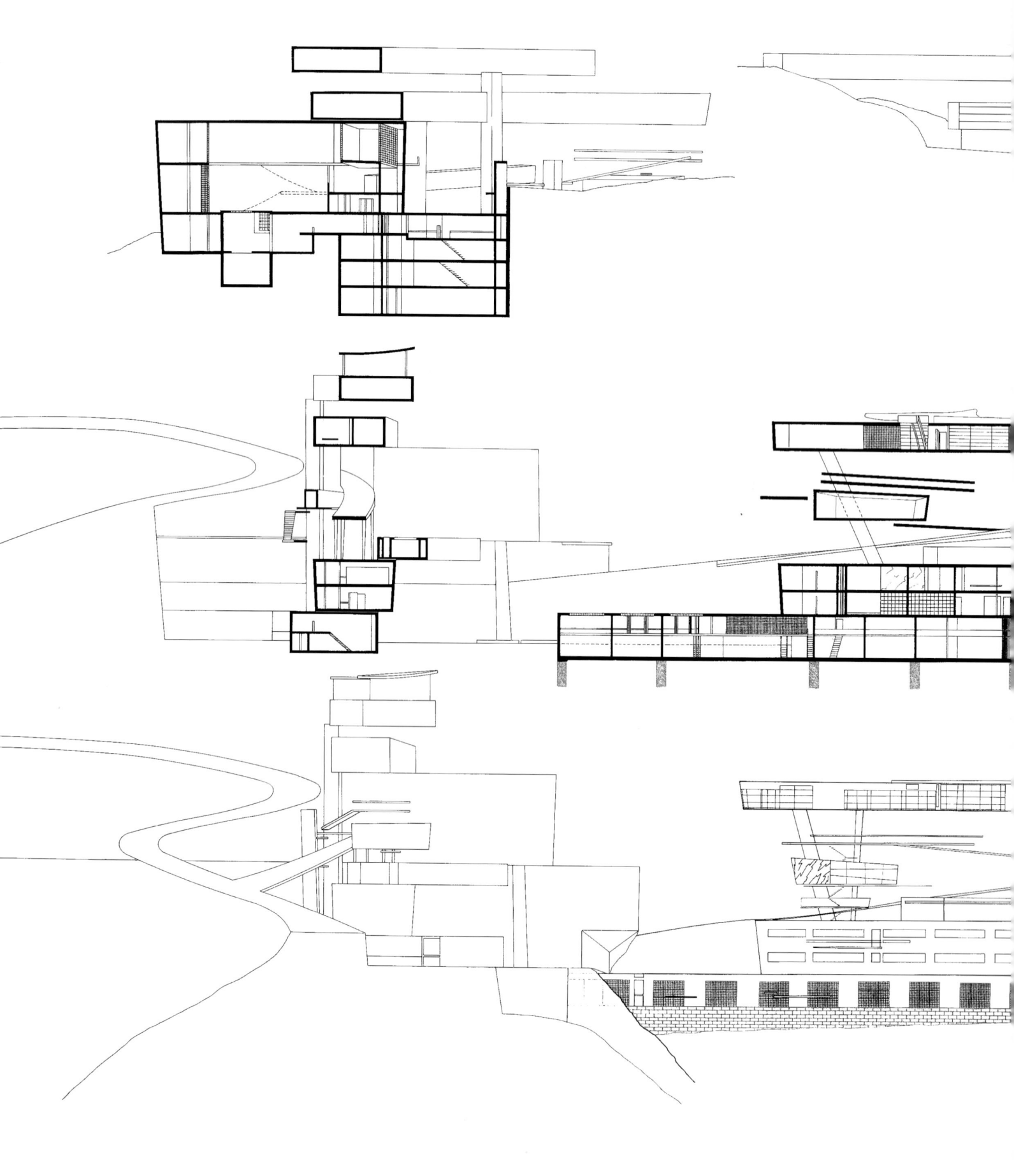

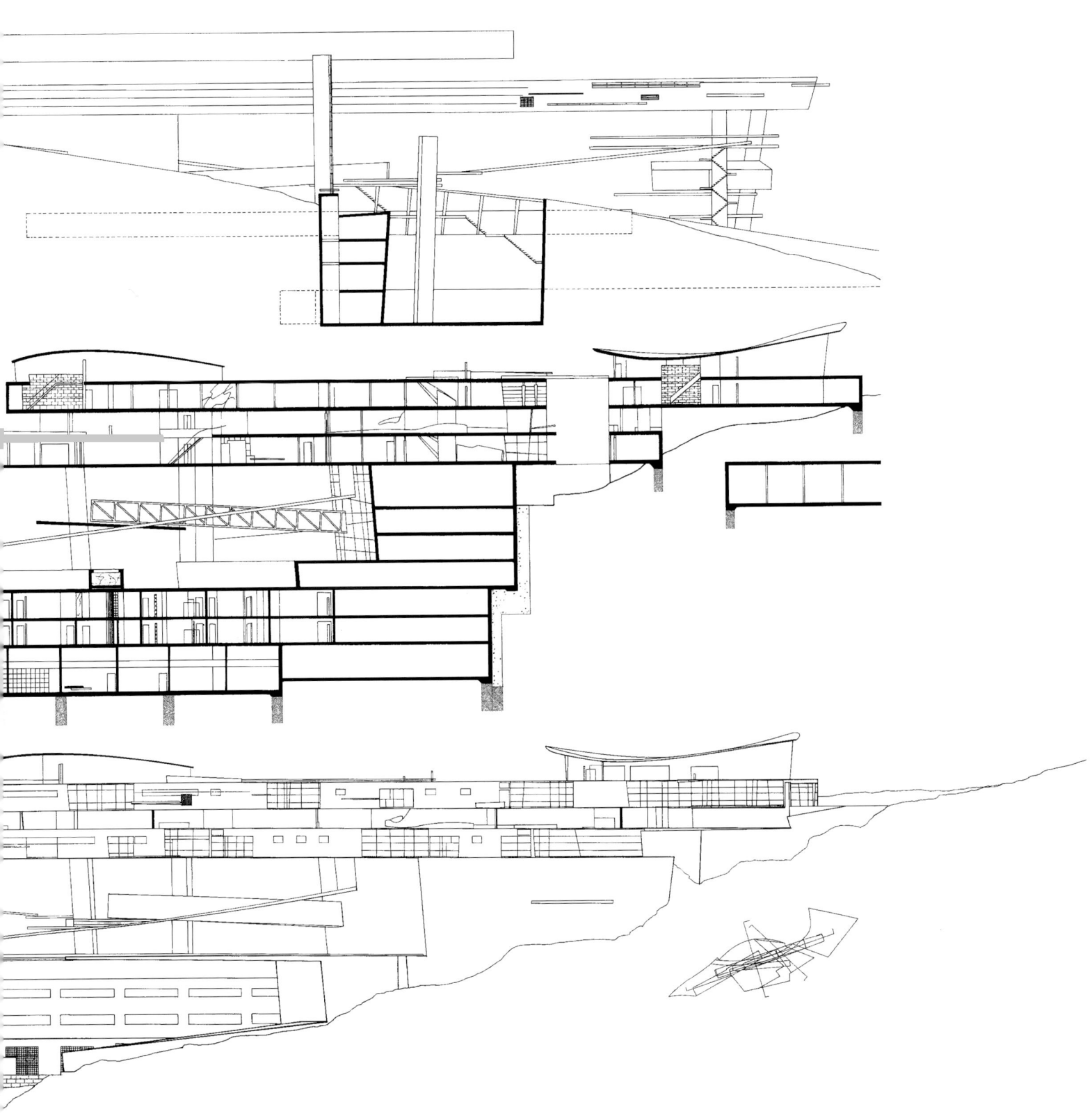

Sections 断面

The Peak

029

The divers　ダイバー

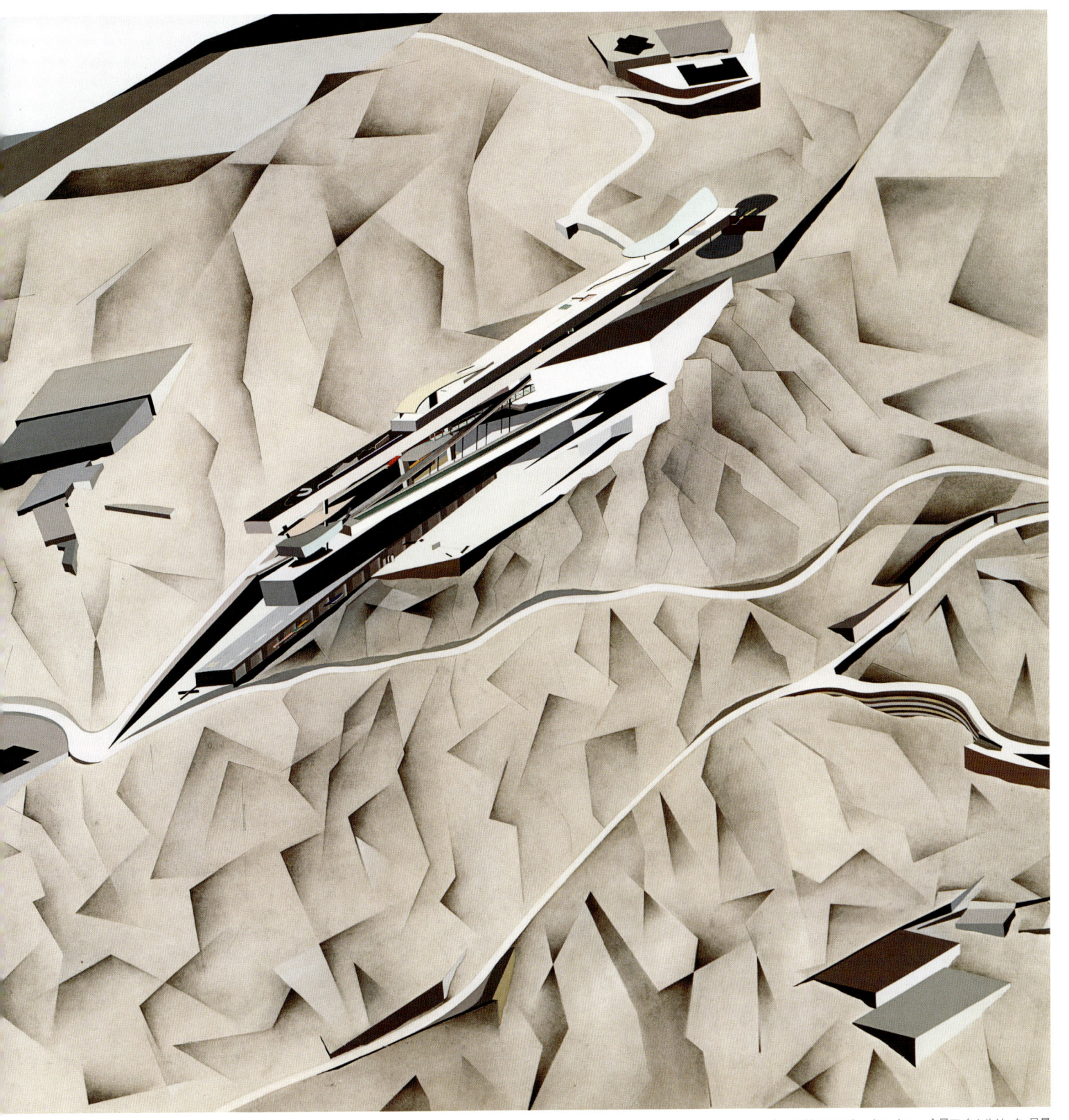

Overall isometric, day view　全景アイソメトリック, 昼景

The Peak

香港のような大都会にランドマークとなる建物をデザインすることは，現時点において，形態的には必ずしも難しい課題ではないが，20世紀の建築デザインの歴史との関連という点において，コンセプトの上でも，プログラムの上でも，重要な問題提起となるものである。この敷地は，香港の街そのものの乱雑さとの接近と同時に，それと距離を取ることの取ることの両方の意味で，プログラム上の独創性と圧倒的な意味性を必要とする。

全般的な状況は多彩である。香港と九龍半島の繁栄とバイタリティを受け止める。文字通り，丘の上，街の上高く位置するこの敷地は，この都市の過密な環境からは解放されているが，依然として，下方に広がる大地と水に結びついている。劇的に展開する視界，その自然のもつ動脈状の地形を強調するために，さまざまな材料から成る建物の構成要素は，垂直方向，水平方向に飛び交い，敷地上に突き刺さる──ひとつのシュプレマティストの地質学ともいえようか。この建築は敷地を切り裂くナイフのようであり，伝統的な構成原理を切り裂き，新しい原則を再構成する。自然に挑戦するが，自然を破壊するものではない。

クラウン・ランドの南側にあたる地域を掘削し，敷地の最高部を最低部の高さへと揃える。掘り出された石は磨いて敷地内の各所へ敷き込み，磨かれた御影石でできた人工の山を形づくる。この新しく生まれた御影石の山は屹立し，敷地の最高部へと合体していく。丘の中に広がる掘削の跡には，クラブの快楽の諸施設がおきかわる。

ビームは水平に重なり合い，一連のプログラムを構成する。第1の層には，前面がガラス張りの2階高のスタジオ型アパート15戸が入る。第2層は第1層の上に重なり，20戸のアパートを収容し，その屋根が上に位置するクラブ施設のメインの基壇を構成する。

クラブは，第2層の屋根とペントハウス層の下側との間に吊るされた13メートル高のヴォイドである。クラブの諸施設は，物理的にもプログラム上も，人工の山の中に延び広がっている。さまざまな高さにクラブを構成するエレメントのすべてが宙吊られたこのヴォイドは，新しい建築風景となる。クラブを構成するヴォイドの上部には第4層が重なり，完全に独立したペントハウス4戸が収容される。

敷地の最高部に位置する最上階（第5層）のペントハウスはプロモーターのアパートで，北端にプールがある。デッキ上に独立したエレメントとしておかれているダイニングと広いリビングは，プロモーター一家の専用である。

香港市街から見ると，余暇活動と知的活動が共に空中に浮かべられ，この山崖が背景となっている。この建築は，そこに組み込まれているプログラムにエネルギーを与える，贅沢で〈ハイ〉な生活のコンデンサーである。最終的に立ち現われるのは，山裾から見えてくるプログラムを内包したビームの複合体であり，これら宙吊られた人工衛星のような構造物は，現代の地質学を構成する。華やかな生活の頂点を提案し，象徴することによって，ザ・ピークのビームやヴォイドは，不動の量塊上のゆるやかな断層になる。

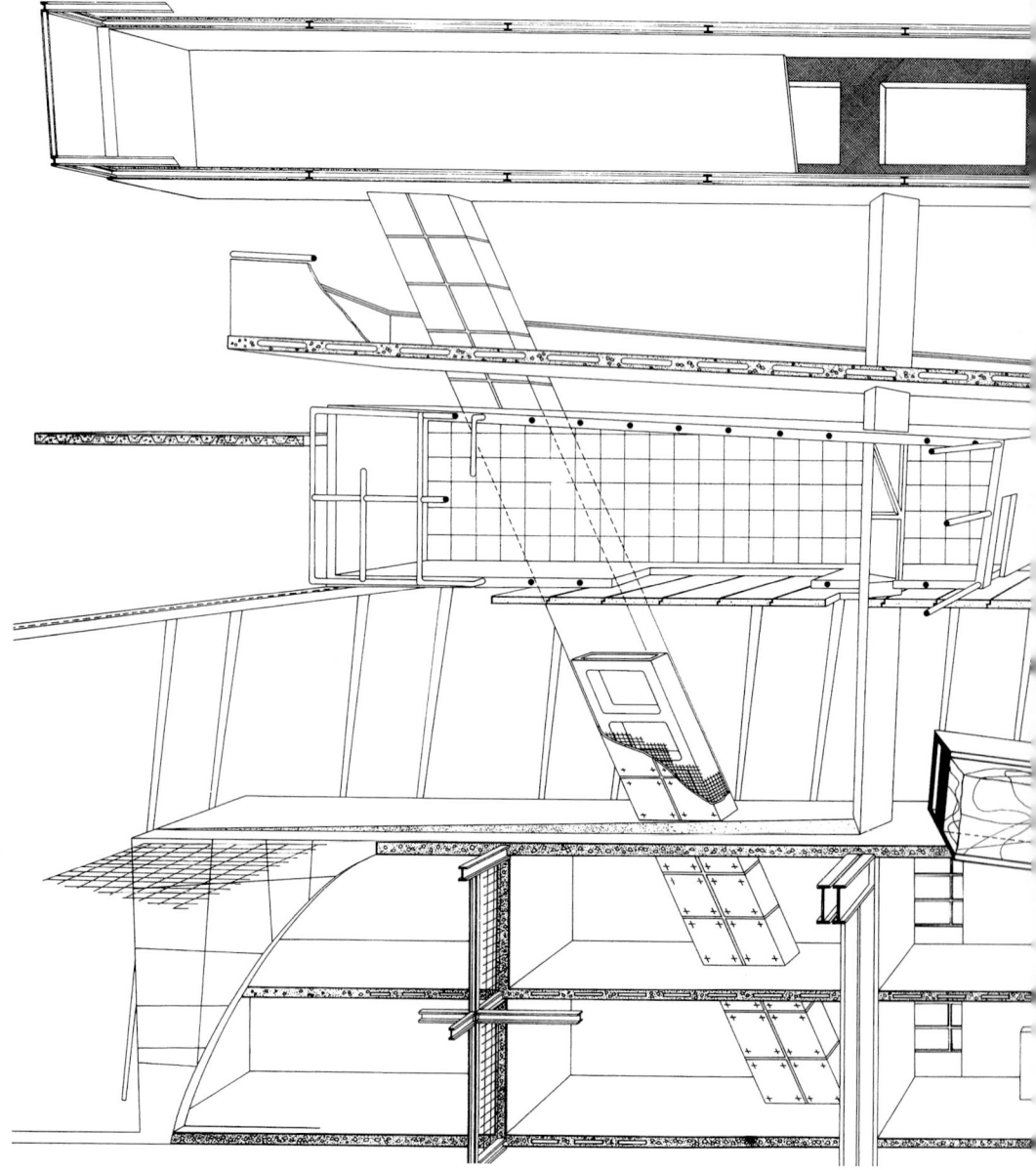

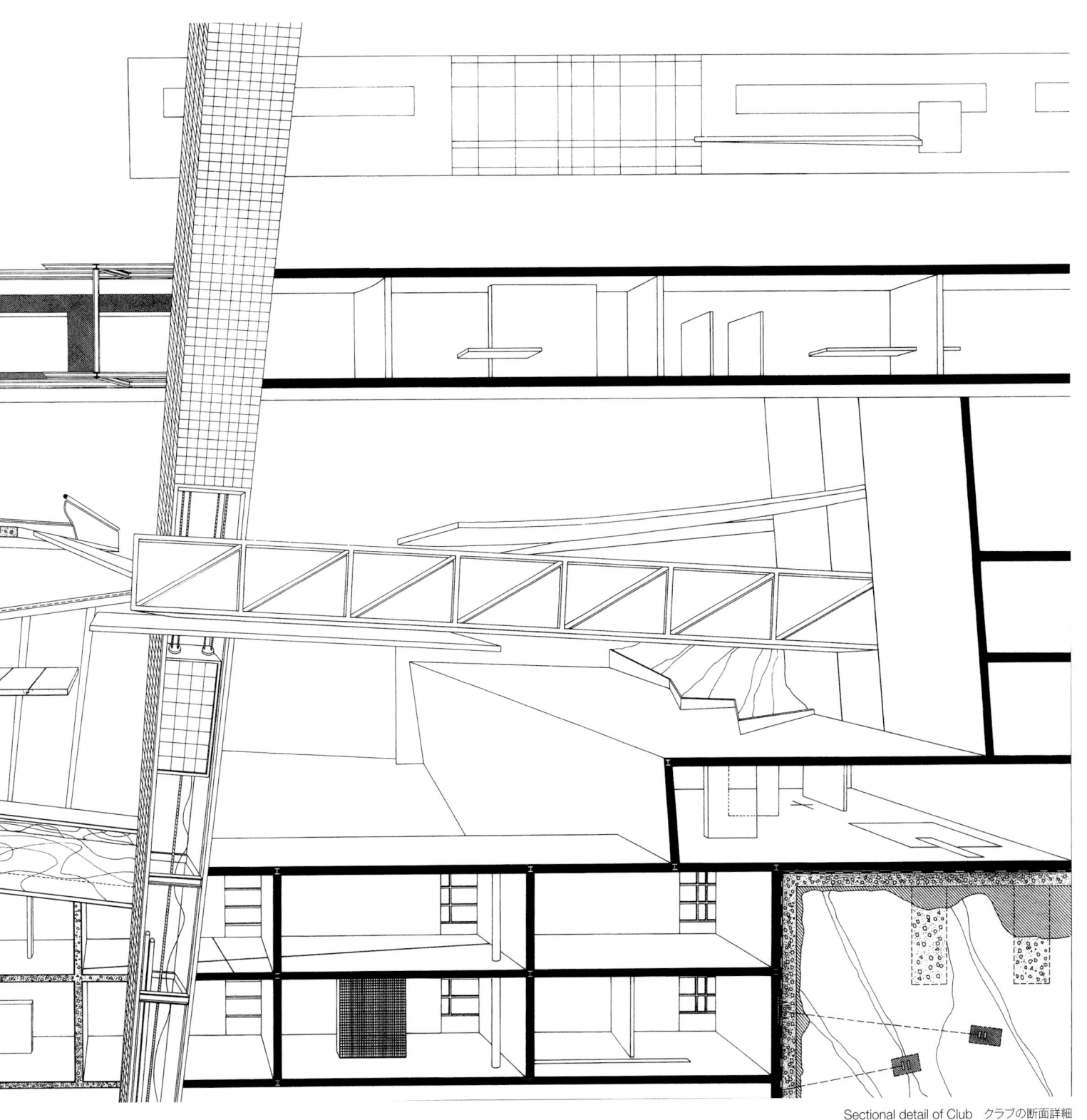

Sectional detail of Club　クラブの断面詳細

The Peak

1983
THE WORLD (89 DEGREES)
ザ・ワールド（89°）

This painting represents the culmination of a seven-year exploration into architecture's uncharted territories that began with my work as a student at the Architectural Association.

Technology's rapid development and our ever-changing lifestyles created a fundamentally new and exhilarating backdrop for building, and in this new world context I felt we must reinvestigate the aborted and untested experiments of Modernism—not to resurrect them, but to unveil new fields of building. Here, projects that I had carried out over the last seven years have been compressed and expanded.

このペインティングは，私の7年間にわたる建築の未知なる領域への探究の極致を表している。それはAAスクールの学生時代の制作活動に端を発するものであった。

テクノロジーの急速な発展と，絶えず変化する我々のライフスタイルは，建築の本質においては新しく刺激に満ち溢れた存在であった。そのような来るべき世界のなかで，私はこれまでに試みられることなく頓挫したモダニズムの数々の実験に——近代の復権としてではなく，建築の新しいフィールドの発見として——改めて光を充てる必要性を理解していた。この作品は7年間にわたる数々のプロジェクトを凝縮し，発展させたものである。

The World (89 Degrees)　ザ・ワールド（89°）

The World (89 Degrees)

1985
GRAND BUILDINGS, TRAFALGAR SQUARE
トラファルガー広場計画

London, U.K.

View of site with London skyline　ロンドンのスカイラインと敷地を見る

Grand Buildings, Trafalgar Square

Building rotating
建物を回転させる

Worm's eye view of ramp and towers　タワーと坂道を仰視する

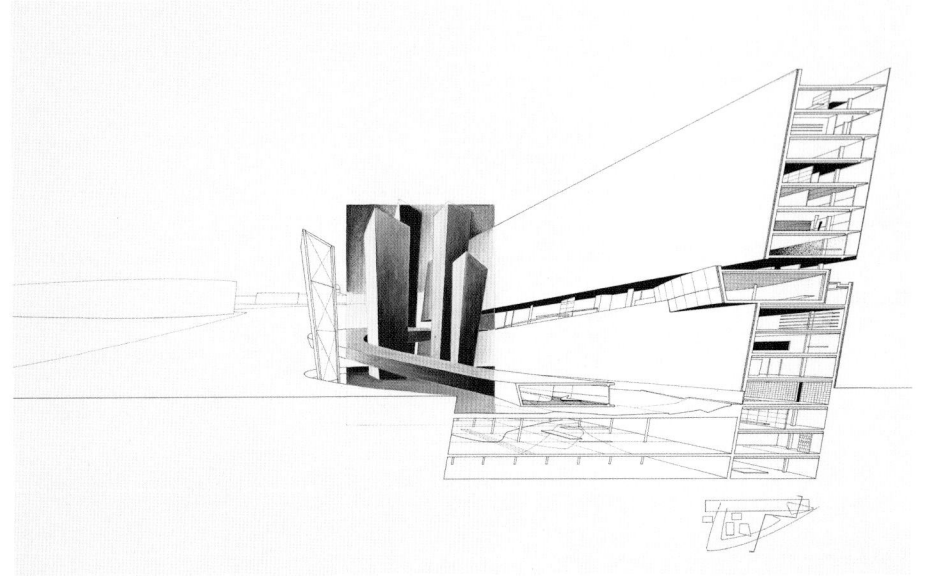

Section 断面

Schemes to recapture London's most famous square continue to this day. In the hope that outdated planning restraints might be abandoned, a proposal that celebrated the dynamic possibilities of the urban landscape was presented.

It aimed at extending the public realm into the quality of city life. A public podium, slabs of offices and towers are central characteristics of the buildings. Beneath the towers topped by penthouses, are subterranean lobbies. A shopping concourse peels up, gently curving around the site's perimeter and enclosing a new public domain as it winds up to the roof, which features the public terrace that overlooks the mire of cars below. As one's vantage-point moves around the square, the towers appear to mutate from the shards that penetrate the square's surface into a single solid mass.

今日までロンドンで最も名の知られた広場を取り戻す計画である。時代にそぐわない建築規制から解き放たれることを期待し,都市的ランドスケープのダイナミックな可能性を祝福する提案を行った。

その目的は公共領域を都市生活の質へと拡張することにあった。基壇部の公共空間,オフィスフロア及び高層棟が,この建築の中心的特徴である。高層棟の頂部にはペントハウスが,地階にはロビーが設けられている。商業空間のコンコースは,敷地周辺に沿って緩やかなカーブを描きながら屋根まで巻き込むように浮かび上がり,新しい公共領域を囲み,その下を走る車の渋滞を気にしない公共のテラスを特徴づける。広場の周りのあちこちから良い眺めが得られるので,高層棟群は広場に表面的に広がる断片から,一つの立体的なまとまりへと変化して感じられるだろう。

Grand Buildings, Trafalgar Square

1986
TOMIGAYA BUILDING
富ヶ谷のビル

Tokyo, Japan

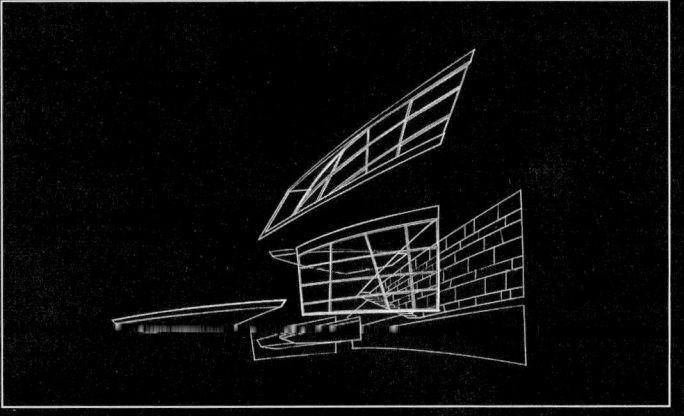

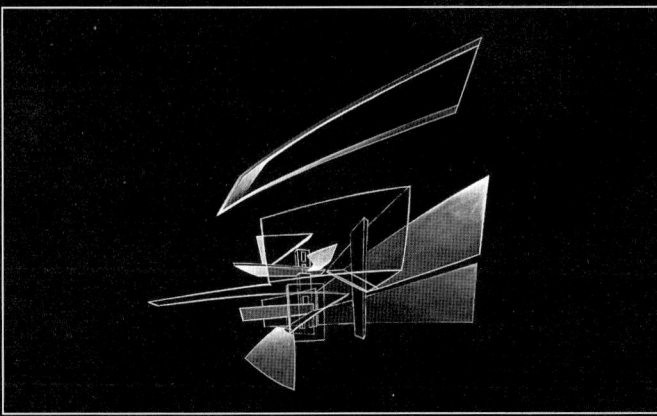

Perspective パースペクティヴ

Plan 平面

Section 断面

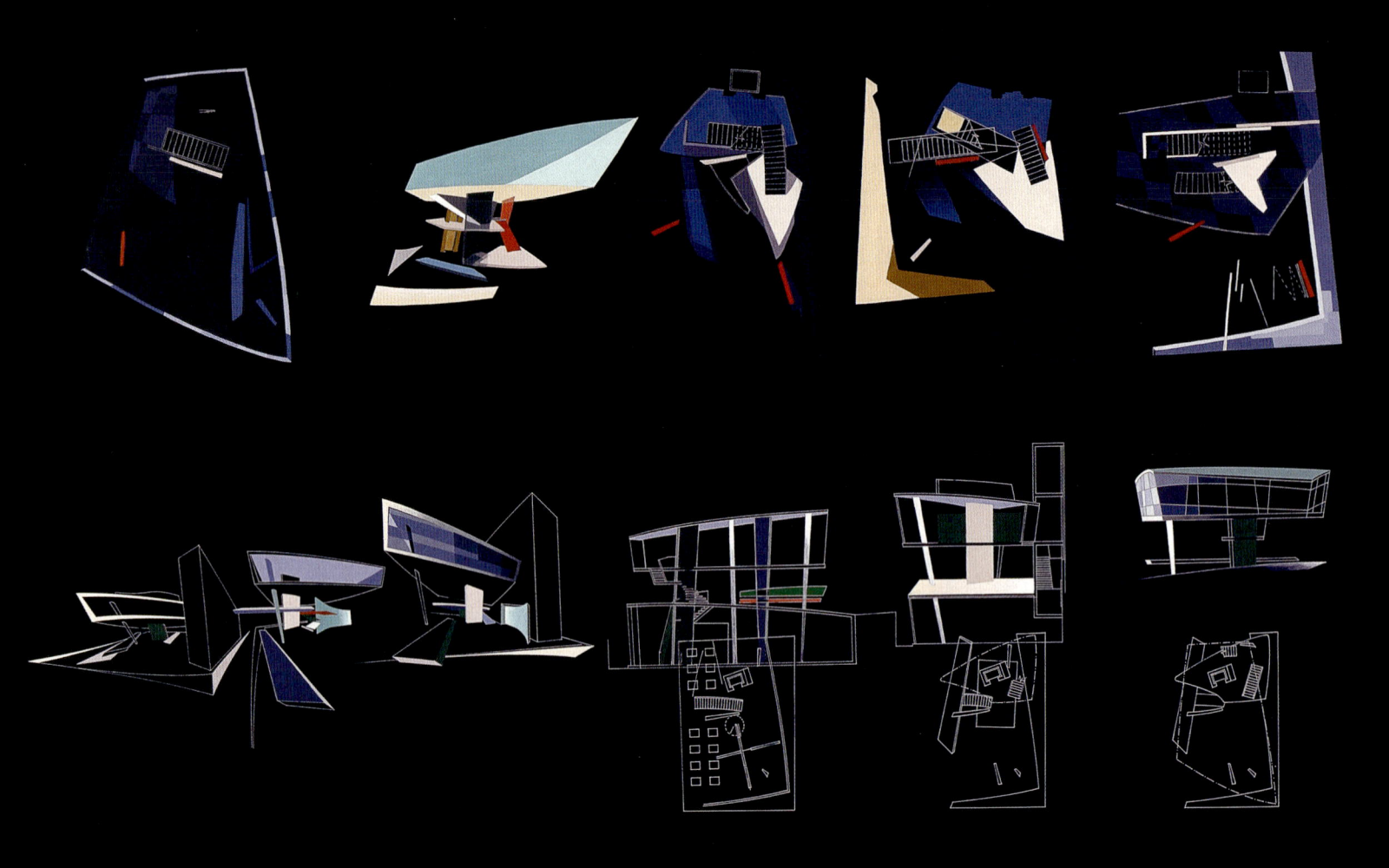

The relationship of this building to the site and street is unusual one in the crowded city. A light glass pavilion is elevated to create a small urban void providing relief from the clutter of the surrounding neighbourhood. This void is a compressed space suspended between two horizontal planes. A major part of the programme is sunk below the curving first floor which is pulled back from the edges on two sides and holds a tall glass wall in a channel which is allows light to filter into the lower space. The entrance stairway steps down to a mid-level platform and an external court within the lower space. This provides views up past the ground level to another platform and the belly of the pavilion above.

The generous proportions of the lower space enable complete flexibility, as either one continuous floor or a series of platforms, allowing this space to be used for retail and office activities. The raised pavilion, although completely independent, is an integral part of the whole building concept. It is a light, one-storey structure which hovers above the open ground, with a curving roof line and full height windows on three sides. The design offers flexibility for office studio or retail use. Areas of the ground will be of a translucent glass paving, lighting a path in the evening light and filtering daylight, while creating a soft defuse light for the space below.

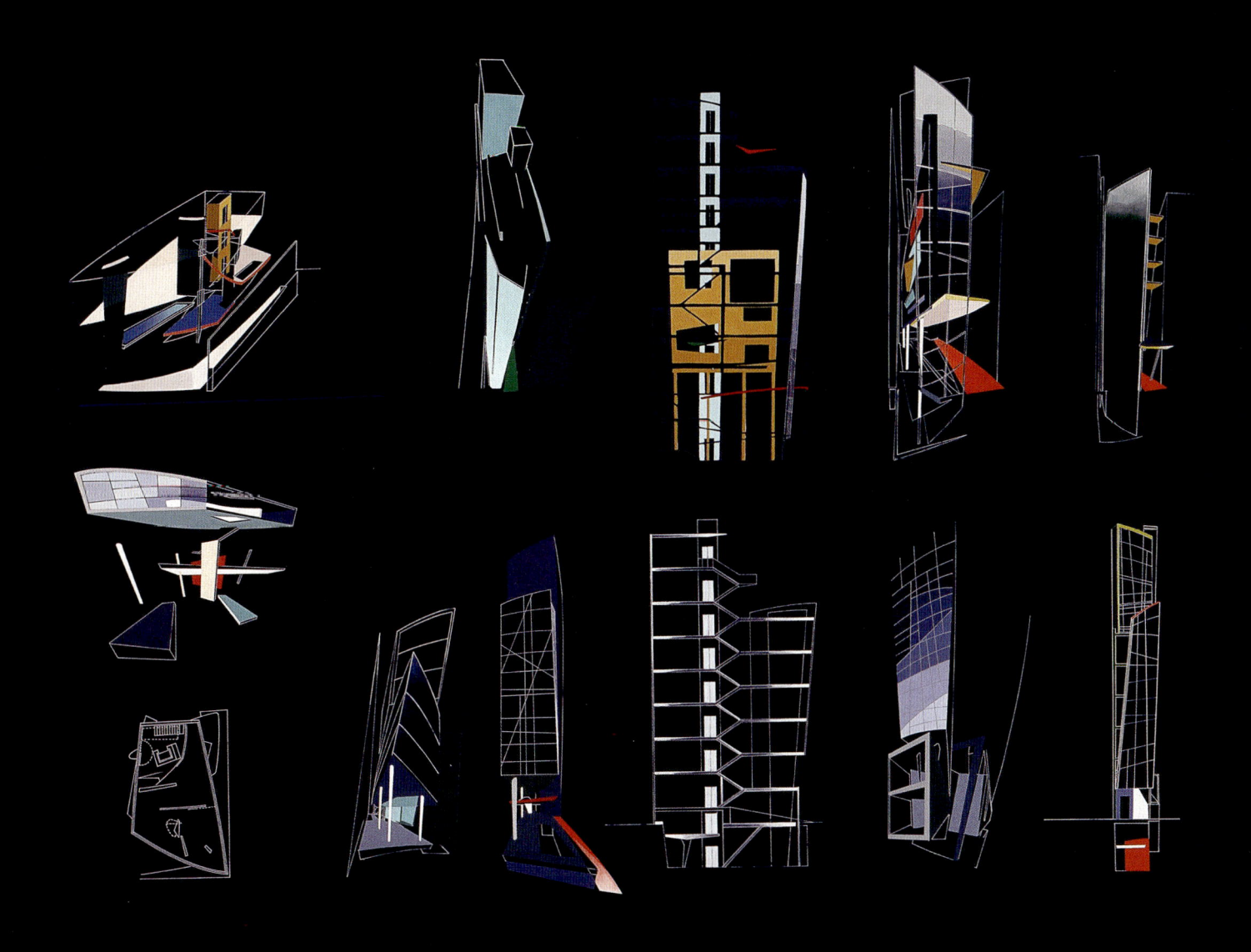

Studies　スタディ

敷地と道路に対するこの建築の関係は，過密した都市において類稀なものである。ここでは周辺の雑踏を和らげるため，軽やかなガラスのパヴィリオンを浮かせることにより小さな都市的ヴォイドが生み出された。ヴォイドは2枚の水平面によって挟まれ，空中へと凝縮されている。プログラムの主要部分は弧を描く1階の下へと埋め込まれた。1階は2面がセットバックし，光を地下空間へと落とす溝を通る背の高いガラスの壁を支持する。エントランスの階段は中間階のプラットフォームを通り，地階に設けられた屋外の中庭へと下る。そのため下から見上げると，地上，中間プラットフォーム，および上階のパヴィリオンの腹部を見ることができる。

ワンフロア，あるいはひとつながりのプラットフォーム，そして広大な下部空間は完全にフレキシブルである。そのため，これらの空間は店舗やオフィスとして利用することができる。空中のパヴィリオンは完全に独立し，建築全体のコンセプトにとっては不可欠な存在である。パヴィリオンは単層の構造体として，軽やかに地表の上空を浮遊する。カーブした屋根を持ち，天井高いっぱいのガラスが三つの面を囲む。オフィス・スタジオや店舗は自由に利用することができるように計画された。地表面は半透明のガラスによって敷き詰められている。そのため夜間は動線を照らし，昼間は光を透過することによって，地下の空間は柔らかい拡散光で満たされることになった。

Tomigaya Building

1987
AZABU JYUBAN BUILDING
麻布十番のビル

Tokyo, Japan

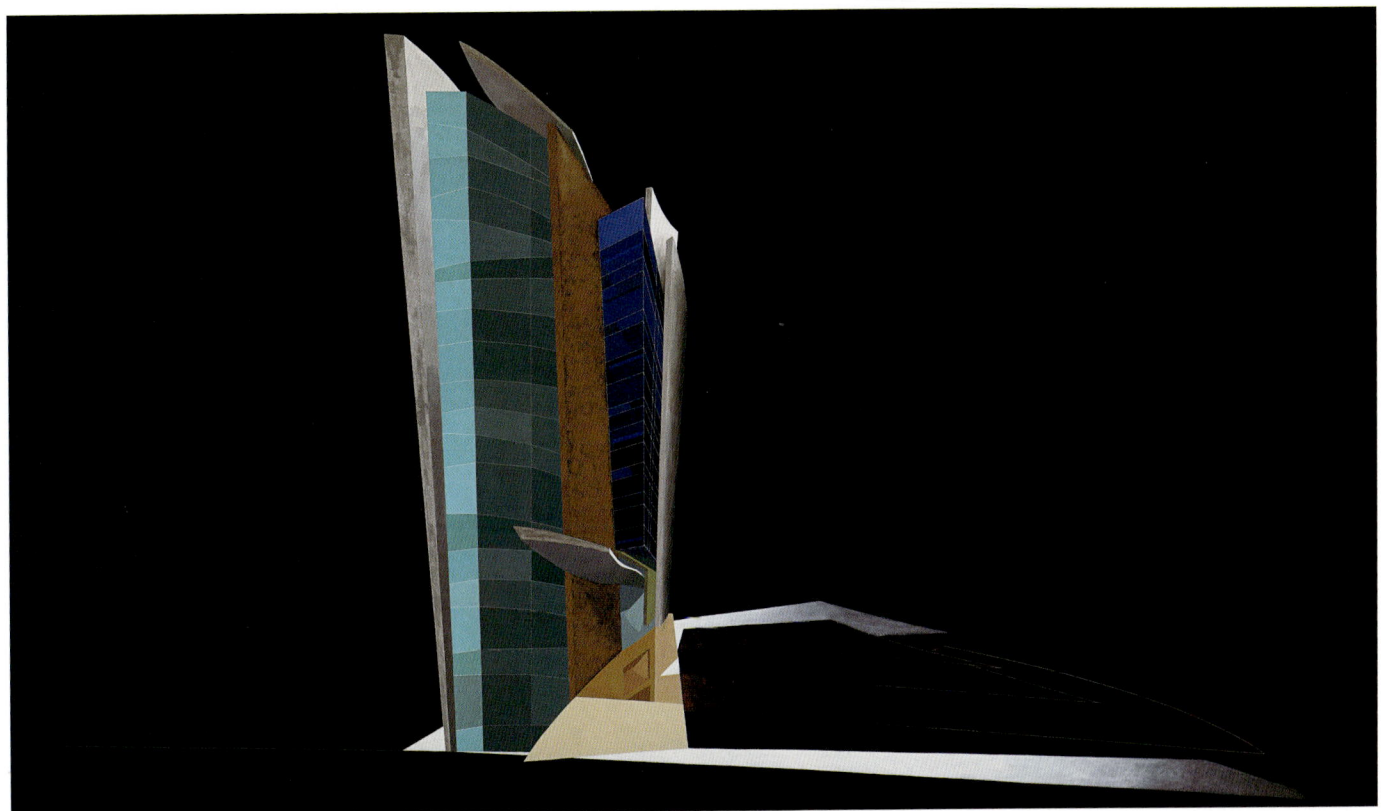

View toward entrance　エントランスを見る

Entrance　エントランス

Drawing on the experience of the Ku'Damm Project in 1986, we realised the great potential for releasing space. In Tokyo—Blade Runner territory—most sites are beyond the boundaries of space, and many buildings only increase the city's stifling congestion.

Slicing into the landscape and piercing the earth, the building exaggerates the pressure of its narrow site in a canyon of random building near the Roppongi district. The pristine glass structure is compressed between a tall metal wall and a reinforced concrete wall punctured by jewel-like windows. Between the walls are two curtain walls—one of blue glass, the other clear—that tilt out, rising to the terrace's parapet walls. Inside, the full impact of the releasable space is immediately apparent in the three-storey entrance space. A vertical stairway runs from the building's heart all the way up to the top, exploding into dramatic balconies.

Azabu Jyuban Building

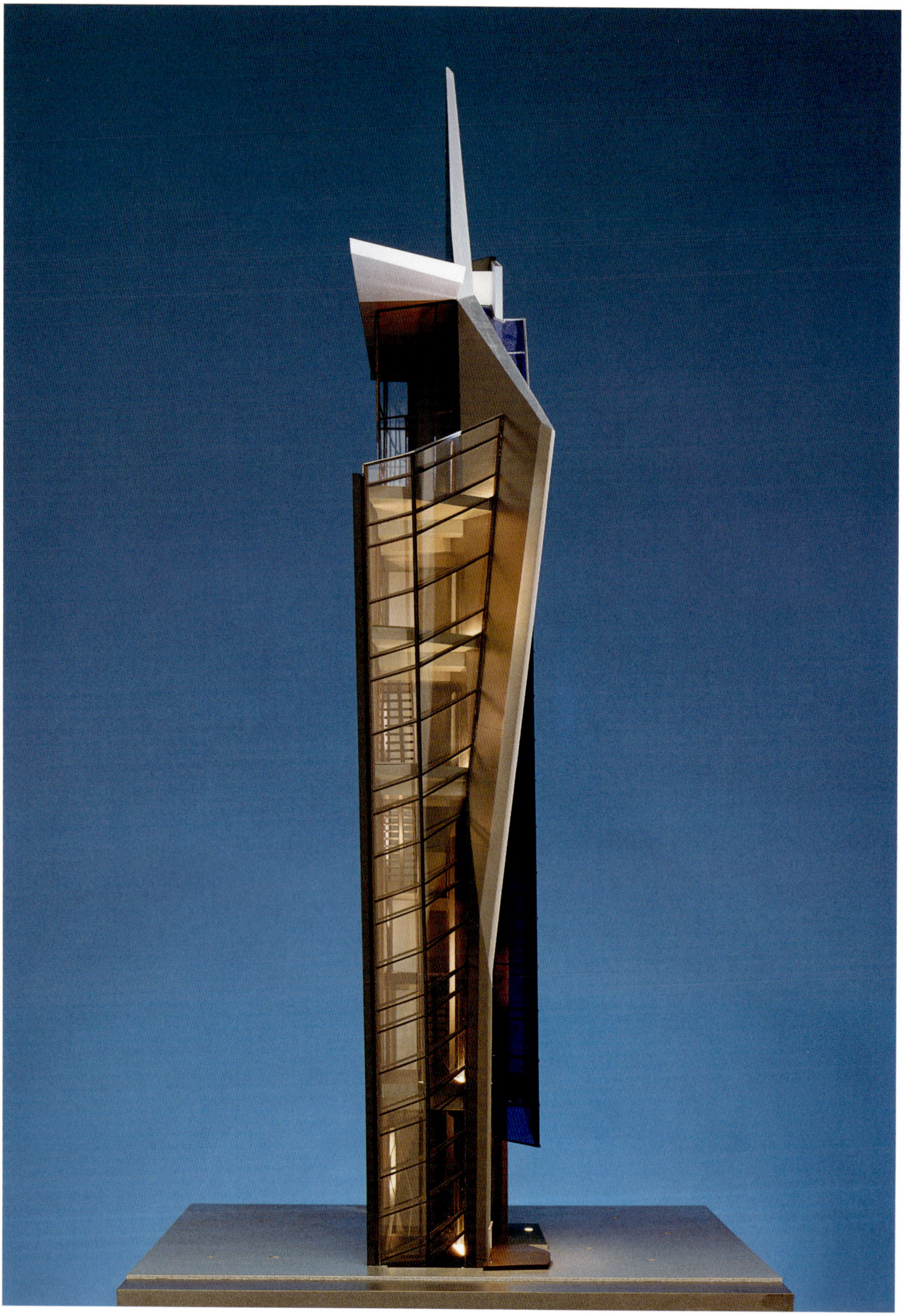

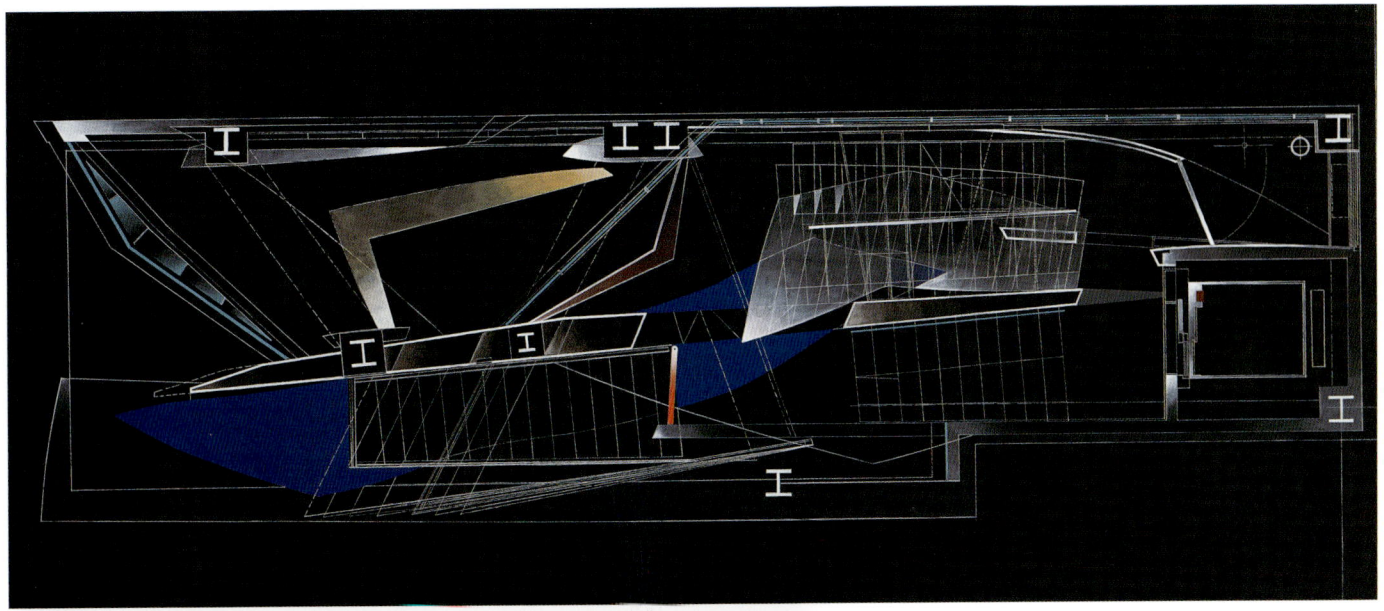

Plan　平面

Sectional model　断面模型

　我々は1986年のクーダム計画から，空間を解放することによる素晴しい可能性を発見していた。このドローイングはそのような経験に基づくものである。東京では——ブレードランナーの世界である——多くの敷地が空間の境界を突破すると共に，建築は息苦しい都市の過密を加速させている。
　この狭い敷地は六本木から程近く，無作為な建築群の峡谷のなかにある。建築をランドスケープへとスライスし，大地に突き差すことにより，抑圧が強く表現されている。背の高い金属壁と宝石のような窓で穿孔された鉄筋コンクリートの壁との間には，純粋なガラスの構造体が圧縮されている。これらの壁に挟まれた2枚のカーテンウォール——片方は青く，他方は透明ガラスである——は上方へ斜めにと伸びて，テラスの腰壁を覆う。内部は3層のエントランス空間に入ってすぐに現れる，解放的な空間が衝撃的である。垂直階段は建築の中心部から頂部へと真直ぐに，印象的なバルコニーまで一直線に走る。

Azabu Jyuban Building

1988
BERLIN 2000

ベルリン2000

Berlin, Germany

Before the collapse of the Berlin Wall in 1989, we were invited to speculate about the city's future. As part of an overall scheme between the axes of Mehringplatz to Bahnhof Friedrichstrasse and Brandenburger Tor to Alexanderplatz, the falling of the Wall offered new possibilities for regeneration. We considered both the expansion and the repair of the city, ranging from corridors of development to 'Wall-zone' building programmes.

The focus of our vision was the Alexanderplatz. Because it represents one of the few attempts to go beyond typical 19th Century urbanism, we decided to leave it free of homogeneous commercial development, to stand in poignant contrast to the vulnerable line that used to demarcate Berlin's division. A series of diagrams shows possible development of these newly released territories. Corridor cities project into the landscape, and new geometries inhabit the former 'dead zone', sometimes rectilinear yet slightly out of sync with the existing order.

In our eyes, the Wall zone could become a linear park. Where were once a concrete ribbon wall and no-go zone, we would lay down a strip of park, decorated with buildings.

我々が未来のベルリンについて考察するためにここを訪れたのは1989年のベルリンの壁崩壊以前の出来事である。計画予定地はメーリンク広場からフリードリッヒ・シュトラーセ駅へと続く都市軸と, ブランデンブルク門からアレクサンダー広場へと続く都市軸に挟まれた地区の一部にあたる。壁の崩壊は再生への新しい可能性を生み出す契機となった。コリドールの開発から「ウォール・ゾーン」の建築プログラムに至るまで, 都市の拡張と修復の両面がここでは検討の対象となった。

計画はアレクサンダー広場を構想の中心に据えたものである。アレクサンダー広場は19世紀型の典型的な都市を超えて企てられた数少ない事例のひとつである。そこで検討されたのは, 均質な商業地開発ではなく, 東西ベルリンを分割した繊細な境界線との強烈な対比を成すことであった。幾つものダイアグラムは新しく解放された領域の発展可能性を示している。コリドール都市はランドスケープへと広がり, 新しいジオメトリがかつての「緩衝地帯」に生まれる。幾つかの場所では直線的に, また, 既存の秩序から僅かに振って計画される。

ウォール・ゾーンはリニア・パークとして再生される。かつてコンクリートの壁と立入禁止区域のあった場所には細長い公園が置かれ, 建築で飾られる。

Berlin 2000　ベルリン2000

1988
VICTORIA CITY AERIAL
ヴィクトリア・シティ・エアリアル

Berlin, Germany

This competition project investigated the development of a central site within the city-core, which used to be West Berlin. It faces a major axis, Kurfurstendamm, with two storey perimeter buildings and leaves its inner space and backside unused. The existing buildings accommodating the famous Cafe Kranzler— are a typical architectural product of the fifties. Designed by Hans Dustmann in 1956 according to the then prevailing concepts of reconstructing the block structure, the existing buildings are on podium level only, with the slab rising high on top or in the back. The planned slab in the back area was never built. The site is cut by a dynamic force of the elevated railway, which curves towards the Bahnhof Zoo.

Before the wall came down, this site epitomised Berlin's state as an urban island. Although on the Kurfurstendamm, it is completely enclosed and virtually inaccessible. To create a building in such a fortified context Zaha Hadid suggested the need to intensify the urban density horizontally exploring the idea of urban foyers. The site was thus divided into new air corridors with three distinct zones that contain the three major functions, shopping facilities, offices and a hotel.

かつての西ベルリンに位置する市街中心部の主要地区開発に関する研究コンペ案。敷地は目抜き通りのクーアフュルステンダムに面している。周囲は2階建ての建築によって囲まれ、内部や背後の空間はそのまま残されている。既存建築には有名なカフェ・クランズラーが入居していたが、建築は典型的な50年代のスタイルであった。これは街区建築の再建といった当時の主流の考え方に基づく、ハンス・ドゥストマンの1956年の計画によるものである。既存部分は基壇レベルが設定され、その上に、あるいは背後にスラブを積層するといったものであった。背後に計画されていたスラブは建設されることはなかった。敷地は動物園駅へとカーブを描く高架の鉄道が横切り、大胆に切断されている。

壁が崩壊する前は、この敷地は島のように孤立した都市というベルリンの状況を縮図的に示していた。クーアフュルステンダムに面するにも関わらず完全に閉鎖され、事実上到達不可能な場所である。要塞化したコンテクストで建築を生み出すために、ザハ・ハディドは都市ホワイエといった概念を水平方向へと拡張し、都市の密度を強化する必要性を提起した。そこで、敷地は商業施設、オフィス、ホテルという主な三つのプログラムに対応する三つのゾーンとして、これまでにない空中回廊へと分節された。

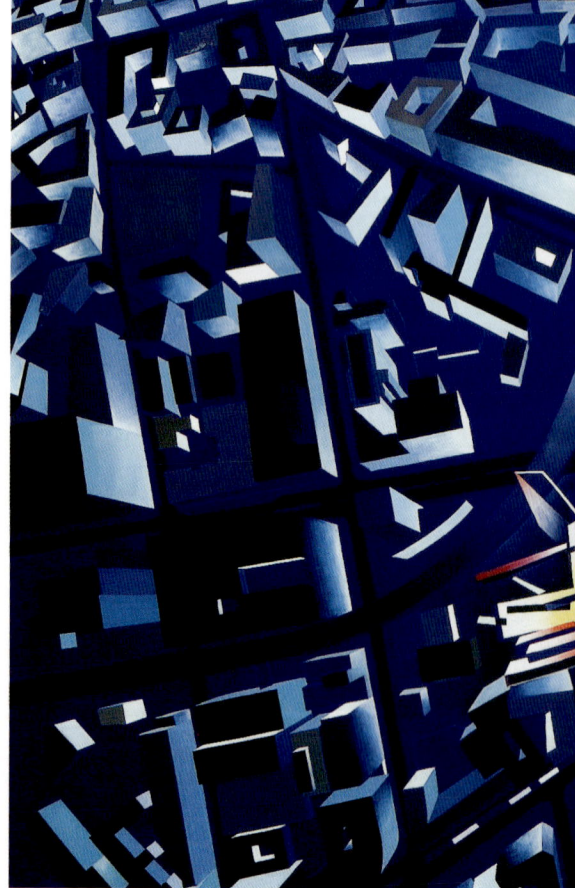

Blue beam (above)　ブルー・ビーム（上）
Aerial perspective (below)　鳥瞰パースペクティヴ（下）

Victoria City Aerial

051

1989
HAFENSTRASSE OFFICE & RESIDENTIAL DEVELOPMENT

ハーフェン通りのオフィス&住宅開発計画

Hamburg, Germany

Hafenstrasse　ハーフェン通り

The two sites (a corner and a middle site) at the old harbour street are gaps in a row of traditional four and five storey houses. The relation to the Elbe river is mediated through a series of parallel strips terracing down to the water: the row of houses, the old street, a small park, the new street, the embankment. The intention was to develop a programmatic links across the strips and to turn the embankment into a beach or sports field. The gaps in the wall of houses will not be filled hermetically but allow permeation to the area behind, e.g. to the school behind the middle site. The corner bends and the in-between space of the middle site receives a series of different slabs like a stack of books. Bernard Nochstrasse and Haffenstrasse meet at an acute corner; the former rises the latter falls. A slab building is proposed which leans forward and twists, while its back opens to the riverfront. The vertical organisation is a sequence of commercial and residential layers. A public space at the first two levels joins the entrance and lobby to the levels above. As one ascends, each floor shifts, creating a different entry space at every level. There are two residential levels followed by two levels of offices. A sky lobby separates the office area from the penthouse above. Sliding sections of the glass curtain wall enable parts of each floor to become outdoor terraces. Two blade columns provide the main structural support. Further stiffening is accommodated by a solid back wall and the floor slabs. A heavy base pad anchors the structural elements. The riverside elevation is a continuous curtain wall, which wraps over and becomes a penthouse roof. The twist of the building creates a hyperbolic surface at the back, which may be constructed using horizontal and diagonal straight members. The geometry of the curtain wall is created by a single curve running at diagonal of the building.

Middle site and elevation studies
中央の敷地と立面のスタディ

二つの敷地（一方は角地，他方は通りの中央にあたる）は，4，5階建ての伝統住宅が建ち並ぶ古い港町の通りの一角にある。町並み，古い道路，小さな公園，新しい道路，および堤防の土手が，水辺に向かって段々とストライプ状に並ぶ。このことが敷地とエルベ川との関係を成立させている。この計画の目的はそのようなストライプをまたいでプログラム的つながりをつくり出し，堤防をビーチやスポーツ・グラウンドに変貌させることである。住宅の外壁との隙間は閉じられることなく，例えば中央の敷地から背後の学校に抜けるといった具合に，空間は後ろの区画へと浸透することが期待された。中央の敷地のコーナーや中間領域には，本が積み上がるように，数多くの床スラブが見えてくる。敷地の角はベルンハルト・ノット通りの上りとハーフェン通りの下りがぶつかる鋭角の交差点にあたる。建築の床スラブは前面にせり出し，捻れるように計画されている。また，背面は川岸に向けて開放されている。鉛直方向の空間構成は商業と住宅のレイヤーを配置したものである。入って最初の2層のパブリック・スペースは，エントランスとロビーを上層階へとつないでいる。登るごとに上層階の床位置は変化する。そのため，各階には個別のエントランス空間が構成される。住宅は2層にわたり，さらに2層分，オフィスが続く。スカイ・ロビーはオフィスとその上のペントハウスを分け隔てる役割を果たす。ガラスのカーテンウォールはスライドさせることで，各々のフロアは一部を屋外テラスとすることができる。ブレード状の2枚の柱が主要構造の支持材にあたる。背後の耐震壁とフロア・スラブが構造を補強する役割を果たしている。重量のある基礎スラブは構造要素を地盤へと定着させている。川岸側のファサードは連続したカーテンウォールが全面を覆い，ペントハウスの屋根となっている。建築は湾曲して背後に双曲線の曲面を構成するが，これは水平や対角線方向に直線部材を架けて建設することができる。カーテンウォールのジオメトリは建築を斜めに走る単純なカーブに沿って生成されている。

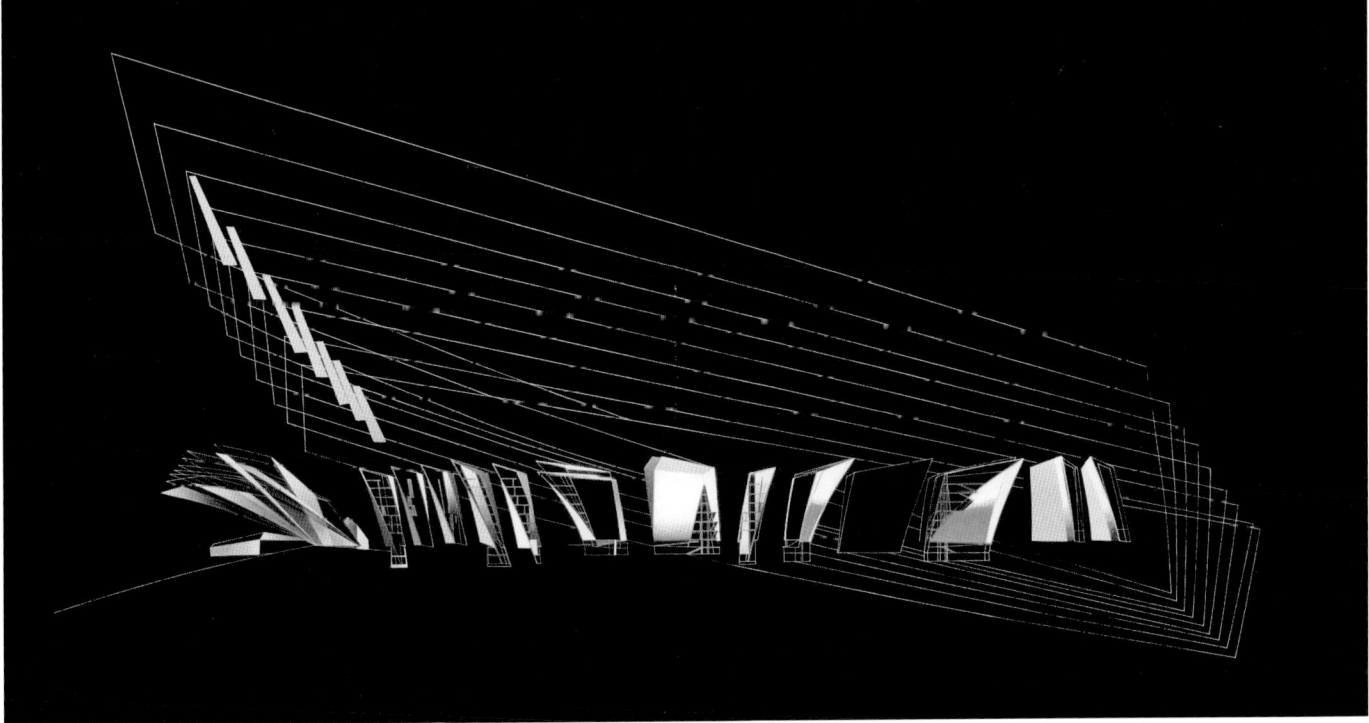

Overall view (above) 全景（上）
Hafenstrasse office (below) ハーフェン通りのオフィス（下）

Hafenstrasse Office & Residential Development

1989-93
KMR, ART AND MEDIA PARK
KMR アート&メディア・パーク

Dusseldorf, Germany

Perspective　パースペクティヴ

The development of this prominent site is the impetus to transform the old Dusseldorf Harbour into a new Enterprise Zone. The programme for the whole area concentrates on providing facilities for the communication business and allied, creative professions. Their offices and studios are interspersed with and supported by shops, restaurants, cultural and leisure facilities. This becomes a strategy for the whole harbour development.

The focus of the area is the river, which is animated with sport and leisure activities. A large, artificially modelled landscape, with one of the planes like a grass wedge, faces the river and becomes an extension of this very public and active part of the site.

This is physically protected by a 90 m long wall of offices. From the river an enormous metallic triangle cuts into the site. It pierces the wall, breaking it, to form an entrance ramp to the street and a sloping plaza below. The adjoining ground planes crack open and reveal technical studios to the north, shops and restaurants to the south. Below ground, a wall of technical services is compressed, which results in part of the wall rising above ground and curving around to form a 320 seat cinema.

On the street side the wall has tiny, linear incisions in its in-situ concrete elevation; while on river side, individual floors are articulated by varying depths of cantilever according to the function of each of the floors. The advertising agency is an even more fragmented series of slabs, set perpendicular to the street. They are glass splinters broken from the wall and have floor to floor full height triple glazed curtain wall. Where the floor slabs converge, a void is carved out for conference rooms and exhibition areas. The cores of lifts and services are separated into detached elements to give dramatic, uninterrupted views across the Agency. The entrance lobby is at the point of intersection of wall and Agency. It is a minimalist glass box surrounded by a family of sculptured feet and heavy, triangular, transfer structures. A grand curved stair leads the way up to the conference rooms through the underbelly of a heavy slab suspended above.

Perspective of executive office　役員室を見る

KMR, Art and Media Park

この重要な敷地の開発は，古きデュッセルドルフ港から新しい企業誘致地区への変換の起動力となる。地区全体のプログラムは，通信業やそれらと提携するクリエイティブ職のための施設を整えることに重きを置いている。彼らのオフィスやスタジオは，店舗やレストラン，文化・娯楽施設の中に散在する形で他のプログラムと共存し，それらに支えられている。この方針は港エリア全体へと展開されるものである。

この地区の焦点は，スポーツや娯楽施設が賑わう河川エリアにある。人工的に造形された大きなランドスケープを構成する面の一つは芝生のようなギザギザな形をしており，川に面したランドスケープは，この最もパブリックで活気のあるエリアの延長となる。

このエリアは，長さ90メートルのオフィスの壁によって物理的に守られている。河川側からは巨大な金属質の三角形が敷地に切り込んでいる。三角形は壁を破り，断絶させることで，街路へのエントランス・スロープを形成し，その下側には斜面状の広場が展開する。隣接する地盤に生じた割れ目は，その隙間から北側の技術スタジオや，南側の店舗やレストランをあらわにする。地下では，機械設備がひとつの壁に押し縮められ，その結果，地上に出現した壁の一部が，カーブを描き，320席の映画館を形成する。

街路側では，現場打ちのコンクリート壁に小さな線形の切り込みが見られる。一方，河川側では，それぞれの機能に適した異なる深さのキャンチレバーによって各階が分節されている。広告代理店の事務所は，さらに細かく分節されたスラブの集合であり，街路に対して垂直に配置されている。それらスラブは壁から飛び散ったガラスの破片であり，階高いっぱいに三重の複層ガラスカーテンウォールが張られている。スラブが重なる部分ではヴォイドがくり抜かれ，会議室や展示空間となる。エレベータや設備のコアは，独立したエレメントとして切り離され，ダイナミックな景観を遮られずに事務所のどこからでも臨むことができる。エントランス・ロビーは，壁面と広告代理店の交差する場所にある。それはミニマルなガラスの箱であり，彫刻の施された柱脚や重厚な三角形の構造体の間に配置されている。エントランスからは，壮大なカーブ状の階段が上方に吊された重厚なスラブの下をくぐり，会議室へと上がっていく。

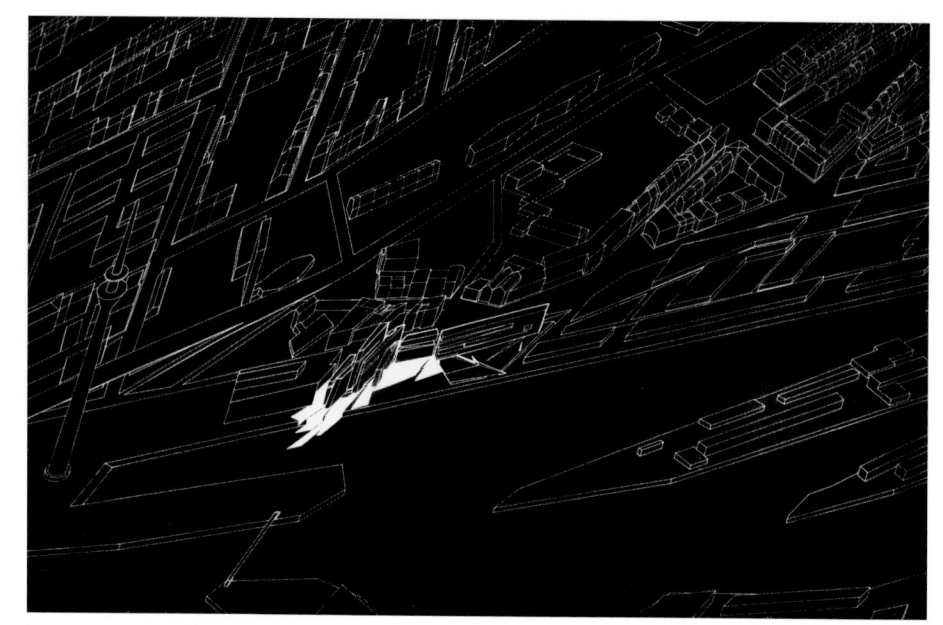

Perspective of site　敷地を俯瞰する

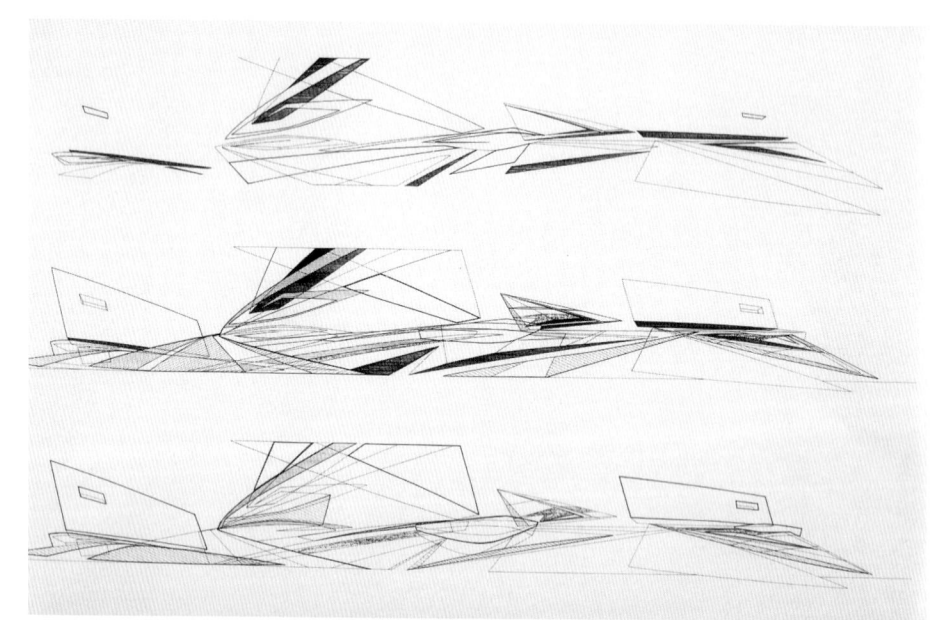

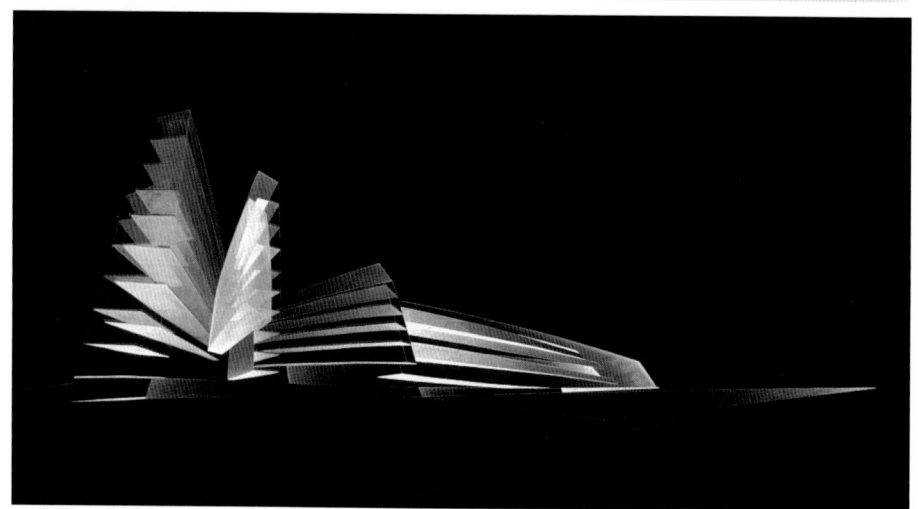

Landscape sequence through block A (above)　ブロックA：ランドスケープのつながり（上）
Perspective (below)　パースペクティヴ（下）

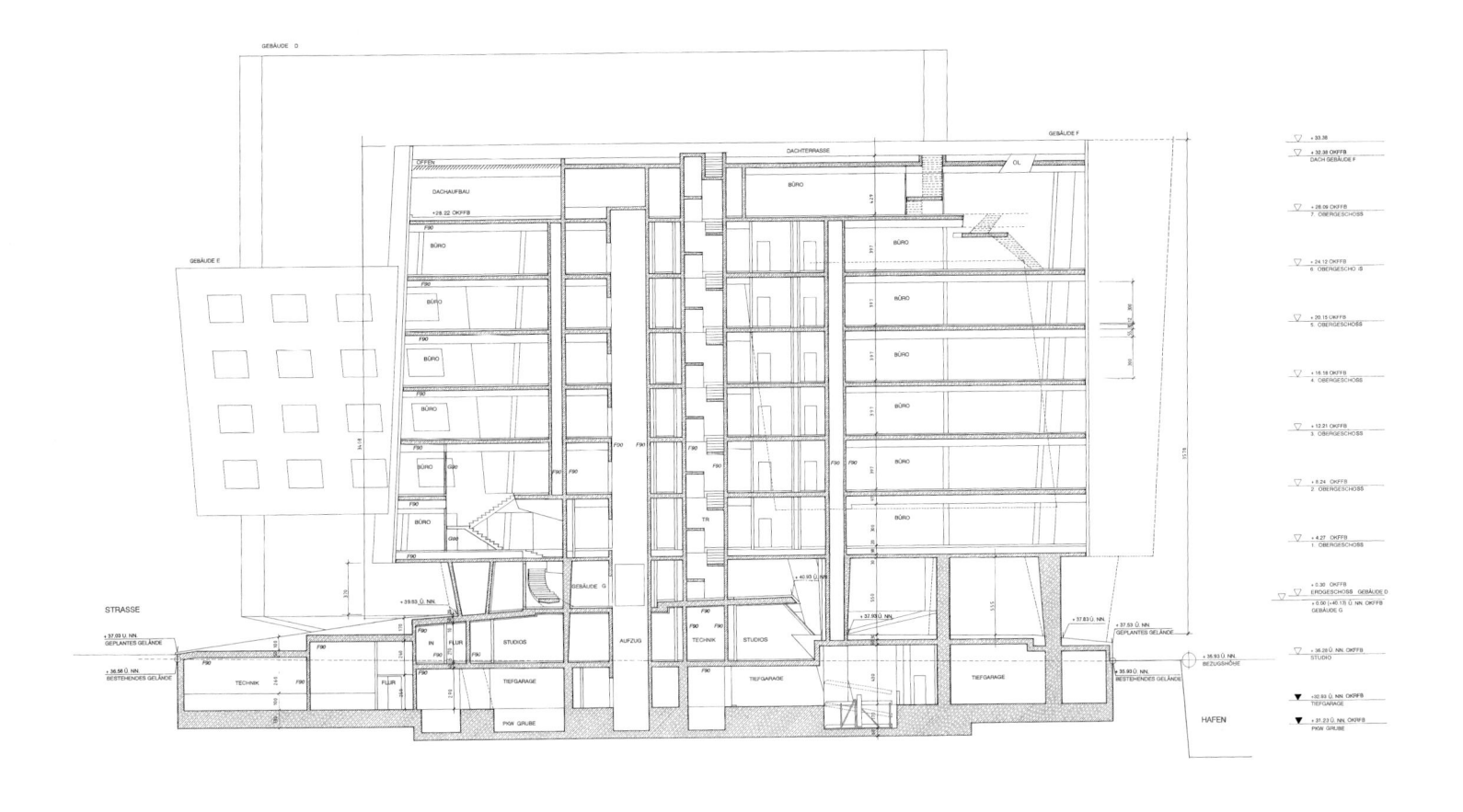

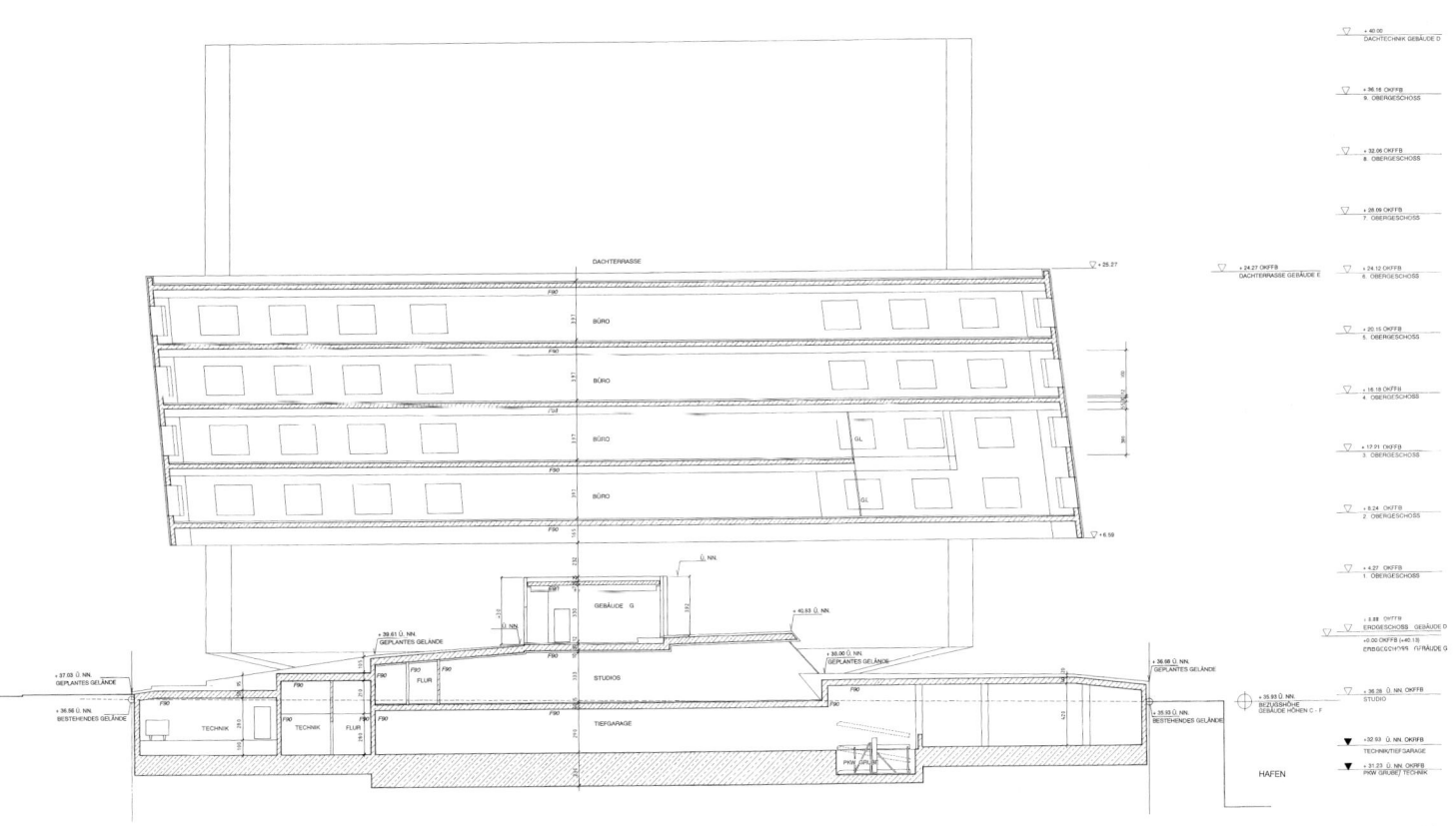

KMR, Art and Media Park

Sections　断面

1989-90
MOON SOON
ムーンスーン

Sapporo, Japan

For a two-fold programme of formal eating and relaxed lounging an opposition of moods was created. The result is two synthetic and strange worlds: fire and ice. Inspired by the seasonal ice buildings of Sapporo, the first floor features cool greys materialised in glass and metal. Tables are sharp fragments of ice: a raised floor level drifts like an iceberg across the space.

Above the ice chamber whirls a furnace of fire, rendered in searing reds, brilliant yellows and exuberant oranges. A spiral above the bar tears through the first floor ceiling, curling up to the underside of the upper-level dome like a fiery tornado bursting through a pressure vessel. A plasma of biomorphic sofas accommodates eating and lounging and allows an infinite configuration of seating types with movable trays and plug-in sofa backs.

Ceiling detail on second floor　2階天井部のディテール

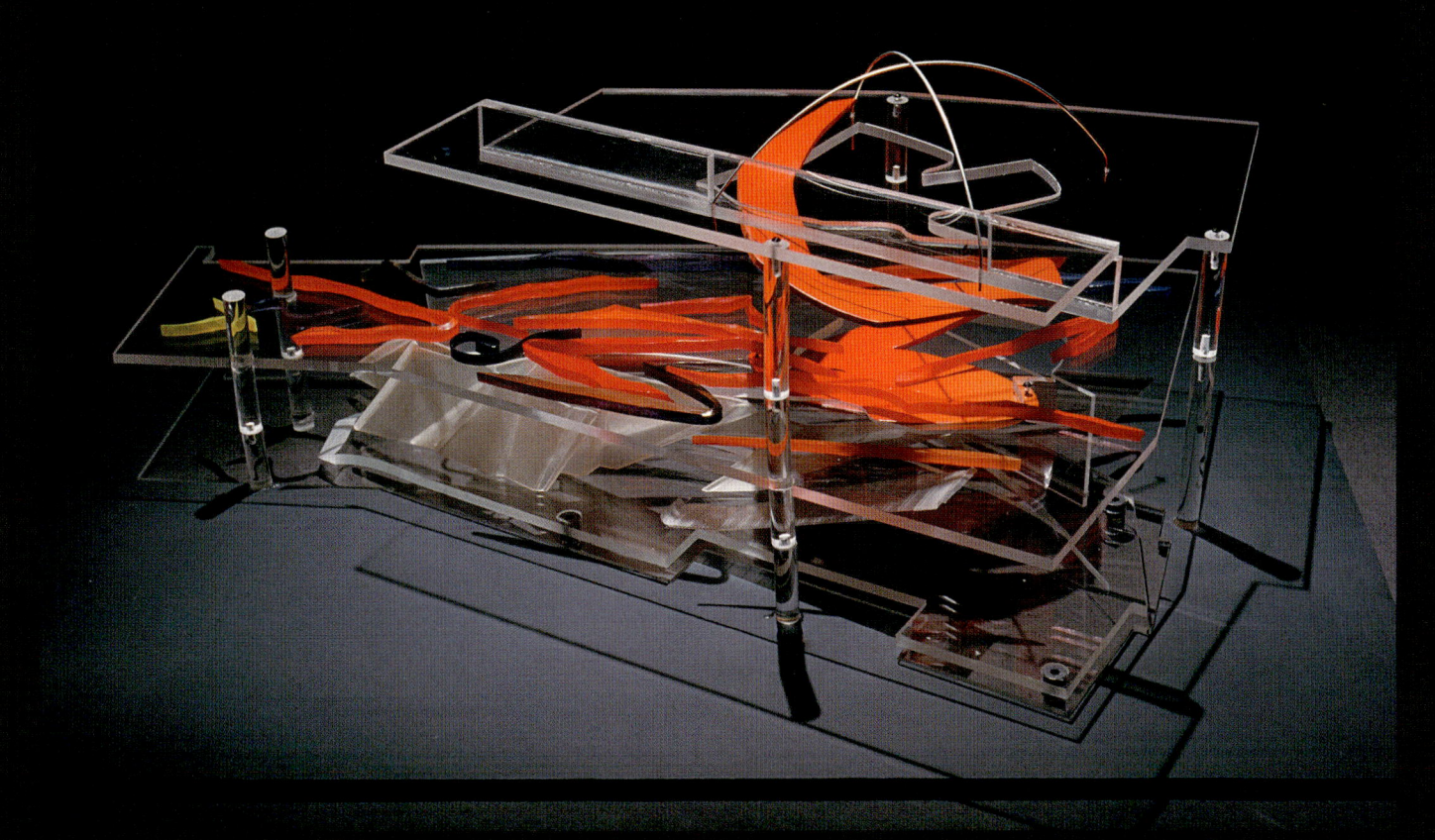

Model　模型

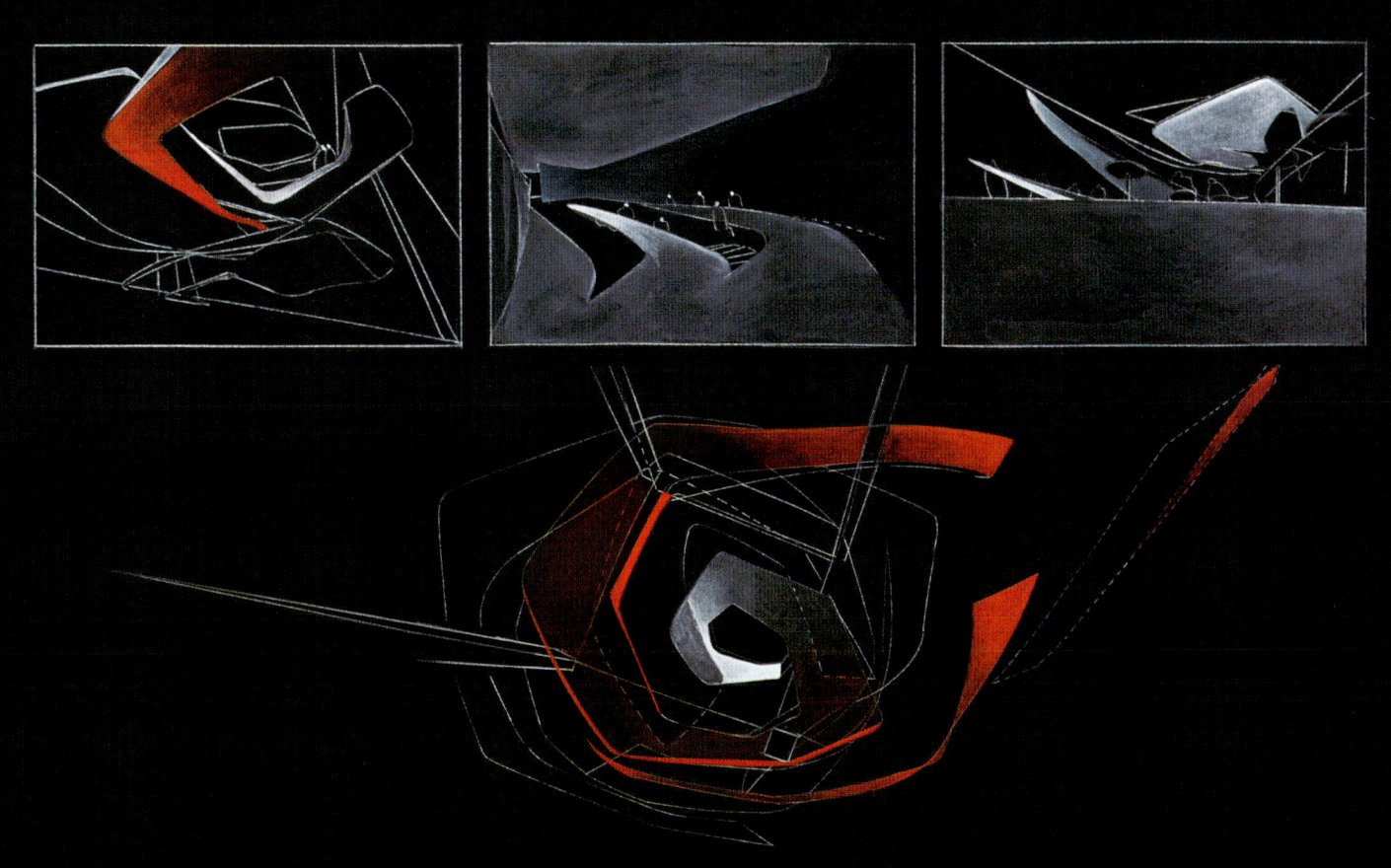

Studies of ceiling "Orange peel" on second floor　2階天井部の「オレンジ・ピール」のスタディ

Reflected ceiling plan: first floor　1階天井伏

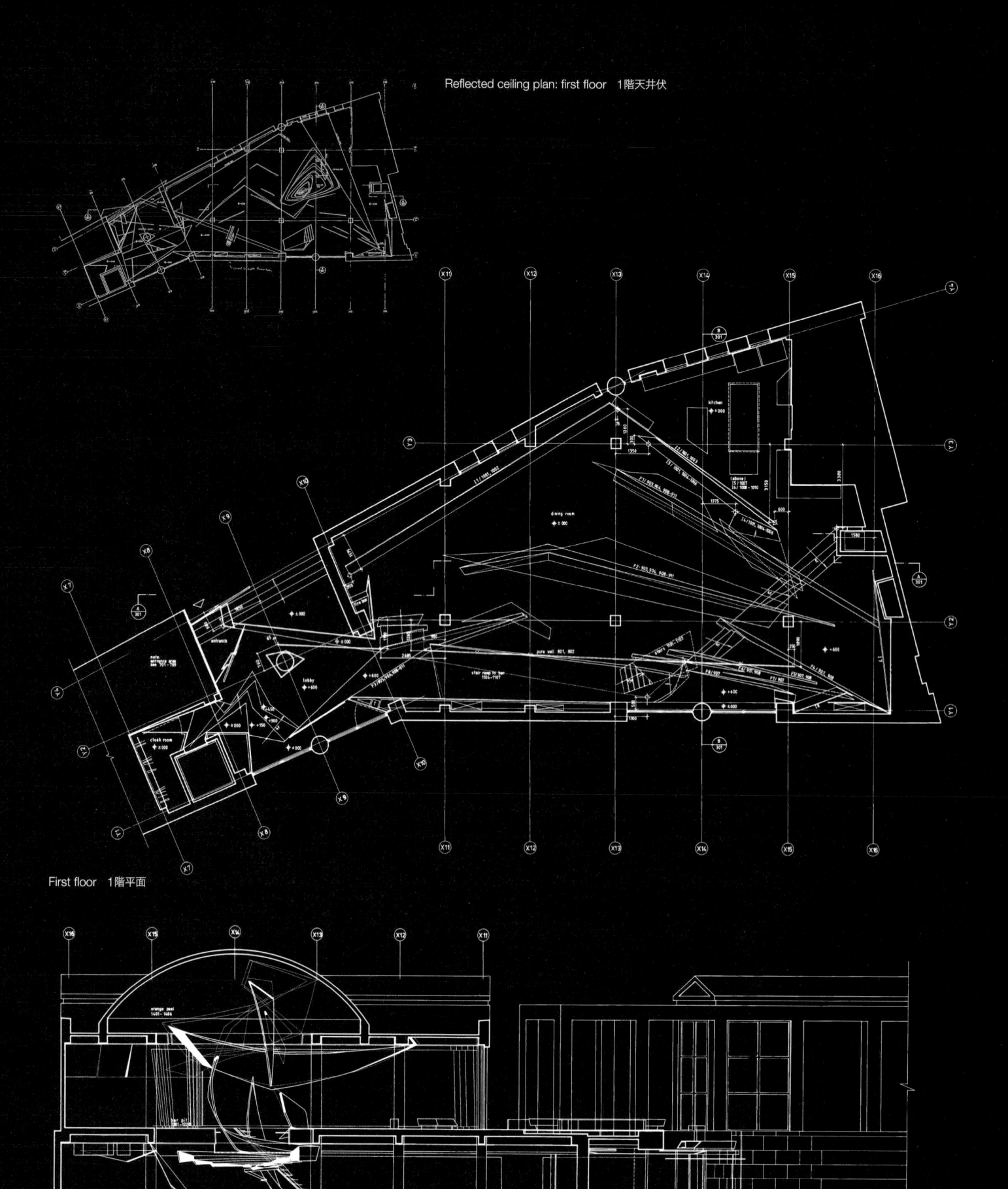

First floor　1階平面

Longitudinal section　長手断面

060

Reflected ceiling plan: second floor　2階天井伏

Second floor　2階平面

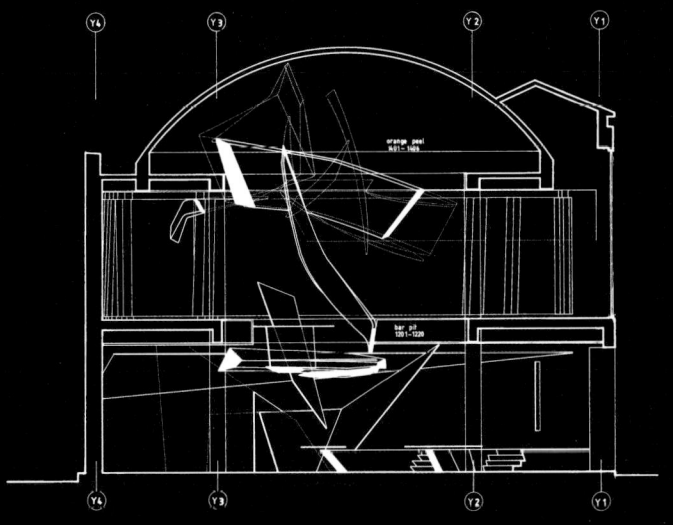

Cross section　短手断面

正式な会食と気兼ねのないくつろぎの場という二重のプログラムを満たすため, 相対する二つの雰囲気が演出された。その二つとは, 炎と氷という統合的で不思議な世界である。冬季の札幌雪祭りで見られる氷像にインスピレーションを受け, 1階はガラスや金属といった素材によってクールグレイの色調が実現された。テーブルは鋭い氷の破片を象徴し, 中2階はまるで氷山のように空間を漂う。

氷室の上方では, 火炉の中で炎が渦巻いており, その様子は焼けるような赤色や鮮明な黄色, 活気溢れるオレンジ色によって表現される。バーの上方に伸びる螺旋は1階の天井を破り, 上階のドームへと巻き上がっていく。その様子はいかにも圧力容器から噴出する炎の竜巻のようである。有機的な造形を持つソファの集合は食事やくつろぎの場を提供し, 着脱のできるテーブルや背もたれは座席の多様な配置パターンを可能にする。

Moon Soon

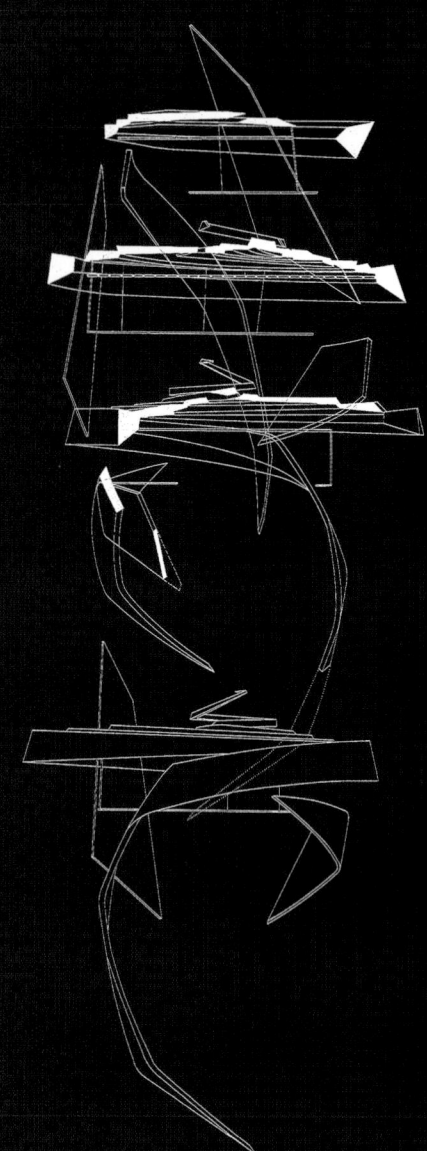

"Orange peel" isometric
「オレンジ・ピール」のアイソメトリック

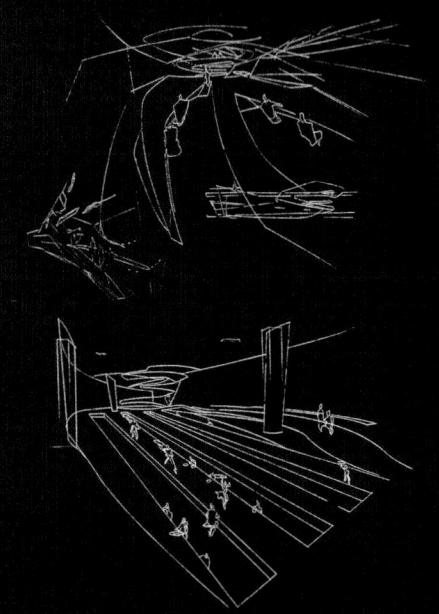

Sketches　スケッチ

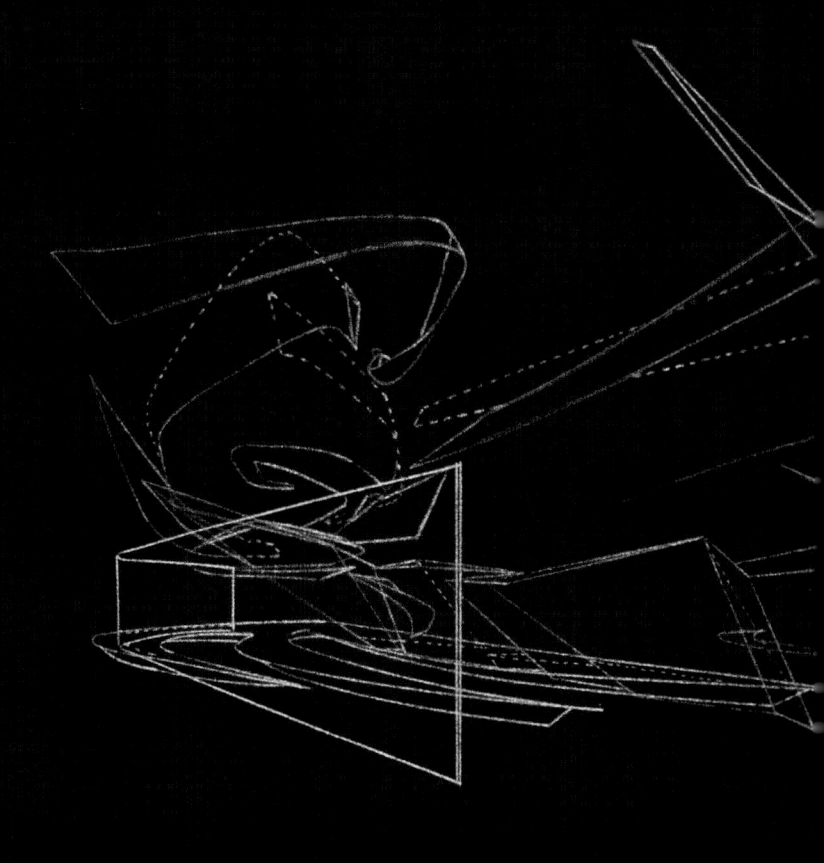

Perspective of first floor (above)　1階パースペクティヴ（上）
Iceberg: image of entrance (below)　アイス・バーグ（氷山）：1階エントランスのイメージ（下）

Entrance area (above) エントランス・エリア（上）
Restaurant on first floor (below) 1階のレストラン（下）

Restaurant レストラン

Moon Soon

"Orange peel" over bar pit (above)　バー・ピット上部の「オレンジ・ピール」(上)
Sofa on bar (below)　バーに置かれたソファ(下)

Bar on second floor 2階のバー

1991-93
VITRA FIRE STATION
ヴィトラ社消防所

Weil am Rhein, Germany

Overall view from east: main entrance and garage under canopy　東側全景：キャノピーの下にはメイン・エントランスとガレージがある

Night view from southwest 夜景。南西より見る

We initiated our design with a study of the overall factory site. Our intention was to place the elements of our commission in such a way that they would not be lost between the enormous factory sheds. We also used these elements to structure the whole site, giving identity and rhythm to the main street running through the complex. This street—which stretches from the chair museum to the other end of the factory site, where the fire station is now located, was envisaged as a linear landscaped zone, almost as if it were the artificial extension of the linear patterns of the adjacent agricultural fields and vineyards. Thus, rather than designing the building as an isolated object, it was developed as the outer edge of the landscaped zone: defining space rather than occupying space. This was achieved by stretching the programme into a long, narrow building alongside the street which marks the edge of the factory site, and which also functions as a screening device against the bordering buildings.

The space-defining and screening functions of the building were the point of departure for the development of the architectural concept: a linear, layered series of walls. The programme of the firestation inhabits the spaces between these walls, which puncture, tilt and break according to functional requirements. The building is hermetic from a frontal reading, revealing the interiors only from a perpendicular viewpoint.

As one passes across the spaces of the firestation, one catches glimpses of the large red fire engines. Their lines of movement are inscribed into the asphalt. Similarly, the ritualized exercises of the firemen will be inscribed into the ground; a series of choreographic nota-

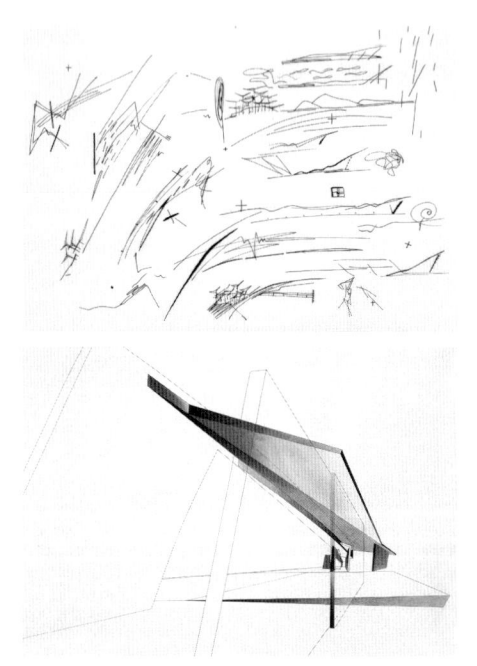

Sketches スケッチ

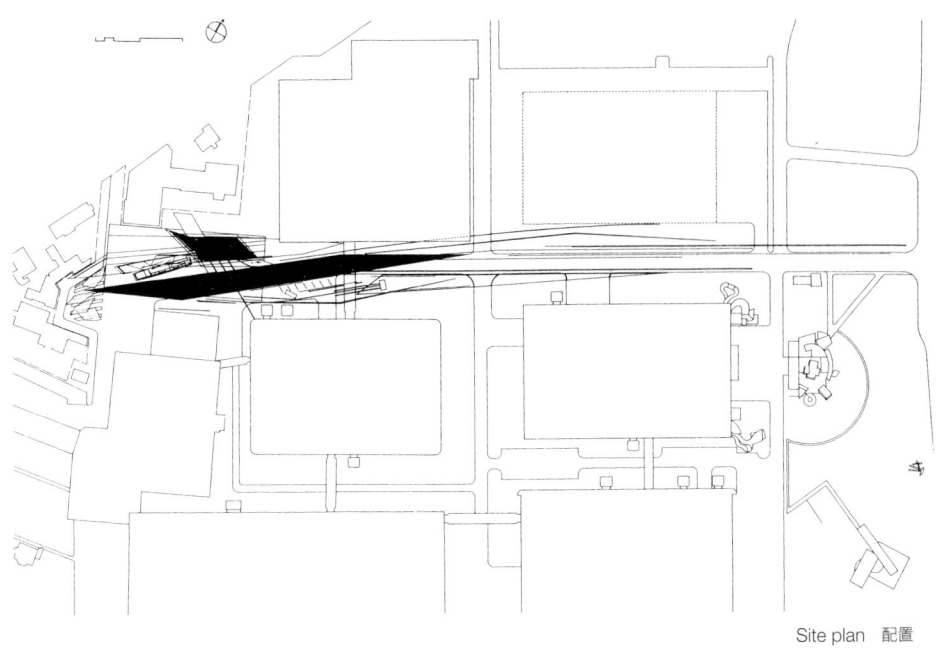

tions. The whole building is movement, frozen. It expresses the tension of being on the alert; and the potential to explode into action at any moment. The walls appear to slide past each other, while the large sliding doors literally form a moving wall.

The whole building is constructed of exposed, reinforced in-situ concrete. Special attention was given to the sharpness of all edges; any attachments like roof edgings or claddings were avoided as they distract from the simplicity of the prismatic form and the abstract quality of the architectural concept. This same absence of detail informed the frameless glazing, the large sliding planes enclosing the garage, and the treatment of the interior spaces including the lighting scheme. The lines of light direct the necessarily precise and fast movement through the building.

Site plan 配置

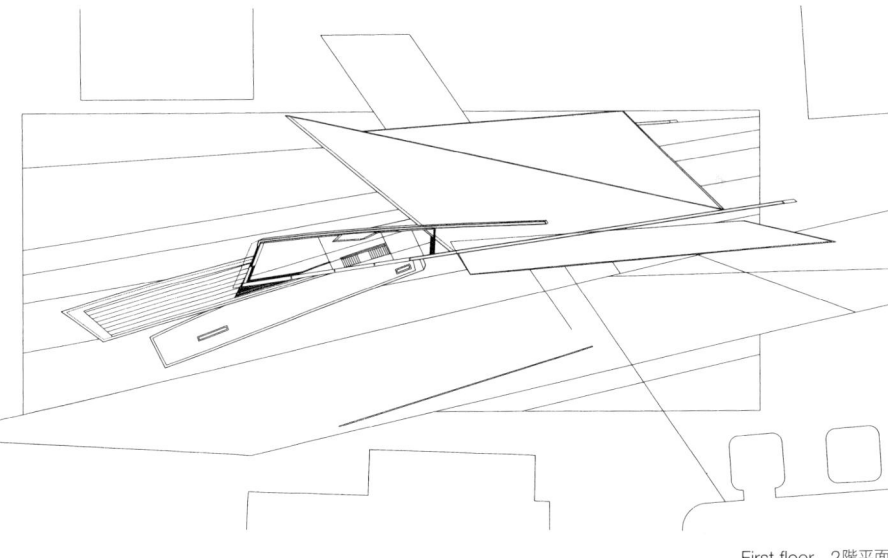

First floor 2階平面

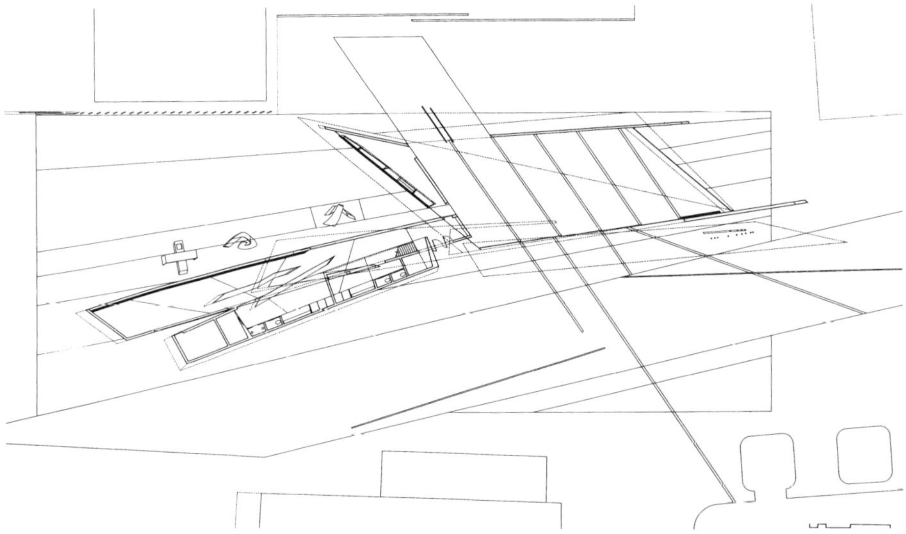

Ground floor 1階平面

Plan studies (above) 平面スタディ（上）
View into corridor (below) 廊下を見る（下）

Aerial perspective　鳥瞰パースペクティヴ

Vitra Fire Station

073

Entrance hall　エントランス・ホール

私たちは，工場敷地全体のスタディをすることからデザインを始めた。私たちの意図は，所定のエレメントが工場の巨大な倉庫の間に埋もれてしまわないよう注意しながら配置することにあった。また，これらを敷地全体を構成するエレメントとして扱うことで，複合施設を貫く大通りにアイデンティティとリズムを与えた。イスの美術館から工場の反対側の端まで伸びる大通りに消防所の敷地があり，隣接する農地やブドウ畑の線状パターンの人工的な延長であるかのような，線形のランドスケープ・ゾーンとして構想された。そのため，この建築は単体のオブジェクトとしてではなく，ランドスケープ・ゾーンの外縁を示すものとしてデザインされた。これは単に空間を占めるものではなく，境界を定めるものである。このことは，所定のプログラムを，通り沿いに配置された細長い建物へと引き伸ばすことで達成された。これは，工場エリアの端を示し，周囲の建物に対して目隠しとしても機能する。

空間の定義や目隠しとしての機能は，直線的で複層的な壁の集合という建築的コンセプトの出発点であった。消防所のプログラムはこれらの壁の間に宿り，壁は機能の要求に応じて裂けたり，傾いたり，途切れたりする。この建物は正面からは密閉されたヴォリュームのように見え，内部の様子は正面に垂直な視点からしか覗くことができない。

消防所の中を横切ると，大きな消防車を垣間見ることができる。消防車の動きはアスファルトに刻み込まれている。同様に，消防士の儀式化された動作も，一連の振付けの記述として地面に刻まれる。建物全体が，ある凍った瞬間として動きそのものを象徴しており，張りつめた空気感や，今にも静寂を破って動き出しそうな臨場感を表現している。壁は滑らかにスライドしているかのような感覚を与え，大きなスライド式のドアは文字通り動く壁となる。

建物全体は，現場打ちの鉄筋コンクリートで構成されている。あらゆるエッジの鋭さには特に注意が払われた。プリズムの形状のシンプルさと建築的コンセプトの抽象的なクオリティから注意を逸らさないように，屋根の縁切りや被覆材といった付属品の使用は避けられた。また，ディテールの不在は，枠のないガラスやガレージを囲い込む可動の平面，照明計画を含む内部空間の扱い方をも定義した。光の筋は，建物全体を通して必然的に正確で迅速な動きを導く。

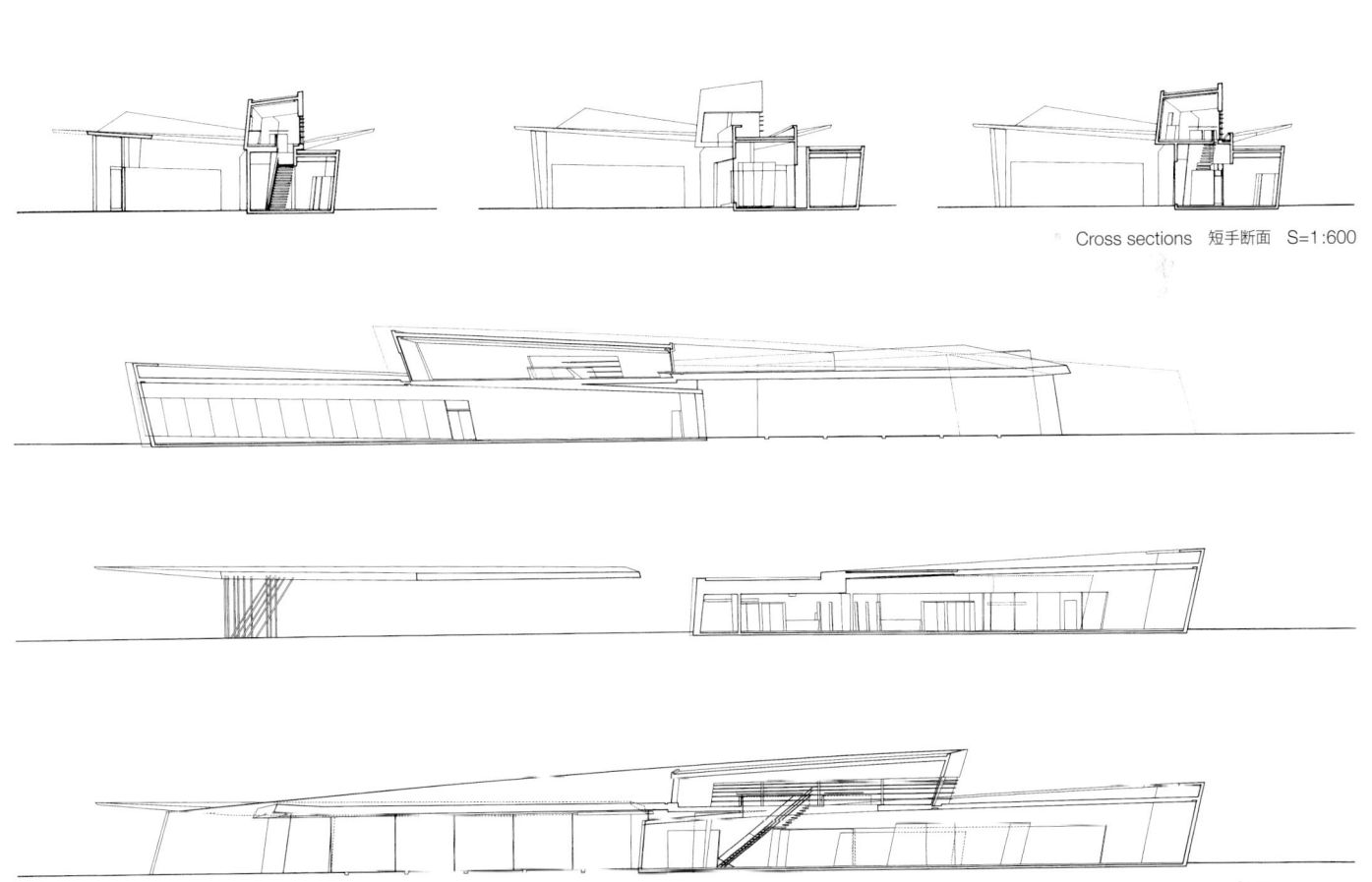

Cross sections 短手断面 S=1:600

Longitudinal sections 長手断面 S=1:600

Vitra Fire Station

View toward entrance from exercise room　エクササイズ・ルームより入口を見る

Club room on first floor (above)　2階クラブ・ルーム（上）
Changing room for male (below)　男子更衣室（下）

Vitra Fire Station

077

1994-96
CARDIFF BAY OPERA HOUSE
カーディフベイ・オペラハウス

Cardiff, Wales, U.K.

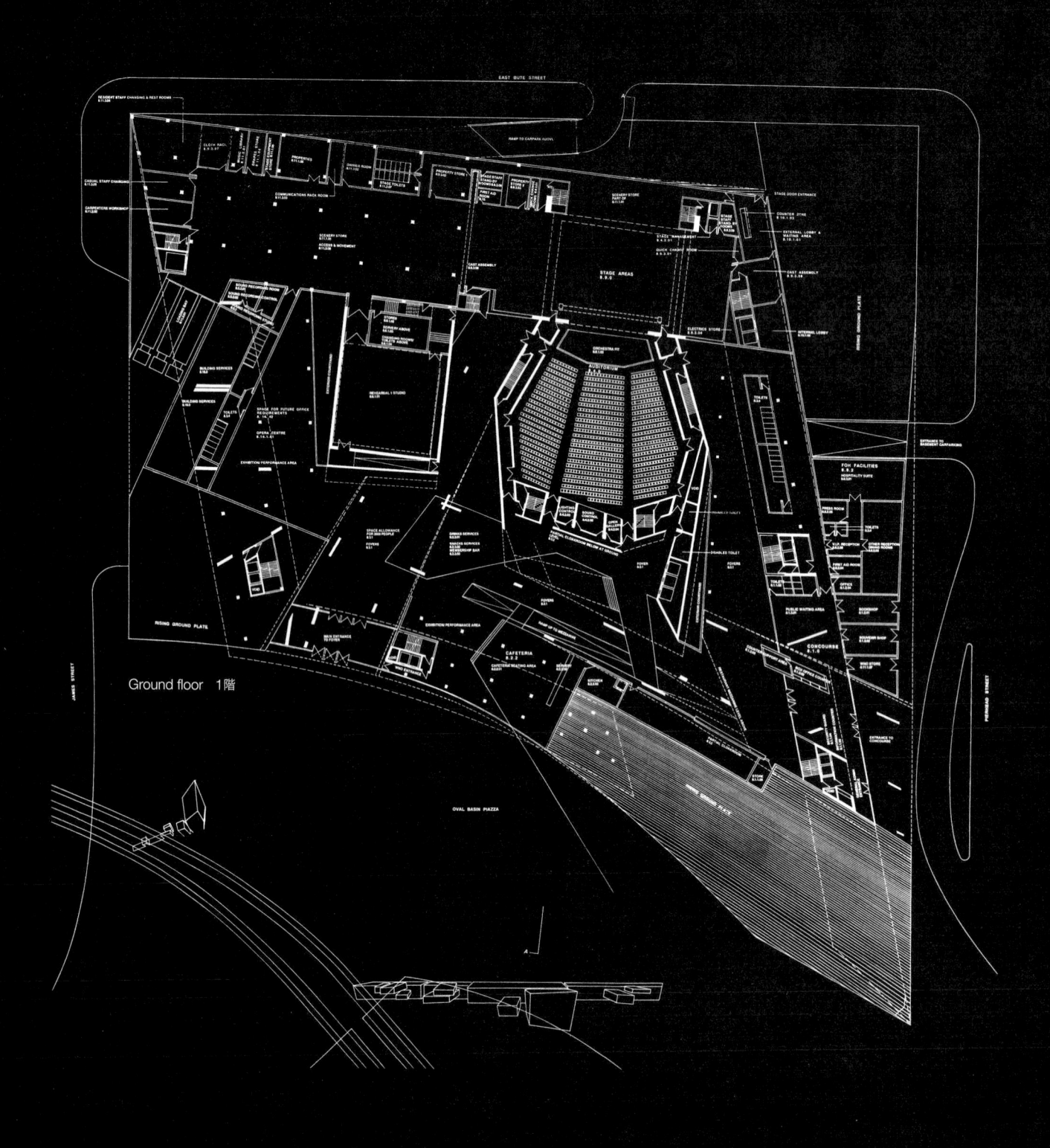

Ground floor　1階

The proposed design for the Cardiff Bay Opera House tries to achieve simultaneity of typically exclusive paradigms of urban design: monument and space. The project takes part in the continuous building mass giving shape to the Oval Basin Piazza as envisioned by the masterplan. At the same time, the building projects a strong figurative landmark against the waterfront.

The dichotomy of the typical perimeter block externally shaping a larger public urban space while enclosing a secluded internal space is dissolved into a continuum between those two types of spaces. This is achieved by three complementary moves: the raising of the perimeter; the opening up of the perimeter at the corner pointing at the pier head and revealing the expressed volume of the auditorium as the main solid figure within the perimeter of the site; and finally, the continuation of the public urban space by means of extending the plaza with a gentle slope into the site establishing a new ground plane over the main foyer areas. Thus, the project provides a raised plaza suitable for outdoor performances and allowing an enhanced vista back into the Inner Harbor and Bay.

The building concept is based on the architectural expression of the hierarchy between serviced and servicing spaces: the auditorium and the other public and semi-public performance and rehearsal spaces spring like jewels from a band of rationally lined-up support accommodations. This band is then wrapped around the perimeter of the site like an inverted necklace where all the jewels turn towards each other creating a concentrated public space between each other, accessible to the public from the center while serviced from the back around the perimeter.

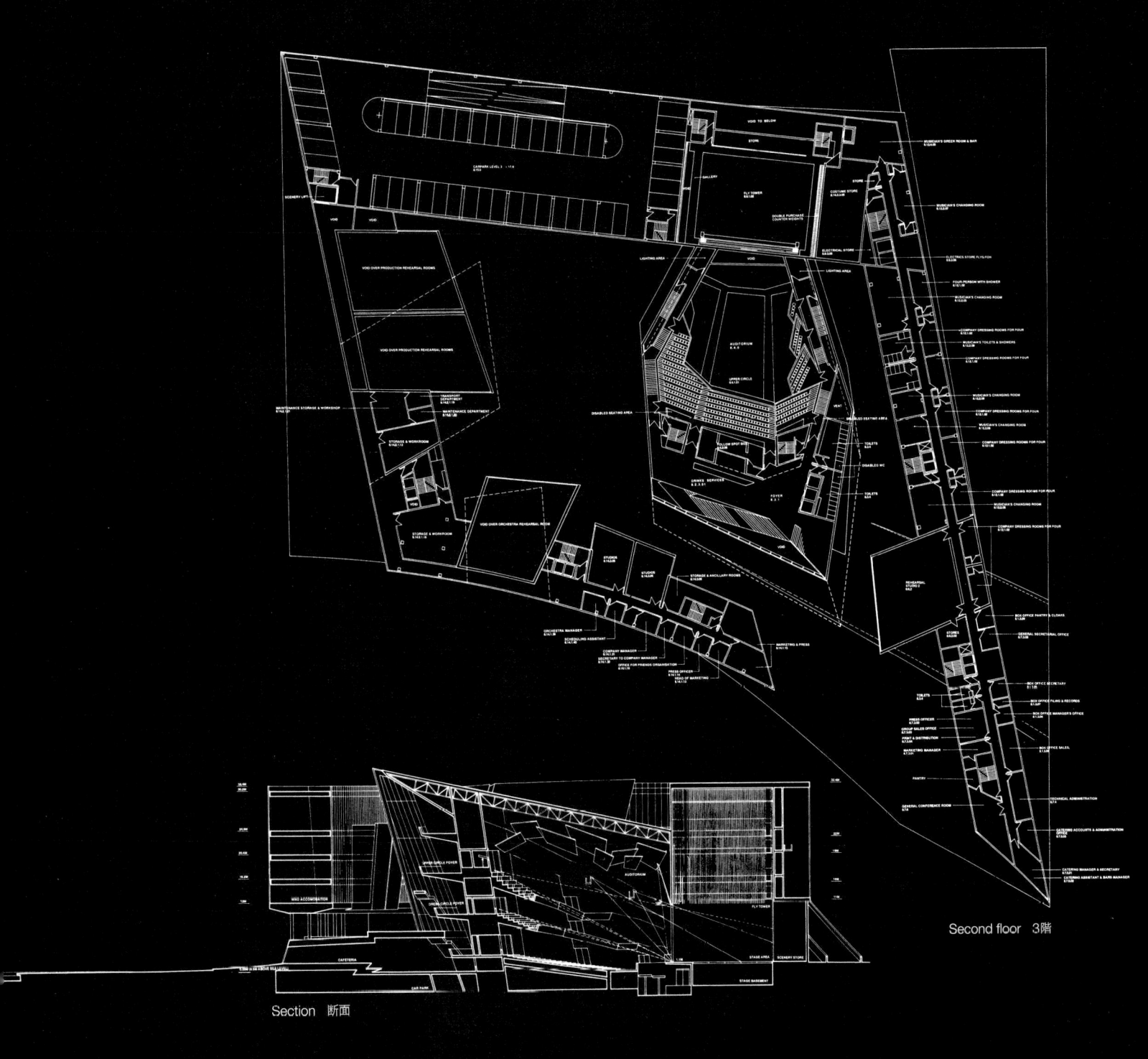

Second floor 3階

Section 断面

Cardiff Bay Opera House

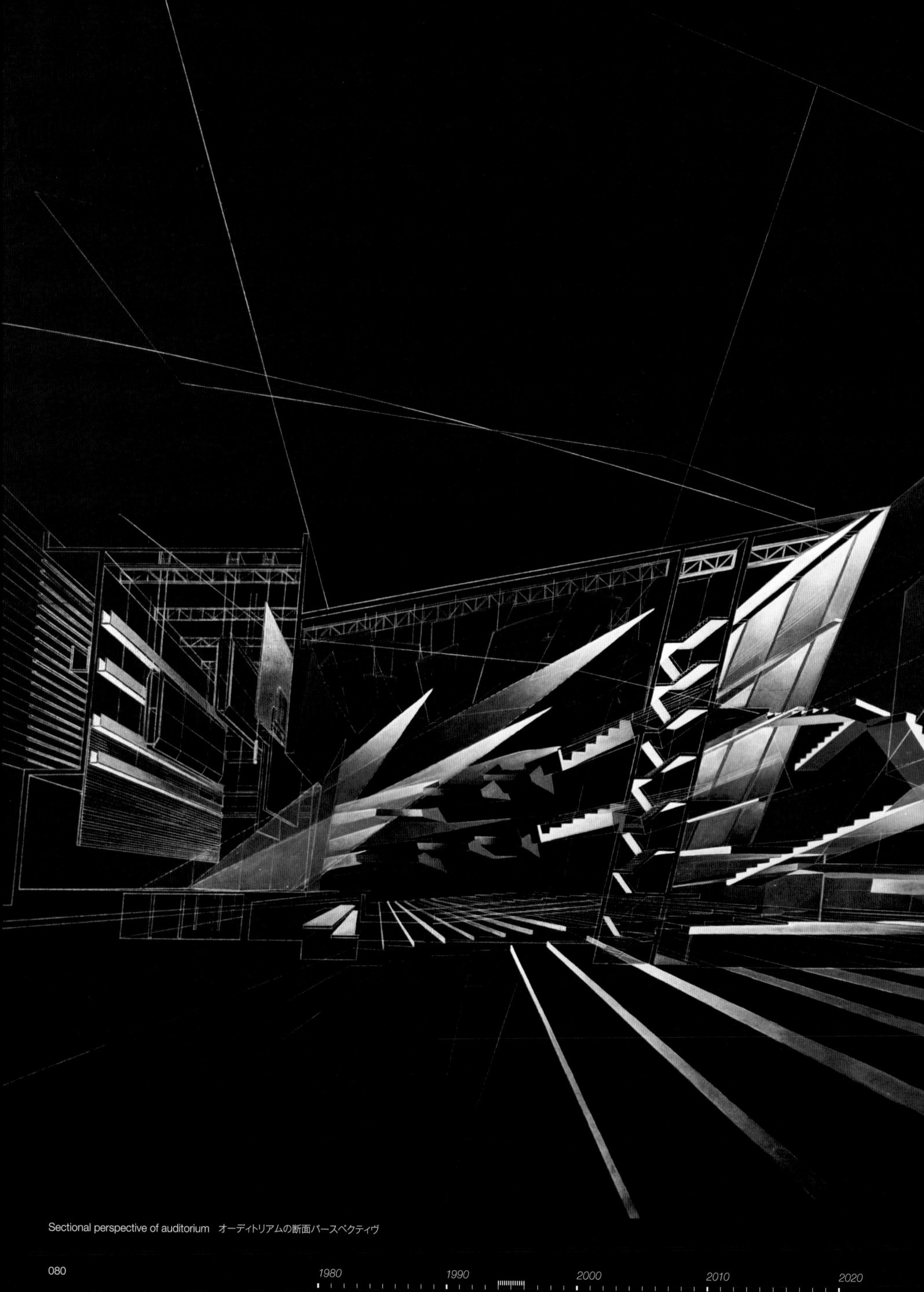

Sectional perspective of auditorium　オーディトリアムの断面パースペクティヴ

Perspectives: composition like jewels　パースペクティヴ：宝石のような空間構成

カーディフベイ・オペラハウスのプロポーザル案ではアーバンデザインにおいてよく見られる独自性の強いパラダイム，すなわち象徴性と空間性を同時につくろうと試みた。建物はマスタープランで示された通り，オーヴァルベースン広場へその姿を見せるように，連続的なひとつながりのヴォリュームとしてつくられている。また同時に港湾地区に対して象徴的なランドマークとなる。

外側の大きなパブリック・スペースと内側の遮断された空間を外側のヴォリュームが二分するという典型的な考え方は，ここでは一つの連続体として一体的に解かれた。この連続性は以下の三つの操作により実現される：外周部の建物を高くすること。港の端部に位置する建物の角の部分を開き，特徴的なオーディトリアムのヴォリュームを硬質な形を持つ象徴として見せること。そして最後に，広場をスロープによって敷地内部へと引き込み，ホワイエの空間へと続く新たな地面を形成することで連続的な都市のパブリック・スペースをつくること。このことによって建物には屋外パフォーマンスに適した広場が高く持ち上げられ，港や海岸の景色をより強調する。

建物のコンセプトは，サーブド・スペースとサーバント・スペースの建築的なヒエラルキー表現に基づいている。オーディトリアムやその他のパブリック，セミパブリックな空間，また演技・リハーサル室といった空間が，合理的に配置された帯状のサポート・スペースの列から宝石のように飛び出している。この帯は，また敷地の外周部をぐるりと囲み，まるで裏返しになったネックレスのようになっている。ネックレスについている宝石は互いに向かい合い，それらの間に濃密なパブリック・スペー

1997-2003
ROSENTHAL CENTER FOR CONTEMPORARY ART
ローゼンタール現代美術センター

Cincinnati, Ohio, U.S.A.

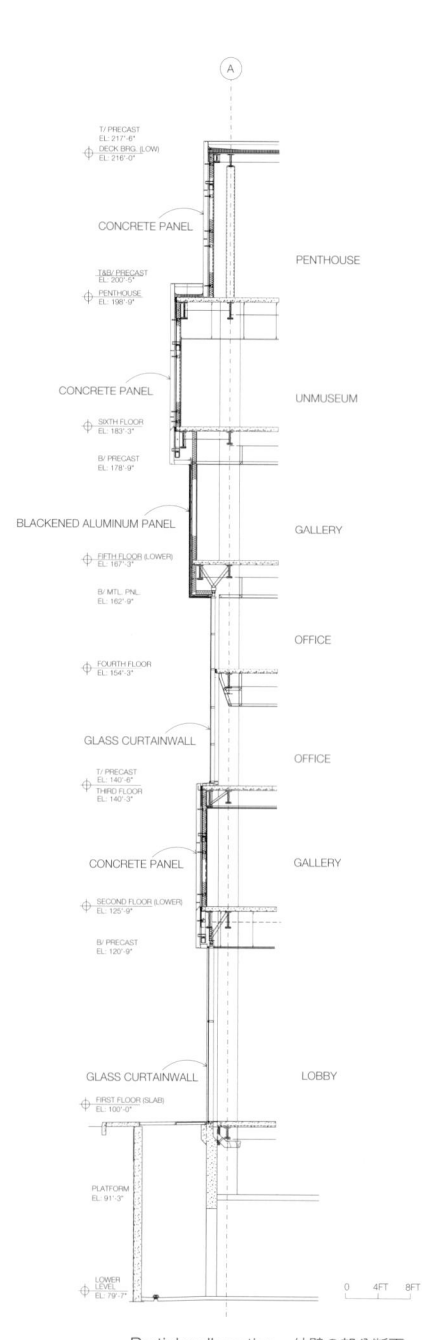

Partial wall section　外壁の部分断面

Site plan 配置 S=1:3000

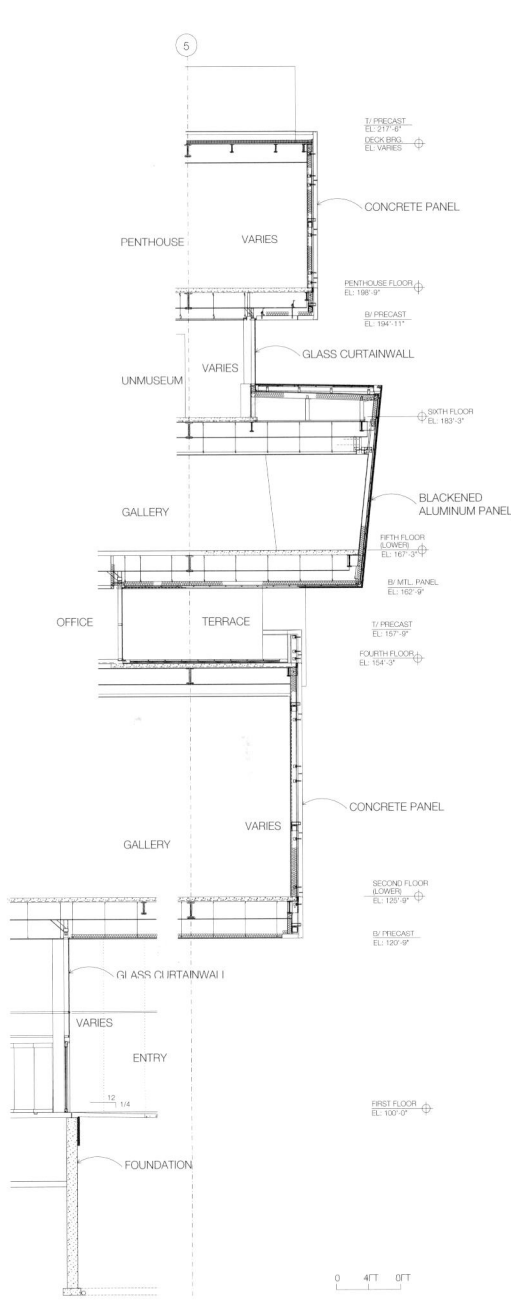

Partial wall section 外壁の部分断面

South elevation on East 6th Street 東6番通り側南面

Rosenthal Center for Contemporary Art

View from Walnut Street on east　東側ウォルナット通りより見る

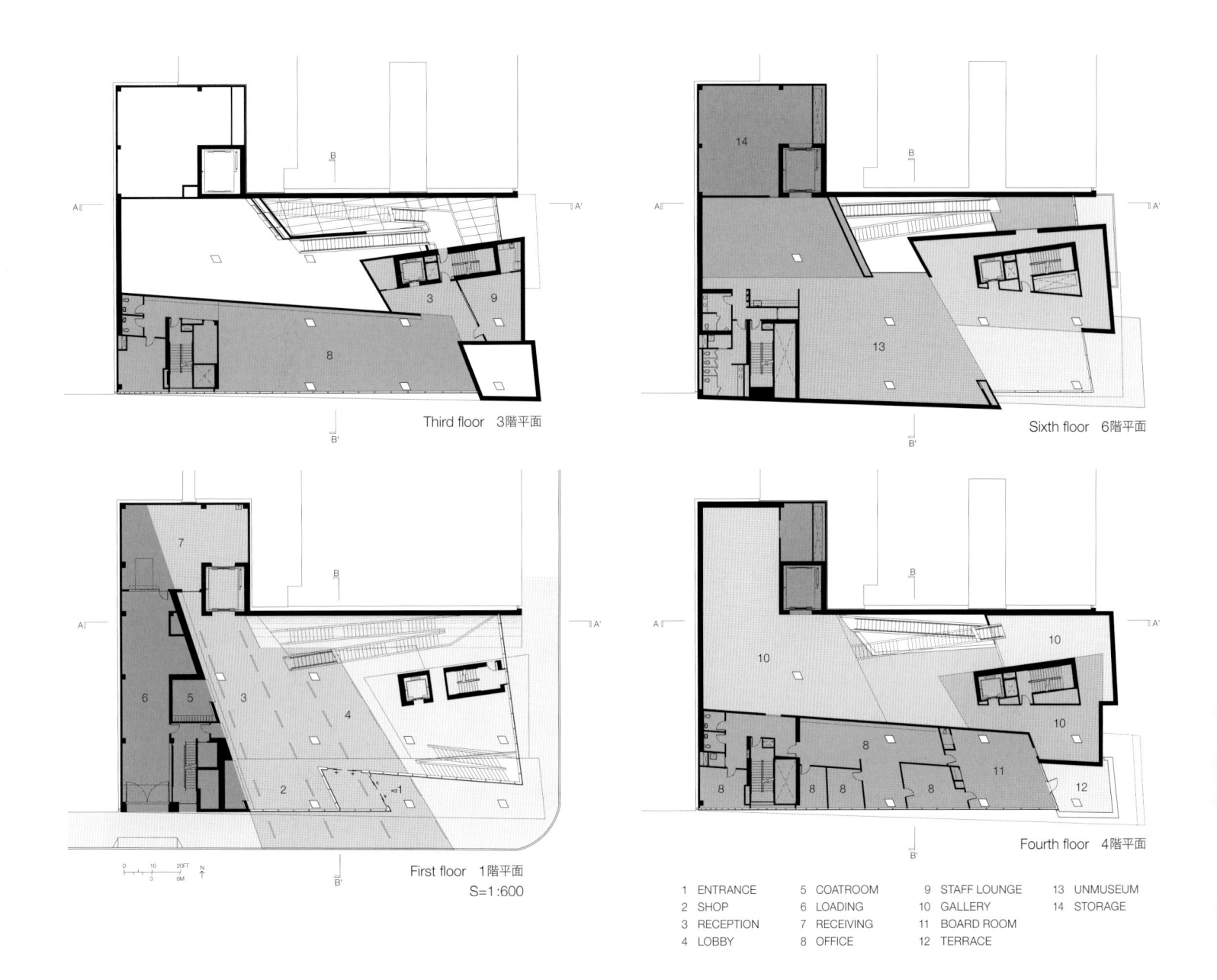

Third floor 3階平面

Sixth floor 6階平面

First floor 1階平面
S=1:600

Fourth floor 4階平面

1 ENTRANCE	5 COATROOM	9 STAFF LOUNGE	13 UNMUSEUM
2 SHOP	6 LOADING	10 GALLERY	14 STORAGE
3 RECEPTION	7 RECEIVING	11 BOARD ROOM	
4 LOBBY	8 OFFICE	12 TERRACE	

The first freestanding building for The Contemporary Arts Center, founded in Cincinnati in 1939 was one of the first institutions in the United States dedicated to the contemporary visual arts. The new CAC building will provide spaces for temporary exhibitions, site-specific installations, and performances, but not for a permanent collection. Other program elements include an education facility, offices, art preparation areas, a museum store, a cafe and public areas. To draw in pedestrian movement from the surrounding areas and create a sense of dynamic public space, the entrance, lobby and lead-in to the circulation system are organized as an "Urban Carpet." Starting at the corner of Sixth and Walnut, the ground curves slowly upward as it enters the building, rising to become the back wall. As it rises and turns, this Urban Carpet leads visitors up a suspended mezzanine ramp through the full length of the lobby, which during the day functions as an open, day-lit, "landscaped" expanse that reads as an artificial park. The mezzanine ramp continues to rise until it penetrates the back wall, on the other side of which it becomes a landing at the entrance to the galleries.

Jigsaw Puzzle
In contrast to the Urban Carpet, which is a series of polished, undulating surfaces, the galleries are expressed as if they had been carved from a single block of concrete and are floating over the lobby space. Exhibition spaces vary in size and shape, to accommodate the great range of scales and materials in contemporary art. Views into the galleries from the circulation system are unpredictable, as the stair-ramp zigzags upward through a narrow slit at the back of the building. Together, these varying galleries interlock like a three-dimensional jigsaw puzzle, made up of solids and voids.

Skin/Sculpture
The building's corner situation led to the development of two different, but complementary, facades. The south facade, along Sixth Street, forms an undulating, translucent skin, through which passersby see into the life of the Centre. The east facade, along Walnut, is expressed as a sculptural relief. It provides an imprint, in negative, of the gallery interiors.

Rosenthal Center for Contemporary Art

East elevation: stacked blocks of concrete　東面：積み重なるコンクリートのヴォリューム

Entrance hall　エントランス・ホール

Rosenthal Center for Contemporary Art

Landing between second and third floor: step-ramp connecting floors　2階と3階の間の踊り場：段状の斜路が階をつなぐ

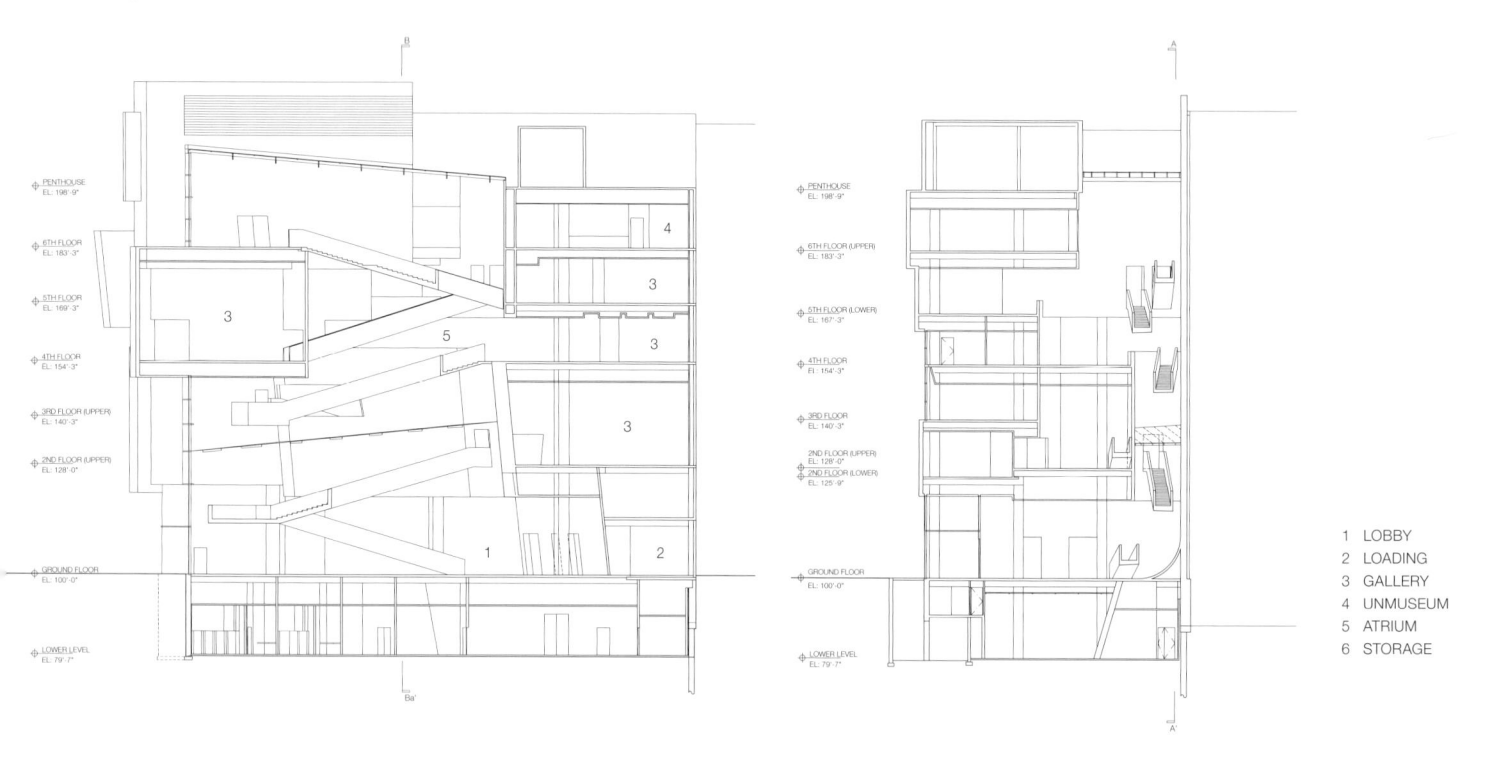

1 LOBBY
2 LOADING
3 GALLERY
4 UNMUSEUM
5 ATRIUM
6 STORAGE

Fourth floor: view of step-ramp　4階：段状の斜路を見る

1939年にシンシナティに設立された現代アートセンター（CAC）は，アメリカが現代視覚芸術に力を入れはじめた初期に設立した組織の一つであり，このプロジェクトは現代アートセンターにとって初の独立した建物である。新たなCACの建物は常設のコレクションを持たず，企画展やサイトスペシフィックなインスタレーション，パフォーマンスのための空間で構成されている。その他のプログラムとしては教育施設やオフィス，準備室，ミュージアムショップ，カフェ，パブリック・エリアなどがある。周辺エリアからの歩行者の動線を引き込んでダイナミックなパブリック・スペースを創出するために，エントランスやロビー，動線部への導入部分などは「アーバン・カーペット」として計画される。6番通りとウォルナット通りの交差する角から始まる歩道の路面がゆるやかにカーブして建物へと入り込み，そのまま建物背後の壁と同化する。アーバン・カーペットは上へとカーブしながら，ロビー全体を大きく横切って来館者を宙に浮かぶ中2階のスロープへと誘導する。ロビーは日中明るく開放的で，擬似的な公園としてランドスケープ化されている。中2階のスロープは建物背後の壁を突き抜け，その裏側のギャラリー入口へと着地する。

ジグソーパズル

滑らかに磨かれて波打つようにうねるアーバン・カーペットとは対照的に，ギャラリーはコンクリートの塊から削りだされたかのような表情を持ち，ロビーの上部に浮いている。
各展示室はそれぞれに大きさや形が異なり，さまざまな大きさや素材の現代アートを受け入れることができる。通路からギャラリーを眺めると思いもよらない光景が見られ，ジグザグと折れ曲がるスロープが建物裏側の狭い隙間の間を上階へと登っていっている。こういった様々なギャラリーが一体となって，立体とヴォイドによる3次元的なジグソーパズルのように組み合わされている。

外皮／彫刻

この建物は街区の角に位置しているため，互いに異質な，しかし補完しあうような二つのファサードを形成している。6番通りに面する南面のファサードは，波打つ透明な外皮を成し，その前を通る人々はセンター内部の活動を見通すことができる。また東面のウォルナット通りのファサードは彫刻のレリーフのように表現されている。この面ではギャラリーの内部形状がネガ／ポジのように反転してファサードに浮き出ている。

Rosenthal Center for Contemporary Art

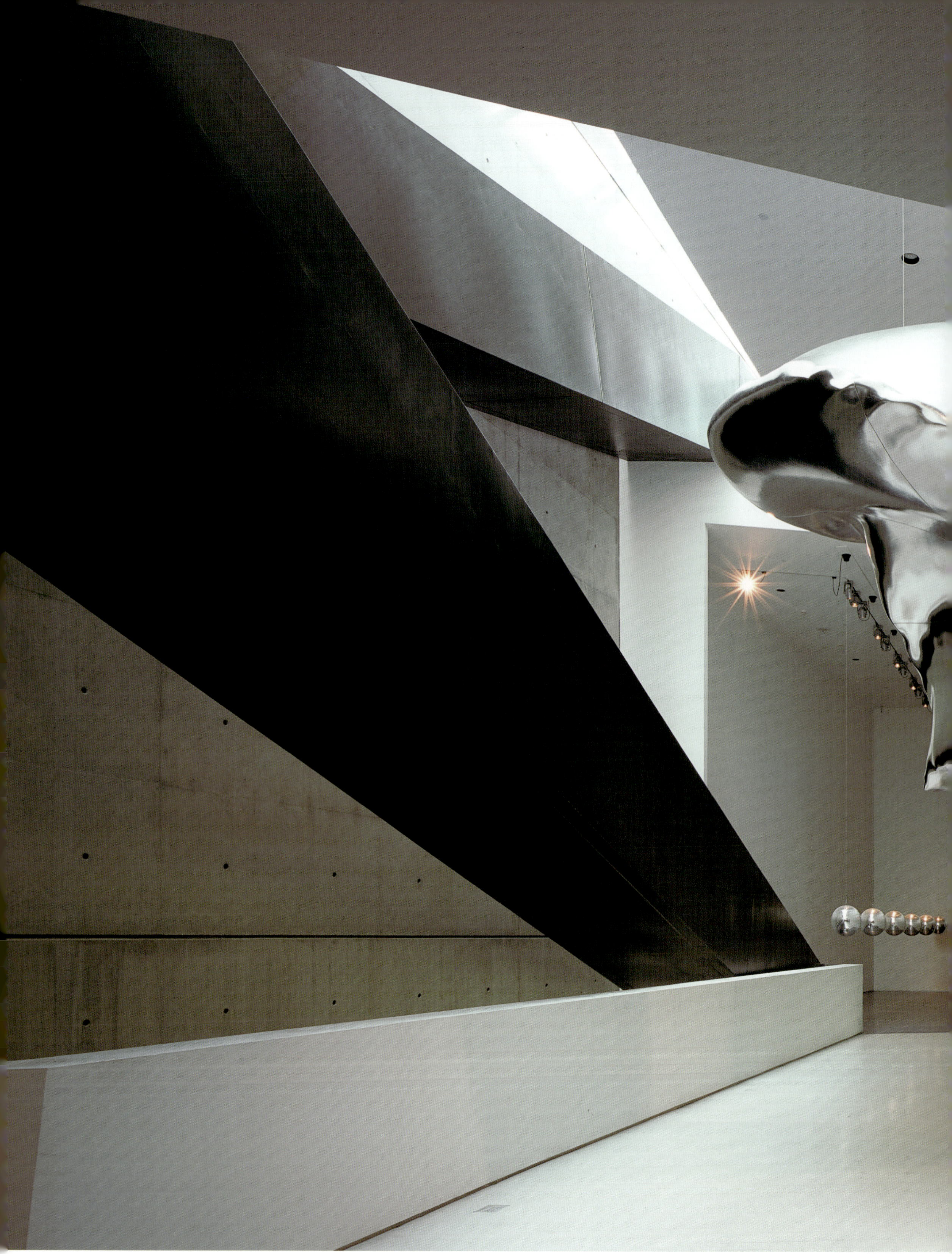

Fourth floor: looking east　4階：東を見る

Rosenthal Center for Contemporary Art

View from fifth floor　5階より見る

Skylight over step-ramp　斜路上のスカイライト

Rosenthal Center for Contemporary Art

1998-2009
MAXXI: MUSEUM OF XXI CENTURY ARTS
MAXXI 国立21世紀美術館

Rome, Italy

Architectural Concept and Urban Strategy: Staging the Field of Possibilities

The MAXXI design addresses the question of its urban context by maintaining an indexicality to the former army barracks. This is in no way an attempt at topological pastiche, but instead continues the low level urban texture set against the higher level blocks on the surrounding sides of the site.

In this way, the Centre is more like an 'urban graft', a second skin to the site. At times, it affiliates with the ground to become new ground, yet also ascends and coalesces to become massivity where needed. The entire building has an urban character: prefiguring upon a directional route connecting the River to Via Guido Reni, the Centre encompasses both movement patterns extant and desired, contained within and outside.

This vector defines the primary entry route into the building. By intertwining the circulation with the urban context, the building shares a public dimension with the city, overlapping tendril-like paths and open space. In addition to the circulatory relationship, the architectural elements are also geometrically aligned with the urban grids that join at the site. In thus partly deriving its orientation and physiognomy from the context, it further assimilates itself to the specific conditions of the site.

Space vs Object

The design offers a quasi-urban field, a world to dive into rather than a building as signature object. The Campus is organised and navigated on the basis of directional drifts and the distribution of densities rather than key points. This is indicative of the character of the Centre as a whole: porous, immersive, a field space. An inferred mass is subverted by vectors of circulation.

The external as well as internal circulation follows the overall drift of the geometry. Vertical and oblique circulation elements are located at areas of confluence, interference and turbulence. The move from object to field is critical in understanding the relationship the architecture will have to the content of the artwork it will house. Whilst this is further expounded by the contributions of our Gallery and Exhibitions Experts below, it is important here to state that the premise of the architectural design promotes a disinheriting of the 'object' orientated gallery space. Instead, the notion of a 'drift'

View from plaza on east 東側広場より見る

takes on an embodied form.

The drifting emerges, therefore, as both architectural motif, and also as a way to navigate experientially through the museum. It is an argument that, for art practice is well understood, but in architectural hegemony has remained alien. We take this opportunity, in the adventure of designing such a forward looking institution, to confront the material and conceptual dissonance evoked by art practice since the late 1960's. The path lead away from the 'object' and its correlative sanctifying, towards fields of multiple associations that are anticipative of the necessity to change.

Aerial view 上空より見る © Iwan Baan

MAXXI: National Museum of XXI Century Arts

Plaza and pilotis: view toward main entrance　広場とピロティ：メイン・エントランスを見る

Pilotis on main entrance　メイン・エントランス前のピロティ

Plaza: projected exhibition room　広場：突き出した展示室のヴォリューム

MAXXI: National Museum of XXI Century Arts

Entrance hall　エントランス・ホール

View toward entrance hall　エントランス・ホールを見る

MAXXI: National Museum of XXI Century Arts

建築的コンセプトと都市ストラテジー：
可能性のフィールドを演出する

現代美術館は，以前ここにあった兵舎を連想させるような性格を維持することで，その都市文脈に対する問題提示を行う。これは，地形の寄せ集めをしようというのではなく，敷地を囲む高層の建物が並ぶ街区側に対抗させて，低層の都市構造を連続させるのである。

この方法においては，センターは「街の接ぎ木」，敷地の第2の皮膚のようなものである。時々，それは地とつながって新たな地を形成するが，必要な箇所では，立ち上がり合体してマッシブなものとなる。建物全体は都市的な性格をもつ。川とグウィド・レーニ通りをつなぐ方向への道筋を想定しつつ，センターは，既に存在するもの，望まれるもの，両方の通路パターンを，内，外に包含する。

このベクトルは建物へ入る主要ルートを規定する。通路を都市文脈と撚り合わせることで，巻きひげのような通路やオープン・スペースが重層しながら，建物は都市の公共的なスケールを共有する。循環的な関係に加えて，建築的要素はまた，敷地に合流する都市グリッドと幾何学的に整列する。こうして，部分的にはコンテクストが備える方位や外形から生まれた建物は，敷地固有の状況にさらに深く同化する。

空間対物体

私たちの提案は，署名入りのオブジェクトとしての建物ではなく，疑似都市，そこに飛び込んでいけるような，ある世界を表現する。方向性をもって漂流し，点的な分布ではなく，密度の配分により空間は構成され，動いてゆく。つまり，センター全体の性格を暗示するのは，多孔性，沈潜性，フィールド・スペースである。埋葬されたマッスは通路のベクトルによって転覆される。

内部同様，外部の通路も幾何学の漂流に従う。垂直方向や斜めに進む通路は，合流，衝突，乱流ポイントに位置する。オブジェクトからフィールドへの移行は，この建築が中に収めることになる芸術作品の内容との関係を理解する上で重要である。これは，ギャラリー／展覧会専門家の尽力によりさらに詳述されることになるが，この建築デザインの前提が，「オブジェクト」指向の展示室という，遺産からの撤退を促進させるものであるとここで述べておくことは重要である。それに代わって「漂流」という概念が具体化された形のなかに取り入れられる。

従って，漂流は，建築的主題にも，館内を経験しながら航行していく道筋にも出現する。それは，芸術作品ではよく理解されているが，建築世界の中では，依然として異質な主張である。この機会をとらえて，こうした先進的な建物をデザインするという大胆な試みのなかに，1960年代後半以来，芸術活動によって喚起されてきたマテリアルとコンセプトの不一致という問題に向き合うことにしたのである。通路は「オブジェクト」とその相互依存関係にある神聖化から離れ，変化の必要が予測される多様な関連フィールドへと導く。

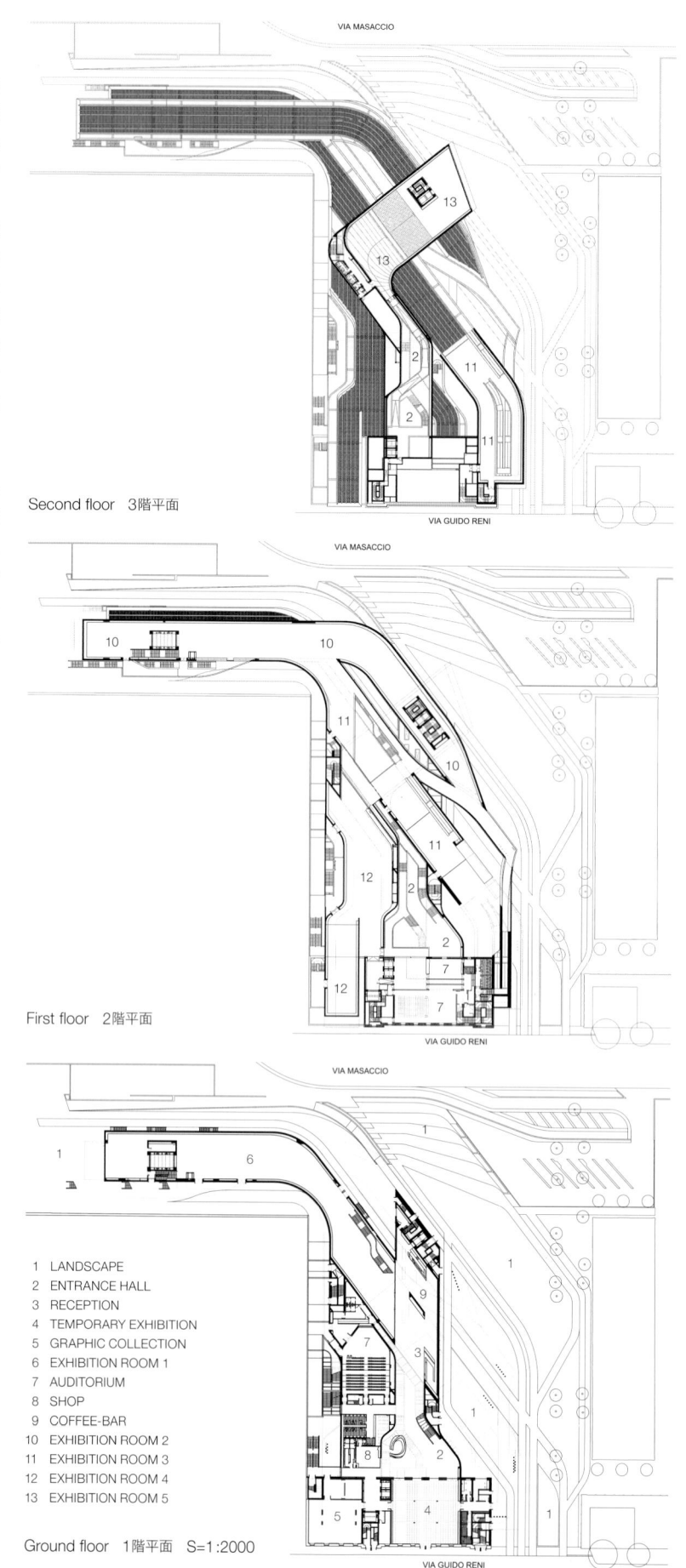

Second floor　3階平面

First floor　2階平面

1　LANDSCAPE
2　ENTRANCE HALL
3　RECEPTION
4　TEMPORARY EXHIBITION
5　GRAPHIC COLLECTION
6　EXHIBITION ROOM 1
7　AUDITORIUM
8　SHOP
9　COFFEE-BAR
10　EXHIBITION ROOM 2
11　EXHIBITION ROOM 3
12　EXHIBITION ROOM 4
13　EXHIBITION ROOM 5

Ground floor　1階平面　S=1:2000

Upper part of entrance hall: view from first floor　エントランス・ホール上部：2階より見る

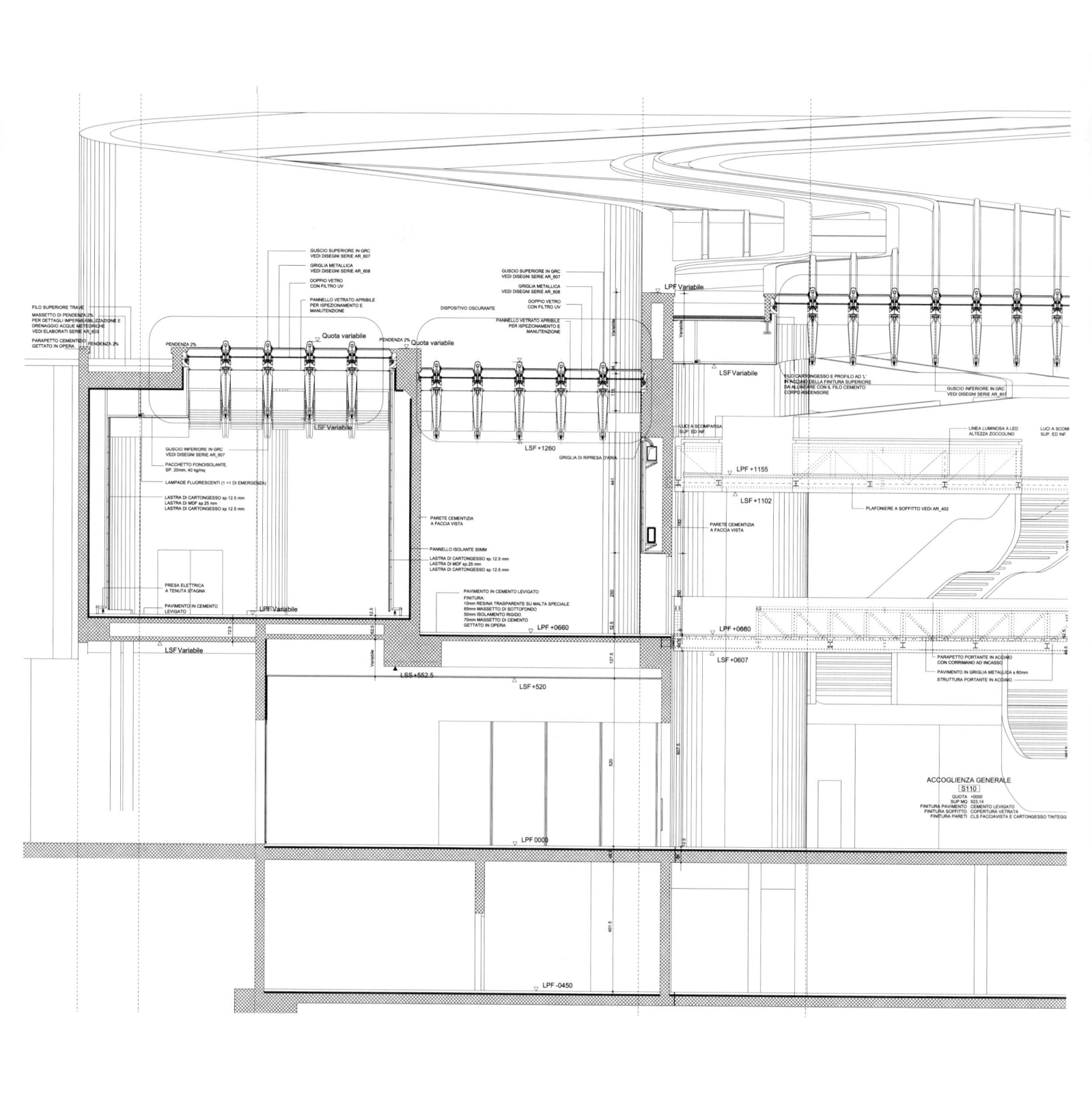

1980   1990   2000   2010   2020

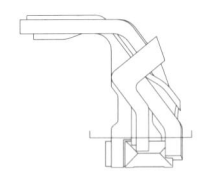

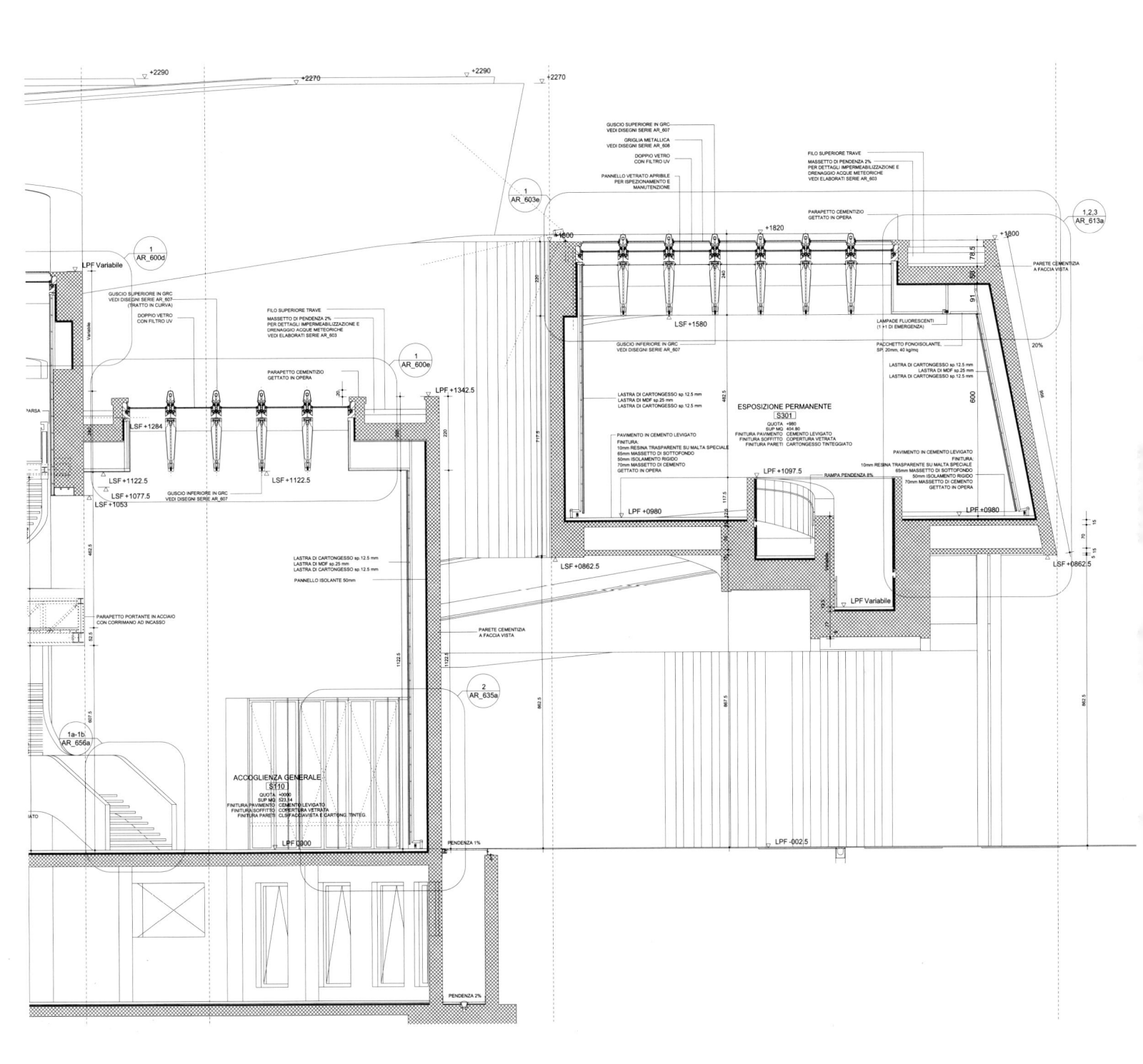

Sectional detail 断面詳細 S=1:150

MAXXI: National Museum of XXI Century Arts

104 | 1980 | 1990 | 2000 | 2010 | 2020

Upward view from entrance hall　エントランス・ホールより見上げる

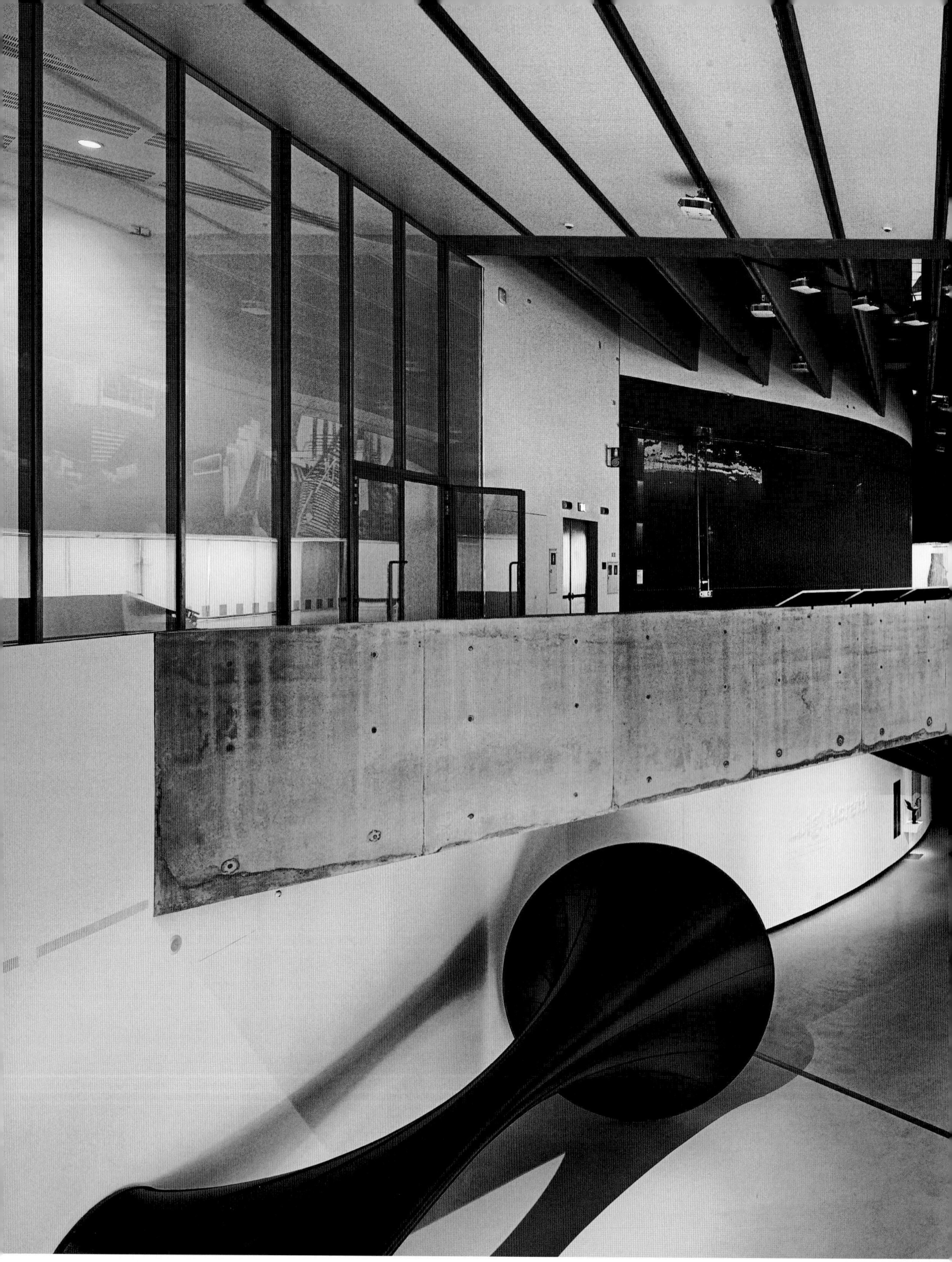

1980 1990 2000 2010 2020

Void: exhibition room 1 (below), exhibition room 3 (above)　吹抜け：下は展示室1，上は展示室3

MAXXI: National Museum of XXI Century Arts

First floor: exhibition room 2 (above), exhibition room 3 (below)　2階：展示室2（上）と展示室3（下）

First floor: exhibition room 4 (above)
First floor: exhibition room 3 on right. Passageway to east end on left and connected to ramp on center (below)

MAXXI: National Museum of XXI Century Arts

2000-05
PHAENO SCIENCE CENTER
フェーノ科学センター

Wolfsburg, Germany

The Science Center, the first of its kind in Germany, appears as a mysterious object, giving rise to curiosity and discovery. The visitor is faced with a degree of complexity and strangeness, which is ruled however by a very specific system of structural organization. Located on a very special site in the City of Wolfsburg it is set both as the endpoint of a chain of important cultural buildings (by Aalto, Scharoun and Schweger) as well as being a connecting link to the north bank of the Mittelland Kanal—Volkswagen's Car Town. Multiple threads of pedestrian and vehicular movement are pulled through the site both on an artificial ground landscape and inside and through the building, effectively composing an interface of movement-paths. Volumetrically, the building is structured in such a way that it maintains a large degree of transparency and porosity on the ground, since the main volume—the Exhibition—is raised thus covering an outdoor public plaza with a variety of commercial and cultural functions which reside in the structural concrete cones. An artificial crater-like landscape is developed inside the open exhibition space allowing diagonal views to the different levels of the exhibitionscape, while volumes, which protrude, accommodate other functions of the science center. A glazed public wormholelike extension of the existing bridge flows through the building allowing views to and from the exhibition space.

North elevation 北立面

Section 断面

Overall view from south: Wolfsburg is town of Volkswagen. Factory area is behind the building　南側全景：ウォルフスブルクはフォルクスワーゲンの町。工場エリアが建物背後に広がる

Phaeno Science Center

111

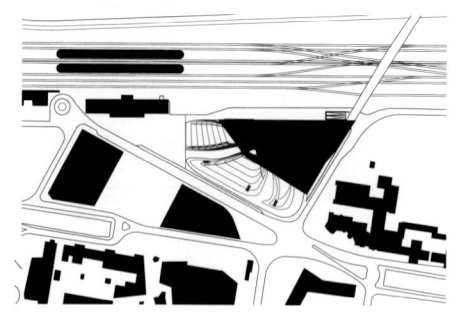

Site plan　配置

Concourse　コンコース平面

1 LANDSCAPE
2 SHOP
3 WORKSHOP
4 MAIN ENTRANCE
5 GROUP ENTRANCE
6 BISTRO
7 AUDITORIUM
8 LABORATORY/LOADING
9 EVENT SPACE
10 COFFEE-BAR
11 RAMP TO BRIDGE
12 ACCESS TO PARKING
13 KITCHEN
14 STAFF ROOM
15 RESTAURANT
16 LABORATORY
17 EXHIBITION
18 BRIDGE TO AUTOSTADT

Ground mezzanine　中1階平面

Reflected ceiling ground　1階天井伏

この種の建物としてはドイツで最初のものとなるフェーノ科学センターでは，好奇心や発見を誘発させるための神秘的なオブジェクトを構想した。来館者は，非常に特殊なシステムに規定された，複雑で，不思議な場と向き合うことになる。

ウォルフスブルク市内でも特別な場所に位置し，ミッテルランド運河の北岸とフォルクス・ワーゲン・カータウンを結ぶだけでなく，（アアルト，シャロウン，シュヴェッガーの設計による）一連の重要な文化施設の終点として建てられた。

歩行者と自動車の複数の動線が，人工地盤のランドスケープ上や建物内部を通り抜けるように引き込まれ，移動経路の接点を効果的に構成している。外部のパブリック・プラザと商業，文化的な機能が入る円錐状のコンクリートの構造体の上に，メインのヴォリュームである展示スペースがある。それゆえ，建物は地面に対して非常に高い透明性や多孔性を保つような方法で量塊的に構成されている。様々な展示風景を斜めに見渡せるように，建物内部のオープンな展示スペースにクレーターのような人工のランドスケープがつくられる一方，突き出たヴォリューム部分には科学センターの他の機能を収容している。既存の橋に増築された虫穴のようなのガラスの公共エリアは，展示スペースを見たり，また展示スペースからも見られるように建物を貫流している。

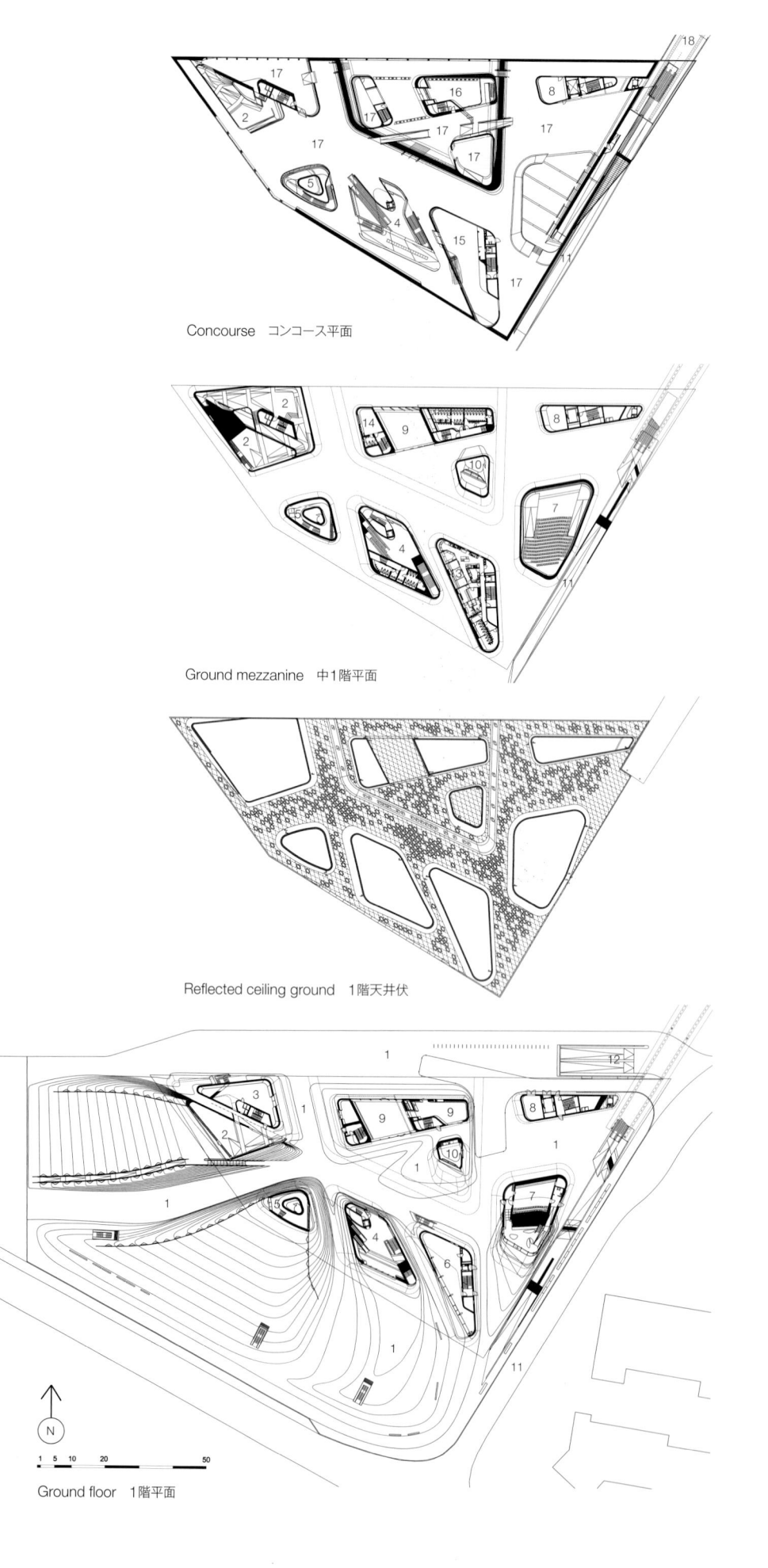

Ground floor　1階平面

Pilotis　ピロティ

Phaeno Science Center

114

View from south: pilotis　南より見る：ピロティ

Ground level: pilotis, looking west 地上レベル：ピロティ, 西を見る

Main entrance　メイン・エントランス

Phaeno Science Center

Void: main entrance below　吹抜け：下はメイン・エントランス

Exhibition area: concave space with undulated floor　展示エリア：緩やかに起伏する床に囲われた窪みのスペース

Phaeno Science Center

120 ・ 1980 1990 2000 2010 2020

Exhibition area　展示エリア

Phaeno Science Center

2005-11/2014
LONDON AQUATICS CENTRE
ロンドン・アクアティクス・センター

London, U.K.

Design Concept

The architectural concept of the London Aquatics Centre is inspired by the fluid geometry of water in motion, creating spaces and a surrounding environment in sympathy with the river landscape of the Olympic Park. An undulating roof sweeps up from the ground as a wave - enclosing the pools of the Centre with its unifying gesture of fluidity, whilst also describing the volume of the swimming and diving pools.

The London Aquatics Centre is designed to have the flexibility to accommodate the size and capacity of the London 2012 Olympic Games whilst also providing the optimum size and capacity for use in Legacy mode after the 2012 Games.

*All photographs are "Legacy mode"　写真はすべて「レガシー・モード」

Site Context
The London Aquatics Centre is located at the south eastern edge of Queen Elizabeth Olympic Park on the new Stratford City Bridge giving pedestrian access to the park from the new Stratford City development and public transportation.

Layout
The Aquatics Centre is planned on an orthogonal axis perpendicular to the Stratford City Bridge. Along this axis are laid out the three pools. The training pool is located under the bridge whilst the competition and diving pools are within a large volumetric pool hall. The overall strategy is to frame the base of the pool hall volume as a podium by surrounding it and connecting it into the bridge.

This podium element allows for the containment of a variety of differentiated and cellular programmatic elements into a single architectural volume which is seen to be completely assimilated with the bridge and the landscape. The podium emerges from the bridge to cascade around the pool hall to the lower level of the canal.

The pool hall is expressed above the podium level by a large roof which arches along the same axis as the pools. Its form is generated by the sightlines for the spectators during the Olympic mode. Double-curvature geometry has been used to create a structure of parabolic arches that define its form. The roof undulates to differentiate the volumes of the competition and diving pools, and extends beyond the pool hall envelope to cover the external areas of the podium and entrance on the bridge.

The roof structure is grounded at three points of the centre (two points at the northwest end on the bridge; and one single point to the south east end). This structural arrangement ensured 7,500 temporary spectator seats could be installed along either side of the pools in Olympic mode (total 15,000 temporary seats) with no structural obstructions. After the 2012 Olympic and Paralympic Games, this temporary seating has been removed and replaced with glazing panels, leaving a capacity of 2,500 seats for community use and future national/international events, with a significantly reduced pool hall volume

Overall view from west　西側全景

Overall view from east 東側全景

Legacy mode

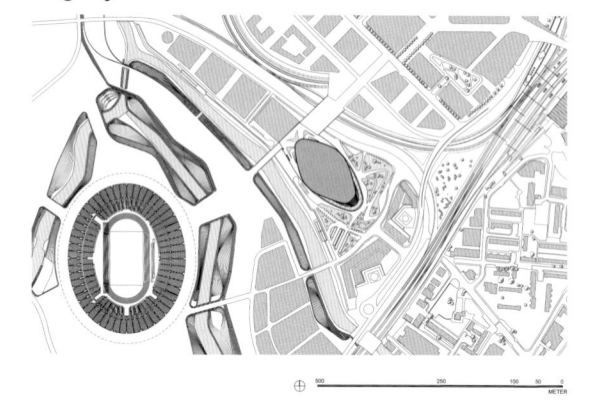

Olympic mode

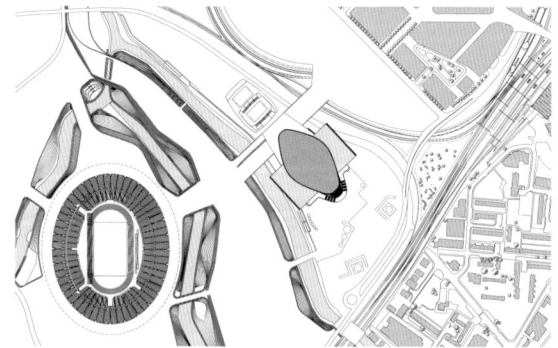

Site plan 配置 S=1:15000

East side 東面

1 MAIN COMPETITION POOL
2 DIVING POOL
3 TRAINING POOL
4 ENTRANCE FOYER & RECEPTION
5 COMPETITION SIDE CHANGING VILLAGE
6 PRE-SWIM SHOWERS
7 TRAINING SIDE CHANGING VILLAGE
8 CRECHE
9 CAFE KITCHEN
10 SWIM TEC AREA
11 TIMING CONTROL
12 PLANT ROOM
13 CHILLER PLANT ROOM
14 UPPER WELCOME ZONE
15 SPECTATOR SEATING
16 PLAZA BRIDGE
17 ATHLETES LOUNGE
18 PHYSIO & MASSAGE AREA
19 ATHLETES CHANGE
20 DOPING CONTROL
21 ATHLETES FINAL CALL ROOM
22 DIVERS WARM UP
23 RESULTS CONTROL
24 ATHLETES MIXED ZONE
25 OLYMPIC FAMILY LOUNGE
26 MAIN ENTRANCE STAIRS
27 CONCOURSE AREA
28 MEZZANINE WHEELCHAIR SEATING
29 GENERAL SPECTATOR STAND
30 MEDIA & SPECTATOR STAND

Olympic mode

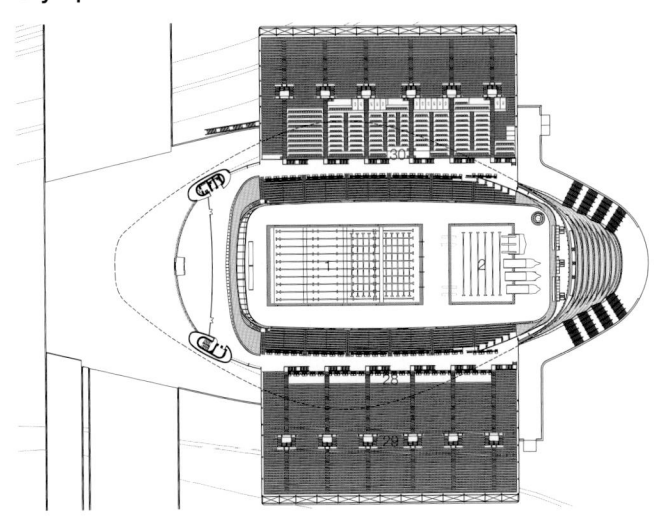

Second floor　3階平面

Legacy mode

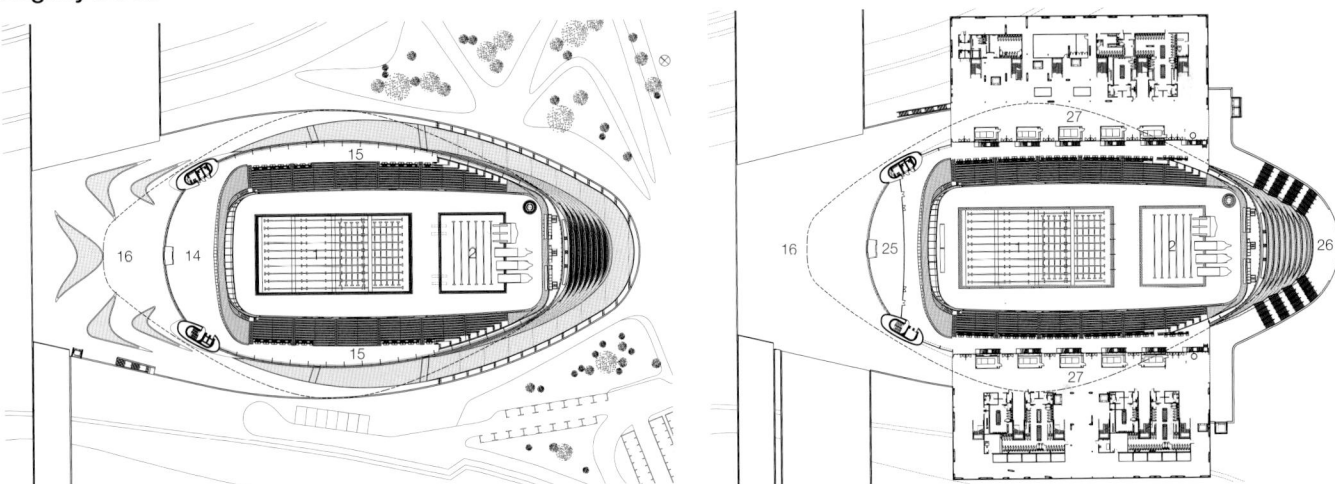

First floor　2階平面

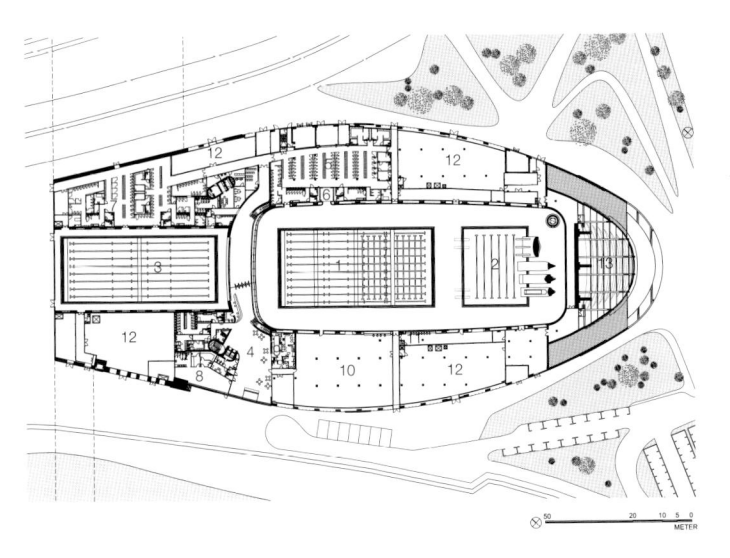

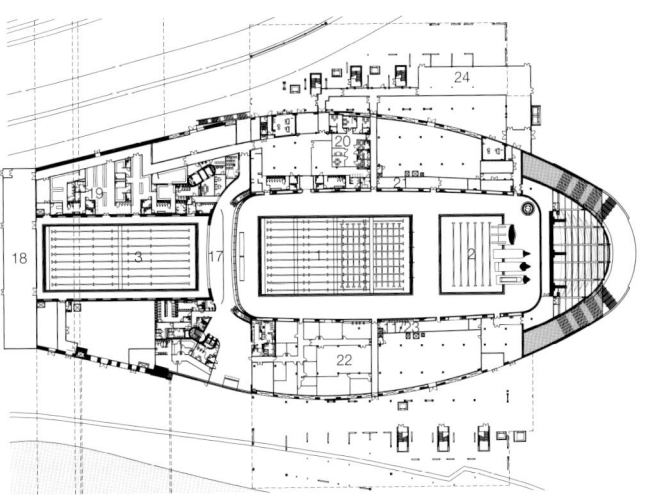

Ground floor　1階平面　S=1:2500

London Aquatics Centre

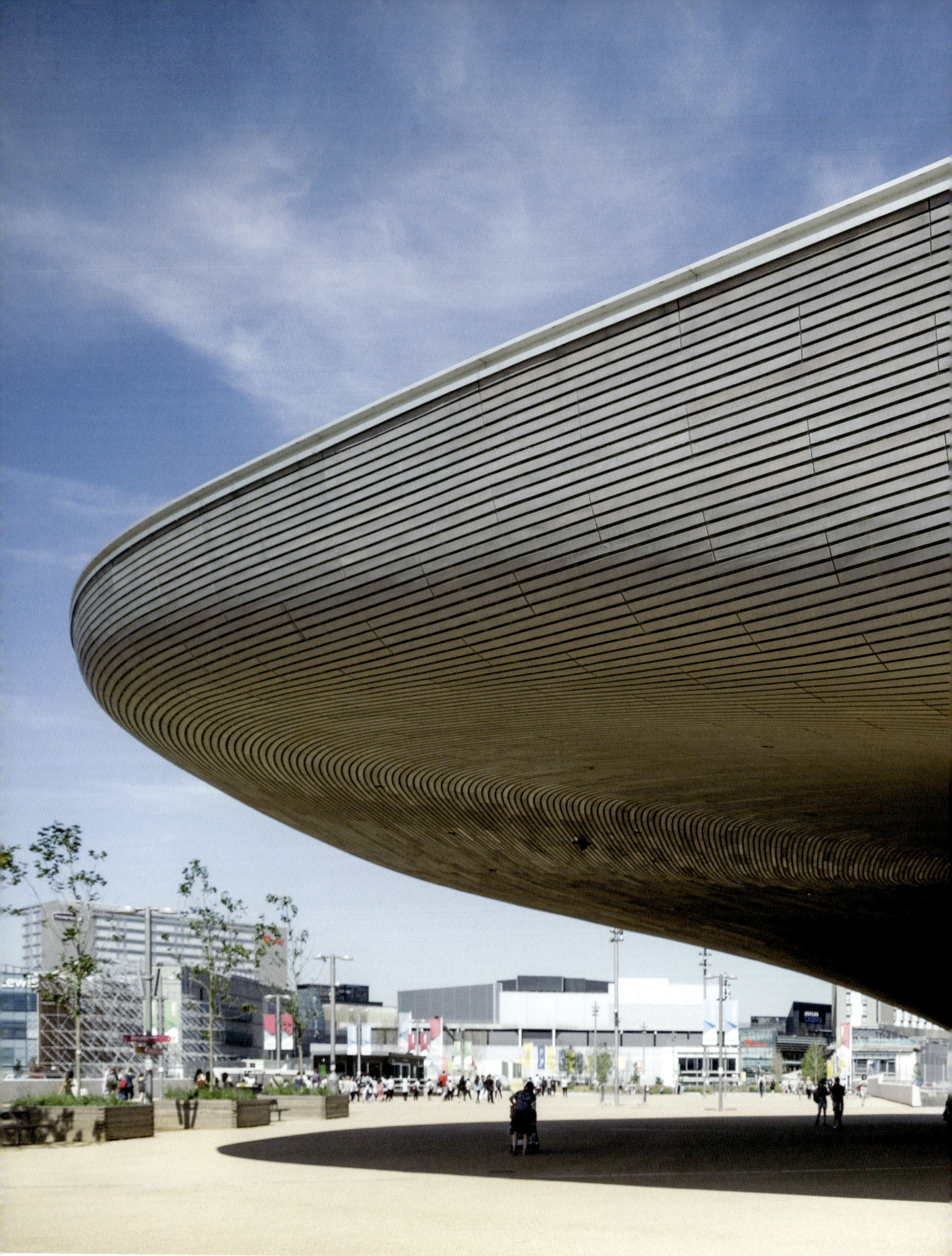

Main entrance　メイン・エントランス

London Aquatics Centre

Legacy mode

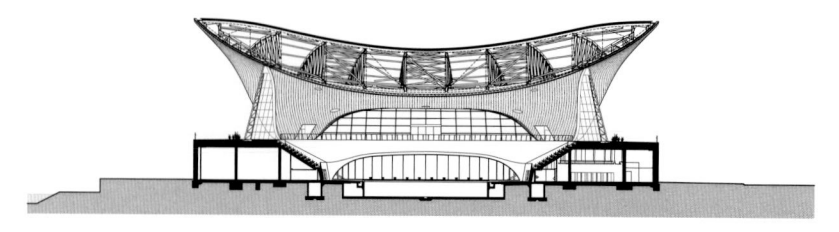

Olympic mode

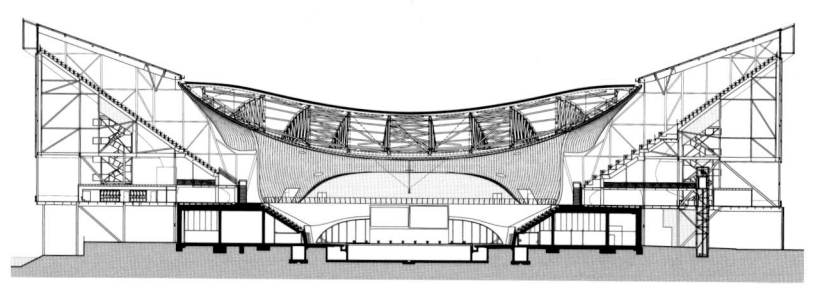

Cross section　短手断面　S=1:1500

設計コンセプト

ロンドン・アクアティクス・センターは流れる水の流動的なジオメトリから着想を得たものである。空間と周辺環境はオリンピック・パークの川辺のランドスケープと調和するように計画された。波立つ屋根は地表面からうねるように起伏して滑らかにプールを包み込む。その一方で, この屋根はスイミングプールとダイビングプールのヴォリュームも表現している。ロンドン・アクアティクス・センターは, 2012年ロンドン・オリンピック大会に対して十分な規模と収容能力を備え, 大会後は引き続き施設として利用できるようフレキシブルに計画された。

敷地のコンテクスト

ロンドン・アクアティクス・センターは新ストラトフォード・シティ・ブリッジに面し, クィーン・エリザベス・オリンピッ

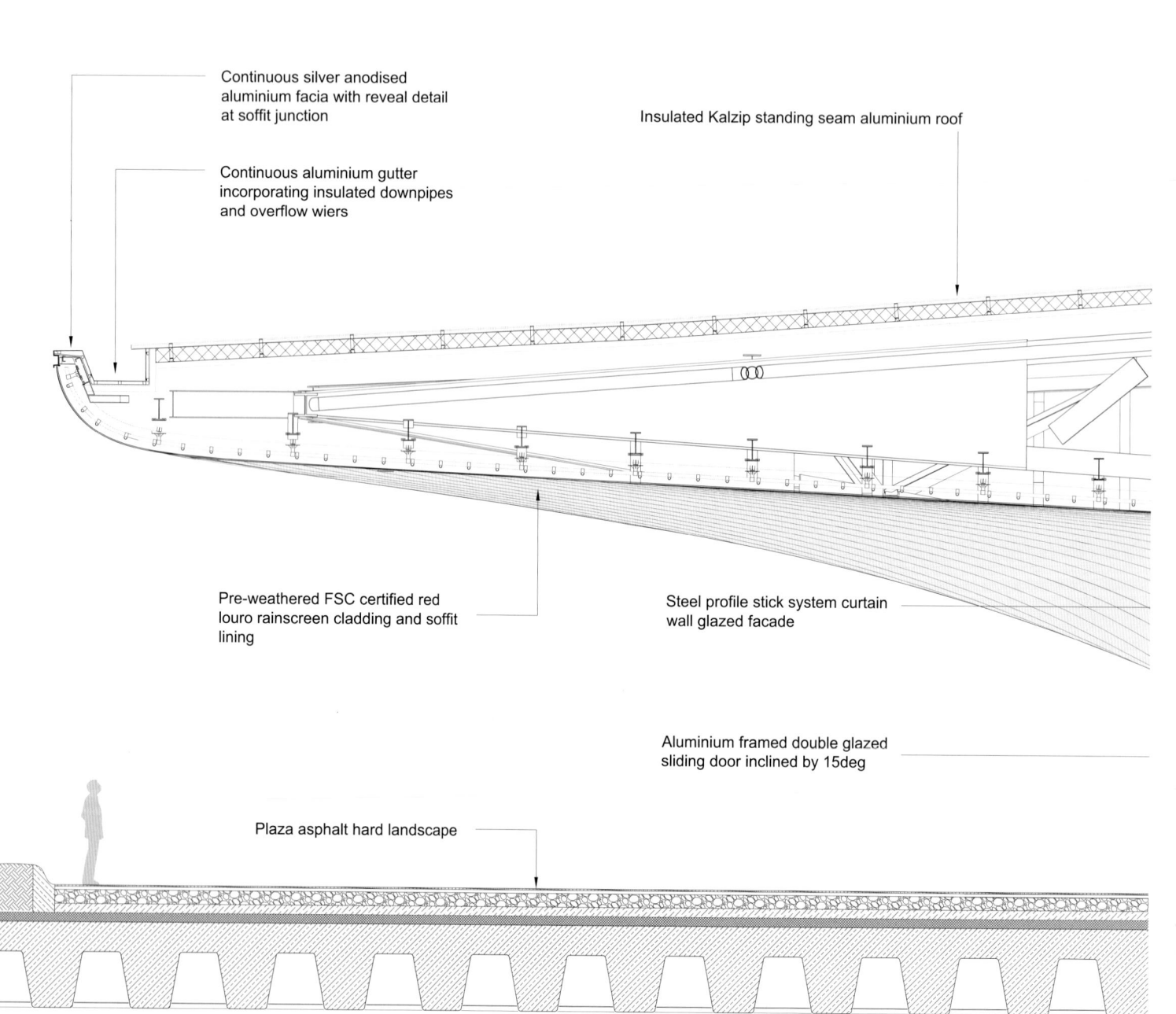

- Continuous silver anodised aluminium facia with reveal detail at soffit junction
- Continuous aluminium gutter incorporating insulated downpipes and overflow wiers
- Insulated Kalzip standing seam aluminium roof
- Pre-weathered FSC certified red louro rainscreen cladding and soffit lining
- Steel profile stick system curtain wall glazed facade
- Aluminium framed double glazed sliding door inclined by 15deg
- Plaza asphalt hard landscape

Sectional detail　断面詳細　S=1:40

ク公園の南東端に位置している。また, 新ストラトフォード地区開発計画の公共交通から公園に抜ける歩行者用動線としても機能する。

配置計画
建物はストラトフォード・シティ・ブリッジに対し, 直交するように計画され, 三つのプールはこの軸線に沿って配置されている。トレーニング・プールは橋の下に, 競技用プールとダイビングプールは巨大なヴォリュームのプール・ホールに計画された。全体の構成は, プール・ホールの基礎をポディウム (基壇) として取り囲み, 橋の中へ接続させている。

ポディウムにはプログラムごとに小分けされ独立した部屋が単体ヴォリュームのなかに収められており, 建築は橋とランドスケープに完全に同化するように見える。ポディウムは, プール・ホールの周りのカスケードの橋から運河の低いレベルまで広がっている。

プール・ホールはプールの軸線に沿って架けられた巨大な屋根によって, ポディウムのレベルから上に現れている。フォルムはオリンピックの観客の視線から生成されたものである。フォルムを規定する放物線のアーチ構造をつくるために二重曲率のジオメトリが採用されている。波打つ屋根は, 競技用プールとダイビングプールを差異化し, ポディウムとブリッジ側のエントランス・エリアを覆うために, プール・ホールの先へ延びている。

屋根構造は3ヵ所で地表に着地している (2ヵ所はブリッジに面した北西端部, もう1ヵ所は南東端部である)。この構造配置計画によって, オリンピックの期間中は構造に障害無く, プールの片側に各々7,500席 (すなわち両側の合計で15,000席) の観客席を仮設として設置することが可能となった。2012年のオリンピック大会とパラリンピック大会が閉幕すると, 仮設の座席は撤去され, ガラスパネルへと交換された。地域コミュニティの利用と国内, 国際規模の将来のイベントのために, 大幅に規模を縮小したプール・ホールのヴォリュームと2,500席の観客席はそのまま残されることになった。

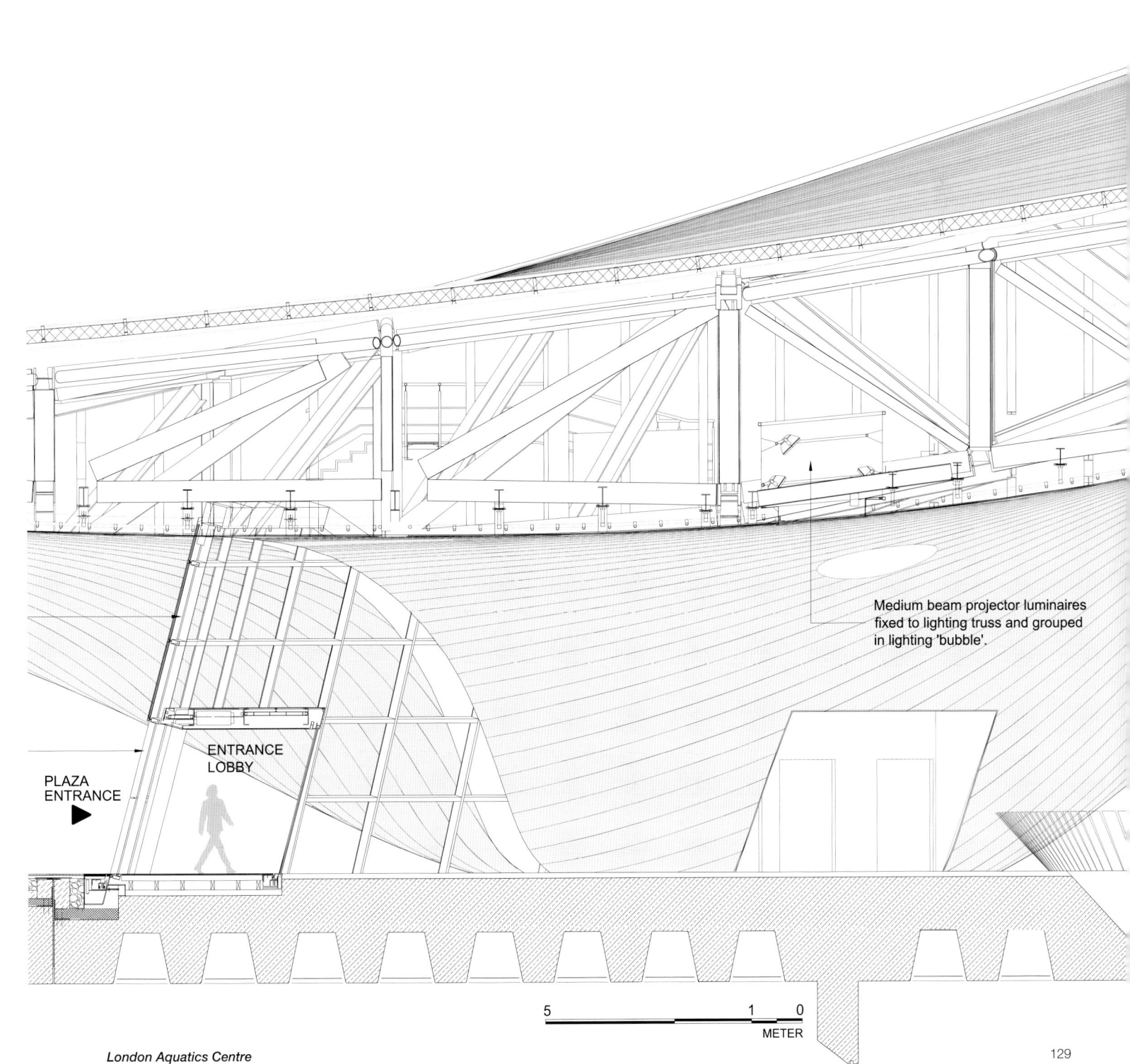

Medium beam projector luminaires fixed to lighting truss and grouped in lighting 'bubble'.

PLAZA ENTRANCE

ENTRANCE LOBBY

London Aquatics Centre

Competition pool (right) and diving pool (left) 競泳用プール（右）と飛び込み用プール（左）

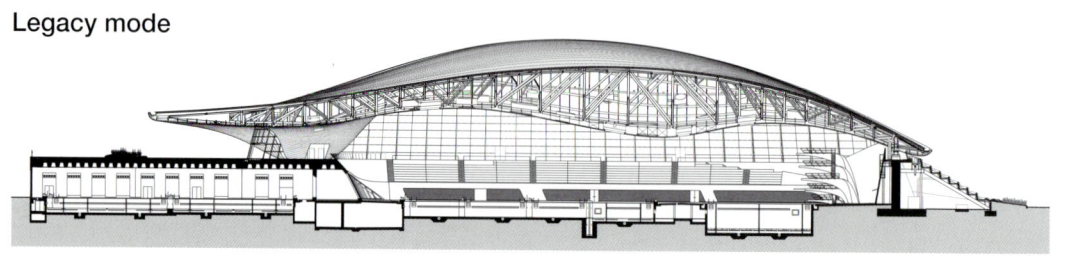

Legacy mode

Longitudinal section 長手断面 S=1:1500

Olympic mode

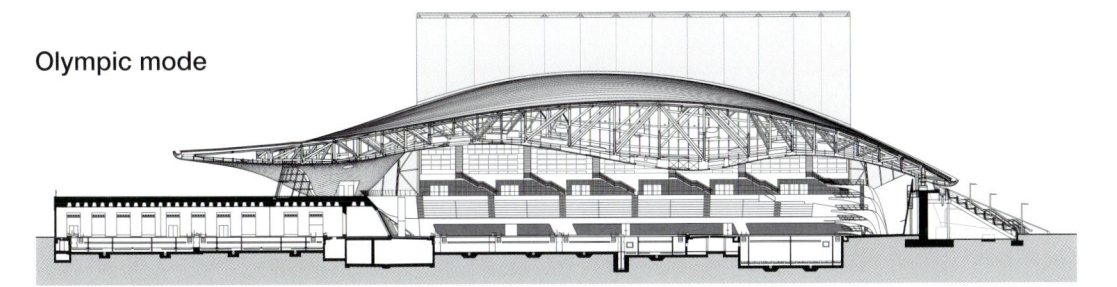

London Aquatics Centre

Diving pool　飛び込み用プール

INTERVIEW 2007
ZAHA HADID

インタヴュー2007
ザハ・ハディド

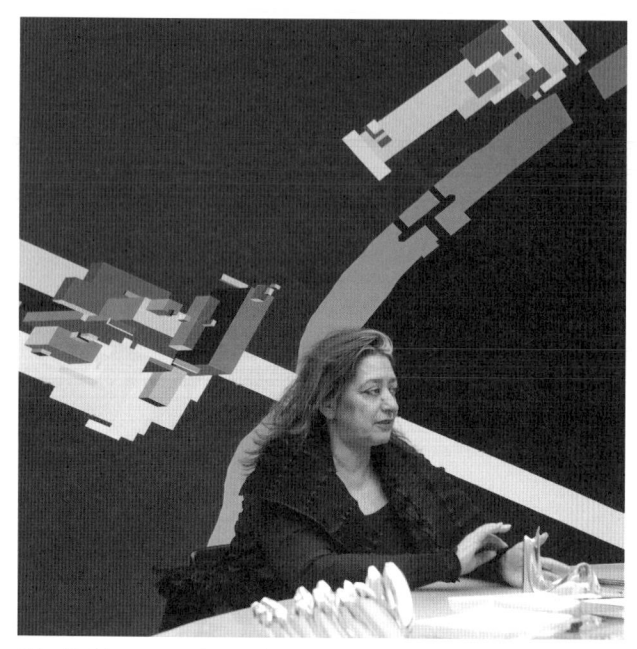

Zaha Hadid (in 2007)　ザハ・ハディド (2007年当時)

Yoshio Futagawa　I'd like to talk about how your practice has evolved since 1994. The projects have become much larger and more complex. You now have an office of more that 200 people here. How do you handle this change in scale?
Zaha Hadid　Every time the office grows it's a difficult transition. The first time we went from twenty to fifty it was very difficult. The next time we went from fifty to a hundred it was very difficult. But now it has settled down. I have very good senior people who are partners now and there are about twenty to twenty-five people here that are very good and capable who direct the others who are still very young and need guidance.
Futagawa　When did you move into your new apartment?
Hadid　About a year and a half ago. I still have the other place. I wanted to renovate it but then I would have to move out and rent. So instead I decided to move here and see if I liked it. It's a nice location and very convenient. I can walk here.
Futagawa　What have you done with your old place?
Hadid　Nothing yet. I will either renovate it or sell it. One or the other.
Futagawa　And how has the design process changed for you now that the work is much more complex? How do you start a design? Years ago the work manifested itself in your beautiful drawings, but now you are doing these concrete buildings and the image of your work has changed a lot. Before you did a lot of sketches, how do you generate early ideas now?
Hadid　I still do sketches. I have a lot of new beautiful sketches. They're next to my desk. A lot of them are about abstract ideas that I would like to try generally and that may be applied to a specific project. When a project is being developed by my staff on the computer I will get print outs and sketch over them again.
Futagawa　How about working in model?
Hadid　We do some models. Now of course the drawings and the

二川由夫　1994年以降の展開についてお伺いします。より大規模で複雑なプロジェクトへとシフトされていますね。今や，この事務所で働くスタッフは200名以上。これほどの規模拡大にはどう対応されているのでしょうか。
ザハ・ハディド　事務所が拡大するたび苦労をしますね。最初20人から50人に増えたときも大変でしたし，その次に50人から100人に増えたときも大変でした。でも今は落ち着いています。パートナーとして参画してくれる優秀な年長者の人材もいますし，指導が必要な若いスタッフたちをとりまとめる有能なスタッフが20～25人いますので。
二川　新しいアパートに移られたのはいつですか？
ハディド　1年半ほど前です。前のアパートも手放してはいません。改装するつもりだったのですが，そのためには中を空にしてどこかを間借りしないとならないので，代わりにここに引っ越して様子を見ることにしたのです。なかなか便利で良い場所ですよ。歩いて通えますし。
二川　前のアパートは，今どうなっているのですか？
ハディド　まだ何もしていません。改装するか売却するか。どちらかでしょうね。
二川　より複雑な仕事を手がけるようになり，デザインのプロセスにはどのような変化が生じましたか？　仕事の取りかかり方は？　以前はあの素晴らしいドローイングからすべてが始まっていたと思うのですが。現在ではコンクリートの建物も多く，かなり作品イメージが変わってきています。以前はたくさんスケッチを描かれていましたが，現在，最初のアイディアはどのように生まれてくるのでしょうか。
ハディド　今でもスケッチはしますよ。新しいスケッチがたくさんあります。ほら，デスクの横に。だいたいは，思い浮かんだアイディアをスケッチした抽象的なもので，特定のプロジェクトのためのものではありません。ほかのスタッフがパソコン上で作業をするようなプロジェクトの場合，プリントアウトをしてもらい，自分でスケッチをし直します。
二川　模型はどうですか？
ハディド　時々，つくります。もちろん，今ではドローイングと模型は同じですよね。以前はドローイングから模型をおこす際，あるいはその逆方向でも，解釈のギャップがつきものでしたが，今は模型はほぼ完璧にプリントアウトできるものですから，解釈自体が不要になり，もっと手早く，ダイレクトになりました。今のテクノロジーはなかなか素晴らしいもので，デザイン・制作プロセスにかかる時間が大幅に短縮されました。例えば，今進行中の曲がりくねった複雑な構造ですが，作業期間は2ヶ月弱です（『リラ』――サーペンタイン・ギャラリーでのインスタレーション，2007年）。驚くでしょう。ヴェニスのビエンナーレには行きますか？　ぜひ私たちのインスタレーションを見てみて下さい。
二川　事務所では，どなたがそういった新しいテクノロジーを導入するのですか？
ハディド　パソコンのプログラムの進化には目を見張るものがあります。若い人には親和性があるようですね。オヴ・アラップ出身で，複雑な構造を扱うのに慣れたスタッフもいます。ご存知の通り，わたしはエンジニアと一緒に仕事をするのが好きです。今のプログラムはすべてがパラメトリックですね。
二川　家具のデザインにぴったりだというのは判ります。一方，建築ではどうでしょう？　内部空間から着手されますか？　それとも外観から？
ハディド　そうですね，パソコンを使うかどうかはあまり関係がないで

models are the same. Before there were always discrepancies that arose out of the translation between drawing and model and vice versa. Now the models can practically be printed. So there is no interpretation. It is more direct, and faster. I think the new technologies available are quite exciting.

It vastly speeds up the design and production process. For example, we're doing a complex structure for the Serpentine Gallery ("Lilas", 2007) in under two months. It's phenomenal. Are you coming to the Venice Biennale? You should see our installation.

Futagawa Who introduces this new technology to your office?

Hadid Computer programs have become incredible and the young people are amazing with them. For example, we have someone who used to work at Arup who is used to working with complex geometry. As you know, I love to work with engineers. The programs are all parametric now.

Futagawa I can see how this would work with furniture. But what about buildings? Do you start with the interior spaces? Or the exterior form?

Hadid Well it's not really an issue with the computer because we are not generating exterior form only. We always consider the design the way we always have which is to design it all at the same time.

Also after a long time, you learn from your own work and develop a repertoire. Sometimes you break this repertoire or add to it. You challenge it. Working with computers hasn't changed this aspect of the practice. The process has not changed in this sense, but the computer does allow you to make these leaps. It is easier to resolve complexity. Before you had to build it, analyze it, slice it. So as a tool the computer has added many dimensions, but it doesn't help you create the ideas. Sure, there are those that use computers to generate form. But for me it doesn't help me make ideas. It is however a tool that helps me think seriously about form.

Futagawa Is there a particular program that you use?

Hadid There are several and they get more and more incredible every year. But you can't just use them on their own. You can't use them without an idea. It's changed the process. For example we used to look at a form by drawing a thousand perspectives. It was time consuming. The computer makes this easier to generate the same number of views. It's made the design process much more elastic.

But in the end you have to make a building stable and stand up. Even a dramatic cantilevered table has to stand up. A building is complex. You have mechanical and electrical and structural engineers. That's what makes architecture very rich. There is a complexity with so many layers. And so it makes creating architecture and thinking about architecture very difficult and very exciting. Not to generalize, but you can always tell when something is not designed by an architect even if a space looks nice, because it will not have a sense of organization.

Futagawa So your office continues to work at a variety of scales.

Hadid Yes. In fact the same people often work on some of the largest projects and then some of the smallest. The ideas have to

す。外形だけをつくるわけではありませんから。デザインについては，以前と変わらず，すべてを同時に考えるというやり方をとっています。また，長年この仕事をやっていると，自然と自分なりのレパートリーができ上がってくるものです。それを壊そうとしたり，新たに増やそうとしたりする。パソコンで作業をする時でもチャレンジ精神は同じです。そういった意味で仕事のプロセスに変わりはありませんが，パソコンのおかげでステップの省略ができることも事実です。以前なら，複雑な形を扱う際，実際に組み立てて，分析して，切断して，という作業が必要でしたが，パソコンでなら簡単に解析ができます。道具としてのパソコンは可能性を広げてくれましたが，アイディアが生まれる場面で使う物ではありません。もちろん，フォルムをつくるのにパソコンを使う人もいるでしょうが，私にとってはクリエイティブな道具ではないのです。フォルムを熟考する際に使うことはありますが。

二川　どんなプログラムを使用されていますか？

ハディド　使用するプログラムはいくつかありますが，毎年どんどん進化していきます。でも，プログラムを使いさえすればいいわけではなくて，はじめにアイディアありき，です。プロセスは変わりましたね。以前は，一つのフォルムに対して膨大な枚数のパースを描くため，非常に時間がかかったものです。パソコンはそういう作業が得意ですから，デザインのプロセスに柔軟性をもたせてくれます。

でも最終的に重要なのは，建物が安定して建ち上がることです。派手なキャンティレバー・スタイルのテーブルでも，ちゃんと自立しないとならない。建物には様々な分野の要素が絡みあっていて，機械，電気，構造のエンジニアの助けが必要になる。それが建築の豊かさなのです。そして，だからこそ建築をつくったり考えたりすることは非常に難しく，面白味のあるものなのです。偏見ではありませんが，建築家がデザインしていないものは，一目でそうとわかってしまいます。見た目は良くても，まとまりに欠けるんですね。

二川　これからも様々な規模の仕事を手がけていかれるわけですね。

ハディド　ええ。同じ人間が大規模なものから小規模なものまでを担当します。アイディアや語法の断絶があってはいけませんから。

例えば，「ヴィトラ社消防所」(1993年, p.068-)では，駐輪場もデザインしました。自転車用の車庫です。キノコと樹木をいっぺんに手がけたようなものです。

二川　家具デザインも不可欠な仕事ですね。

ハディド　ええ。現在とりかかっている家具シリーズをお見せしましょう。アルミ製です。なかなか良いでしょう。このテーブルはアルミの削りだしです（「クレーター」，デイヴィッド・ギル・ギャラリー，2007年）。パソコンを使って，デザインから製作まで数ヶ月ででき上がります。

覚えているかもしれませんが，何年か前に別シリーズの家具を手がけた際，テーブルもつくったのですが，それとこれを比べてみるとほとんど一緒なのです。昔のものの方が直線が多めだったくらいで。

二川　家具デザインの依頼は多いですか？

ハディド　今年は多いですね。エスタブリッシュド＆サンズの仕事をしています（「シームレス・コレクション」，2006年）。

二川　売り上げはいかがですか？

ハディド　好調です。限定モデルは完売しました。

二川　建築と家具の両方ができる人は，あまりいません。心構えは似ていても，まったく別のものだと私は思うのですが。ご自分ではどうお考

relate to each other and be of the same language.

For example when we did Vitra Fire Station (1993, p.068-) we also needed to design bicycle parking——a shed for the bicycles. We did something like mushrooms or trees.

Futagawa Furniture design has always been an integral part of the practice.

Hadid Yes. I can show you some very nice furniture pieces we are developing. They're all done in aluminum. They're very stunning. For instance, we're doing a very nice table, all made of one piece of aluminum ("Crater" for David Gill Galleries, 2007). With the computer these are designed and built in months.

I don't know if you remember but many years ago when I was doing my other furniture I did a table, and when I compare them to this, they are almost identical except the first one had more straight lines.

Futagawa You have a lot of furniture commissions?

Hadid This year we do. We're doing a thing for Established & Sons. (The Seamless Collection, 2006)

Futagawa How are sales?

Hadid They are doing well. The limited editions are all gone.

Futagawa Few people can do both architecture and furniture. I think the attitude is similar but really it is totally different. What do you think about that? How do you go about thinking about tables, chairs and sofas.

Hadid I think about it at the same time. It's all floating in my head. For instance, I want to do a table where the surface becomes a landscape. So I'm thinking of many things and luckily a few things come out and I'm able to focus on it.

Futagawa So this table goes with your architecture.

Hadid Yes, but I think it can work in other houses as well.

Futagawa I see so many iterations of the designs in your studio.

Hadid We vary it until it works just as you would study the geometry of the building.

Futagawa In sketches?

Hadid I still love hand drawing you know. But young people can't draw anymore.

Futagawa There hasn't been much talent after the emergence of your generation.

Hadid I think that will change eventually. It takes a long time to build a career in architecture. It's very competitive. And also there are other social factors. Many things overlap at the same time and produce these generational shifts.

Futagawa How do you feel at school teaching young people?

Hadid I think teaching is interesting because you train people who can move on to different things. There's a lot going on right now that's really exciting. And also there's the opportunity to have these discussions with others.

Futagawa The way of teaching has changed a lot since you were in school.

えですか？　テーブルや椅子やソファーなどをどのように考えていらっしゃいますか？

ハディド　それらを考えるのは同時に，ですね．すべて私の頭の中に浮かんでいるのです．例えばテーブルを考えながら，その表面がランドスケープになればいい，という具合に．いろいろなイメージが頭の中にあって，そこから運良く形になるものがいくつか出て来るので，そこに意識を集中するのです．

二川　だからこのテーブルはあなたの建築にマッチするものだと．

ハディド　ええ，でも他の家にも合うと思いますよ．

二川　最近では，デザインの転用がいろいろな建物で見られるようになってきましたね．

ハディド　建物の形状を決める時と同様に，たくさんのバリエーションを考えます．

二川　スケッチでですか？

ハディド　いまだに手描きのスケッチが好きなんですよ．でも最近の若い人々はスケッチができなくなりましたね．

二川　あなたの世代以降は，才能のある人があまり出てきていません．

ハディド　そんな状況もいずれ変わると思います．建築でキャリアを積むには時間がかかるし，競争も激しい．またそれとは別に，社会的な要因もあります．世代交代というものは，様々な条件が重なり合って起きるものですから．

二川　学校で若い人々を教えることについてはどう思われますか？

BMW Plant Leipzig – Central Building (Leipzig, Germany / 2002-05)　BMWライプツィヒ工場—中央棟（ドイツ，ライプツィヒ）

Hadid Well. It wasn't all digital before.

Futagawa Yes. When we saw the studio we were so surprised by the desks with just a computer. It used to be that you needed drafting tables.

Hadid Well, that's partially because we're renovating. But it's true. Sometimes a computer is all they need. They can't draw and they can't make models. It will take another moment in history for this to change. You can't teach these skills that take ten years to develop in a month or a year.

Futagawa So you don't think it's a problem that there's a lack of skill today?

Hadid I think it's a problem but then again there always new skills that emerge. For instance, for my generation there was a critical moment in the early 80s when some people showed others that there was another way to do things. And that was very subversive. And it was met with resistance from the schools, and the architects and the builders and everyone. But look at how many architects have thrived from that period.

Futagawa Whenever I try to meet architects like you, it's impossible, because everyone is traveling. I would have thought with the internet that communication would be easier, but the opposite has happened for architects. There is more traveling than ever before.

Hadid Yes it's true. The world has opened up a lot. It's really exhausting.

Futagawa You travel a lot lately but haven't been to Japan in

ハディド 人に教えるのは，面白いです。将来様々な方向へ進む可能性を持つ学生を相手にしますから。今はエキサイティングなことがたくさんありますし。それに，学校は他の人々と議論ができる場でもあります。

二川 ご自分が学生だった頃とは教え方もずいぶん変わってきているのでは。

ハディド そうですね。こんなにデジタル化されてはいませんでした。

二川 ええ。スタジオを拝見した時，デスクがとても小さく，パソコンが置いてあるだけで，たいへん驚きました。昔は製図台が必要だったのに。

ハディド 今ちょうど改装中ということもありますが。そうなんです，パソコン一台あれば事足りてしまう。彼らはスケッチもできないし，模型もつくれない。こんな状況が変わるには，もう少し時間がかかりそうですね。本来なら10年かかって習得するスキルを1ヶ月や1年で教えることはできませんから。

二川 では昨今の人材のスキル不足は問題ではないとお考えですか？

ハディド 問題だと思ってはいますが，新しく出現するスキル，というものもあるわけです。例えば，私の世代にとって80年代初頭は重大な節目といえる時期でした。今までとは違う，別のやり方を提示する人々が現れたのです。それは非常に破壊的なパワーを持っていました。学校や建築家や建設業者や，皆からの抵抗にあいましたが，今まわりを見廻してみると当時の混乱の中から成長した建築家がたくさんいます。

二川 あなたのような建築家と会って話をしようとしても，みなさん出張中で，つかまえられません。インターネットの普及でコミュニケーションが楽にとれるようになると思いきや，建築家に関してはその逆のようです。以前よりも出張が増えていますね。

Interview 2007

many years.

Hadid I know. I must go back to Japan. I haven't been in fifteen years, since before Fukuoka in the early 1990s. I will try to go back sometime.

Looking back, I must say that my trips to Asia in the 1980s had an incredible impact on me and my work. This impact stays on even today. It's another universe in a positive way. If you look at Japanese fashion, street fashion, photography and makeup, it's quite interesting and inspiring.

Futagawa How do you keep up with this information?

Hadid Oh, magazines, TV programs. I just think it's incredible. I remember walking around Tokyo looking at all these gadgets. At the time, those kinds of things weren't available in Europe. I think it's a shame there was a recession in the 90s because Japan at the time was very advanced and exciting. I think they were breaking the boundaries and they were hiring architects to do very experimental and interesting work. But then again, when one goes back to these places it's never the same.

Futagawa Where do you get inspiration from these days?

Hadid Right now when I'm traveling it's too hectic to see things. I don't have time to really see the things around me. I would love to go to India because I've never been. I would love to go to Chandigarh. I would love to go to Dhaka by Louis Kahn. It's just fantasies right now. A visit to Japan would be a little easier because I know people there. I would have to plan an agenda for India. But once I was flying over India and the plane was flying very low, the cities were vast and enormous. It made me very curious about them.

Futagawa Now you often go to China don't you?

Hadid No not really. Not in the last year. They've changed a lot of laws about working in China. We are doing the Guangzhou Opera House (2010) which should be open next year.

Futagawa How about the Middle East. You have several projects there currently.

Hadid Yes. In Dubai and Abu Dhabi and we've been approached about a project in Beirut which could be very interesting and even about work in Syria and North Africa.

Futagawa When you work in the Middle East is there a kind of empathy with the culture for you?

Hadid It's the language that ties us together. Of course if I worked in Iraq it would be quite emotional for me since I lived there. But I must say this past year I drove from Beirut to Damascus and I went to see a particular Mosque again and it was very stunning. As a child in Iraq, I went to a nun's school, a Christian school. I used to pass by these things on the bus on the way to, say, a school picnic. These places are, apart from their religious significance, very stunning, and beautiful, with elaborate mysterious interiors. A mosque is very deliberately done and beautiful. It's meant to evoke heaven and it is absolutely stunning. And it's very curious to me the connection between these beautiful worlds and all the geometry and the mathematical roots of the structures. So when I saw them again, I became very curious about it. So I guess these are the kinds of

ハディド その通りです。世界は広がりましたが，その分，体力を消耗します。

二川 近頃は特に出張が多いようですが，日本には数年来いらしていませんね。

ハディド そうなんです。日本にはまた行かないと。もう15年，訪れていません。1990年代初めに福岡に行って以来。いつかまた訪れるつもりです。

振り返ってみると，1980年代にアジア諸国をまわった経験は，自分自身と作品に相当なインパクトを与えています。その影響は今なお残っていると思います。いい意味で，別世界なのです。日本のストリート・ファッションや写真，メークアップなどは，とても興味深く，インスピレーションを与えてくれます。

二川 そういった情報はどのように入手されるのですか？

ハディド 雑誌とか，テレビ番組とか。びっくりするようなものがあります。東京の街を訪れたときに見かけた雑貨やおもちゃ。当時ああいう物はヨーロッパには無かった。90年代の不況は残念なことだったと思います。あの頃の日本は最先端で，とてもエキサイティングでしたから。枠にとらわれずに，建築家を雇って実験的で面白い仕事をさせていました。でも，変わらずにいるものなど無いのは，日本だけではありませんからね。

二川 最近はどのようなものからインスピレーションを受けましたか？

ハディド 今は旅行ばかりでバタバタしていて，周りを見廻す時間がとれません。今まで訪れたことのないインドには興味があります。チャンディガールに行ってみたい。ルイス・カーンのダッカに行ってみたい。現段階ではただの思いつきですが。日本には知人が何人かいるので，行くのはいくぶん簡単なのですが，インドの場合は事前のプランニングが必要です。以前に一度，乗っていた飛行機がインド上空を低空飛行したことがあって，巨大な広がりを持つ市街地を見て，好奇心を大いにかきたてられました。

二川 最近では中国に何度もいらしていますよね？

ハディド いえ，そうでもないです，特に昨年は。中国では仕事をする上での法律がだいぶ変わったようです。来年オープン予定の「広州オペラハウス」(2010年)を手がけています。

二川 中東はいかがですか。現在進行中のプロジェクトがいくつかありますが。

ハディド ええ。ドバイとアブダビで。ベイルートでのプロジェクトについて，かなり面白そうなオファーがありました。シリアと北アフリカのプロジェクトの話もあります。

二川 中東での仕事をされる際，文化的な共感が得られることはありますか？

ハディド 中東諸国と私自身を結ぶ絆は，言語です。もちろん，もしイラクで仕事ができたなら，それはとても感動的なことだと思います。昔住んでいた場所ですので。昨年，ベイルートからダマスカスまで車で移動した際，とあるモスクを見学しに行ったのですが，非常に素晴らしかった。イラクでの子供時代，私はキリスト教の修道女学校に通っていたのですが，学校の遠足などでは，そういった建造物の前をバスで通ることがありました。モスクは，宗教的な意味合いはさておき，それ自体がとても美しく素晴らしい建物で，内部は精巧につくり込まれ，ミステリアスな雰囲気があります。天国を喚起させるよう，非常に美しく緻密につ

Guangzhou Opera House (Guangzhou, China / 2003-10) 広州オペラハウス（中国，広州）

things you get to confirm when you travel.

It is also interesting to see the combinations when you travel. For instance, Moorish Hollywood. When you go to Hollywood there are houses with Moorish influences. Once in Los Angeles, I was visiting a house in Pasadena built for an actor from the 30s. It was this fantastic Hollywood version of Moorish architecture. It was very well done and quite stunning. And now they are doing this hybrid style in Morocco. From Morocco to Los Angeles to Morocco again. They're miles away. The influence comes from the new world back through Spain. It's very interesting how these languages travel in this way. So the process of globalization has been happening for a hundred years.

Futagawa What's the situation with British architecture?

Hadid Well the economy is thriving. London now is like Japan 20 years ago. I don't know Americans. It's double anywhere else. It's double New York prices. A lot of talented architects have become commercial architects. There are not a lot of young architects that stand out. And also unlike America or Europe there are no opportunities to make a name for yourself when you are young. In

くられています。そういった美しい世界と，その構造の幾何学・数学的ルーツの関係性は，とても興味深いところです。久しぶりにモスクを見て，好奇心をかきたてられました。こんな風に，旅行をしたおかげで再確認ができることもあるんですね。

　もうひとつ，旅行につきものなのは，面白いコンビネーションを見つけることです。例えば，ムーア様式とハリウッド。ハリウッドに行くと，ムーア様式の影響を受けた家々を見かけることができます。ロサンゼルスのパサデナに，とある俳優のために1930年代に建てられた家があります。ムーア様式のハリウッド版といったところの，実に立派な建築でした。そして今度はそんなハイブリッド・スタイルをモロッコに持って行くそうです。モロッコからロサンゼルスへ，そしてまたモロッコへと長い距離を渡ってゆく。文化や言語が新世界からスペインを通って戻ってくる。とても面白いですね。グローバリゼーションは，もう100年ほど前から始まっていたのです。

二川　イギリス建築の現状についてお聞かせ下さい。
ハディド　そうですね，経済は上向きです。今日のロンドンは20年前の日

Europe they might win a competition. In America there is always the opportunity to do a family house.

Futagawa Same as Japan.

Hadid I think it's a problem. These kids come out of school. They may go off on their own after one or two years. They have no experience and work on art projects. They don't develop their repertoire. They either don't stay long enough at an office or they stay too long. They aren't very practical.

In Europe at least everything is a competition. So there are a lot of young people who win these projects. There's more opportunity. For example there are lot of young architects that have graduated from the AA School that are building interesting work in Eastern Europe.

Futagawa How about Russia?

Hadid We have a house project in Moscow. But in Russia you have no control over what they might do to it. I love Moscow, but it is crazy. It's an amazing city. The Russians are crazy.

Futagawa Any comments on your contemporaries? Rem Koolhaas, Frank Gehry, Jean Nouvel?

Hadid We are all competitors but also friends. I support them, they support me.

I saw Frank at an event a few weeks ago. I saw Wolf Prix yesterday. I saw Steven Holl in New York and Jacque Herzog in London recently. I don't see Rem much, But we're all very good friends. Architecture is very tough and so it makes you very competitive. It's really difficult.

Futagawa You've been competing with them for a long time.

Hadid It's true. It's amazing that the scene has not changed that much in the last thirty years. The work has changed but the people in the game are the same. So it just means that these people have incredible perseverance and agility at the same time.

Futagawa Do you ever discuss projects with each other?

Hadid No. But for example I'm teaching in Vienna so I was there yesterday with people like Jeff Kipnis and Greg Lynn. And younger people from New York like Jesse Reiser and Ali Rahim. And there's a discussion between us. I give a lecture. So we meet on reviews, but there's no forum really for us to discuss architecture. It's not like when Alvin Boyarsky was here and he would arrange these discussions at the AA School. It does occur sometimes. Like when I was at Yale, Peter Eisenman was on my review. So it happens, but not in any organized way. It's a shame; we're all too busy these days.

June 27, 2007, London

WORKS 2007-

2007-12
HEYDAR ALIYEV CENTER
ヘイダル・アリエフ・センター

Baku, Azerbaijan

Overall view from south　南側全景　© Hélène Binet

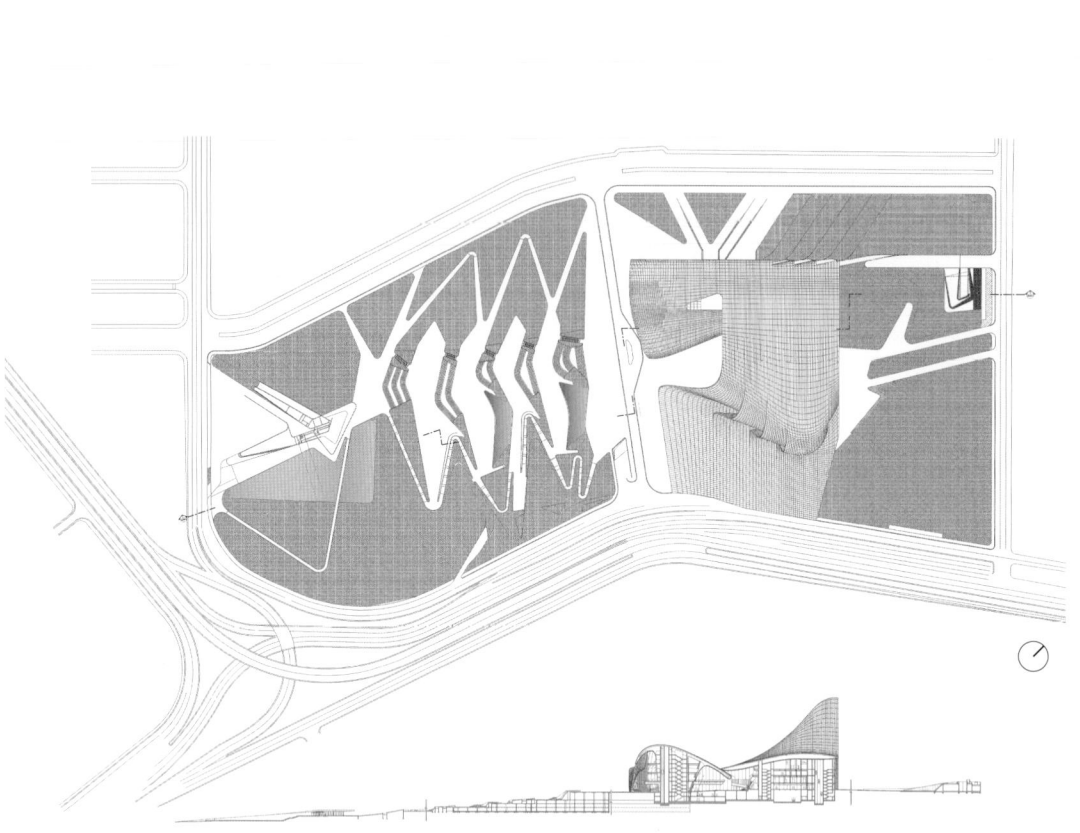

Site plan and section 配置/断面

As part of the former Soviet Union, the urbanism and architecture of Baku, the capital of Azerbaijan on the Western coast of the Caspian Sea, was heavily influenced by the planning of that era. Since its independence in 1991, Azerbaijan has invested heavily in modernising and developing Baku's infrastructure and architecture, departing from its legacy of normative Soviet Modernism.

Zaha Hadid Architects was appointed as design architects of the Heydar Aliyev Center following a competition in 2007. The Center, designed to become the primary building for the nation's cultural programs, breaks from the rigid and often monumental Soviet architecture that is so prevalent in Baku, aspiring instead to express the sensibilities of Azeri culture and the optimism of a nation that looks to the future.

Design Concept

The design of the Heydar Aliyev Center establishes a continuous, fluid relationship between its surrounding plaza and the building's interior. The plaza, as the ground surface; accessible to all as part of Baku's urban fabric, rises to envelop an equally public interior space and define a sequence of event spaces dedicated to the collective celebration of contemporary and traditional Azeri culture. Elaborate formations such as undulations, bifurcations, folds, and inflections modify this plaza surface into an architectural landscape that performs a multitude of functions: welcoming, embracing, and directing visitors through different levels of the interior. With this gesture, the building blurs the conventional differentiation between architectural object and urban landscape, building envelope and urban plaza, figure and ground, interior and exterior.

Fluidity in architecture is not new to this region. In historical Islamic architecture, rows, grids, or sequences of columns flow to infinity like trees in a forest, establishing non-hierarchical space. Continuous calligraphic and ornamental patterns flow from carpets to walls, walls to ceilings, ceilings to domes, establishing seamless relationships and blurring distinctions between architectural elements and the ground they inhabit. Our intention was to relate to that historical understanding of architecture, not through the use of mimicry or a limiting adherence to the iconography of the past, but rather by developing a firmly contemporary interpretation, reflecting a more nuanced understanding.

Responding to the topographic sheer drop that formerly split the site in two, the project introduces a precisely terraced landscape that establishes alternative connections and routes between public plaza, building, and underground parking. This solution avoids additional excavation and landfill, and successfully converts an initial disadvantage of the site into a key design feature.

Geometry

One of the most critical yet challenging elements of the project was the architectural development of the building's skin. Our ambition to achieve a surface so continuous that it appears homogenous, required a broad range of different functions, construction logics and technical systems had to be brought together and integrated into the building's envelope. Advanced computing allowed for the continuous control and communication of these complexities among the numerous project participants.

Aerial view from southwest　南西上空から見る　© Hufton+Crow

In this architectural composition, if the surface is the music, then the seams between the panels are the rhythm. Numerous studies were carried out on the surface geometry to rationalize the panels while maintaining continuity throughout the building and landscape. The seams promote a greater understanding of the project's scale. They emphasize the continual transformation and implied motion of its fluid geometry, offering a pragmatic solution to practical construction issues such as manufacturing, handling, transportation and assembly; and answering technical concerns such as accommodating movement due to deflection, external loads, temperature change, seismic activity and wind loading.

The Heydar Aliyev Center's design evolved from our investigations and research of the site's topography and the Center's role within its broader cultural landscape. By employing these articulate contextual relationships, the design is embedded within this context; unfolding the future cultural possibilities for Azerbaijan.

View from north　北から見る　© Hufton+Crow

Heydar Aliyev Center

Partial west elevation　西面　© *Hufton+Crow*

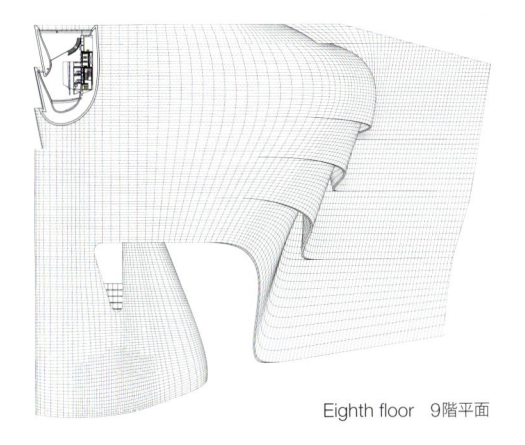

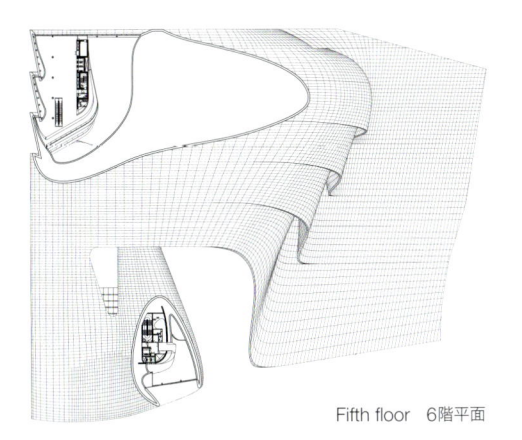

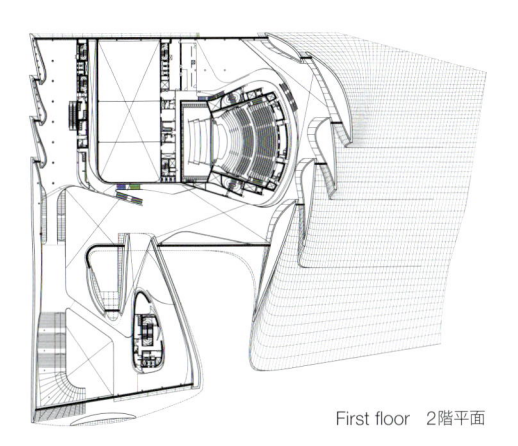

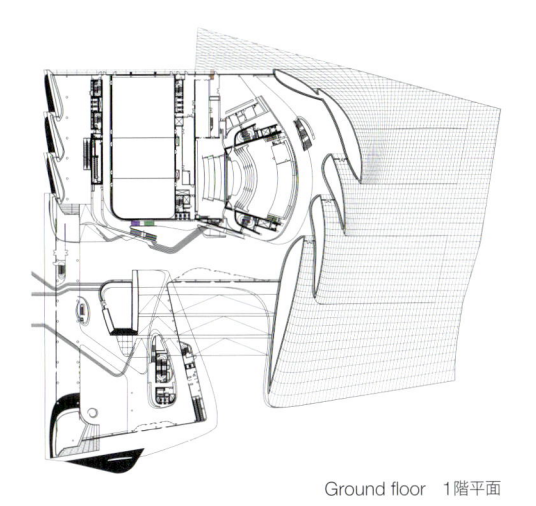

Eighth floor　9階平面

Fifth floor　6階平面

First floor　2階平面

Ground floor　1階平面

Auditorium　オーディトリアム　© Hélène Binet

Heydar Aliyev Center

カスピ海の西岸に位置するアゼルバイジャンの首都バクーは，旧ソビエト連邦だった頃の名残から，当時の計画に強く影響を受けた街や建物が今でも残っている。1991年の独立以降，アゼルバイジャンは厳格なソビエト的モダニズムの遺産を近代化するために重点的に投資をし，バクーのインフラや建物を整備してきた。

ザハ・ハディド・アーキテクツは2007年のヘイダル・アリエフ・センターのコンペにおいてデザインアーキテクトとして指名された。このセンターはアゼルバイジャンの文化プログラムのための中心的役割を担う建物として設計され，バクーに多く存在する硬くモニュメンタルなソビエト的建築を打開し，アゼルバイジャンの文化の繊細さとこの国の明るい未来を象徴するような，野心にあふれた建築となっている。

デザインコンセプト

ヘイダル・アリエフ・センターのデザインは，建物周辺の広場と建物内部をなめらかに繋ぐような，連続的な関係性をつくるデザインとなっている。広場は地面に広がる表皮としてそのまま立ち上がりパブリックな内部空間を包み込み，またアゼルバイジャンの過去から現在までの文化を集めた展示イベントのための空間的なシークエンスもつくっている。またこの広場はバクーの都市構造の一部でもあり，誰にでも開かれアクセスが可能である。なめらかな建物外皮や二つに分岐した形状，折りたたまれ，湾曲する面など，丁寧につくりこまれたデザインがこの広場を建築的ランドスケープへと溶け込ませている。これらは，来館者を迎え入れ，包み込み，異なるレベルへと誘導する。こういった操作により，建築と都市の風景，建物周辺環境と都市広場，建物の形と地面，内部と外部といった様式的な差異を曖昧なものとしている。

流れるような連続性を持った建築はこの地域では決して真新しいものではない。伝統的なイスラム建築では，柱の列やグリッド，あるいはその連続的な並びが無限に続く森のようにヒエラルキーのない空間をつくりだしている。またカーペットから壁，天井，さらにドームまで連続するイスラムの文字や装飾パターンは，建築的な要素と生活の場である地面との境目をシームレスにつなげ，その差異を曖昧にしている。しかし我々はこういった過去の図像にこだわって，それらを模倣したりするのではなく，むしろその歴史性を適切に解釈し直し，現代的な介入に徹することで，歴史的解釈と建築をつなげようと試みたのである。

敷地は急峻な崖によって二分されており，この敷地

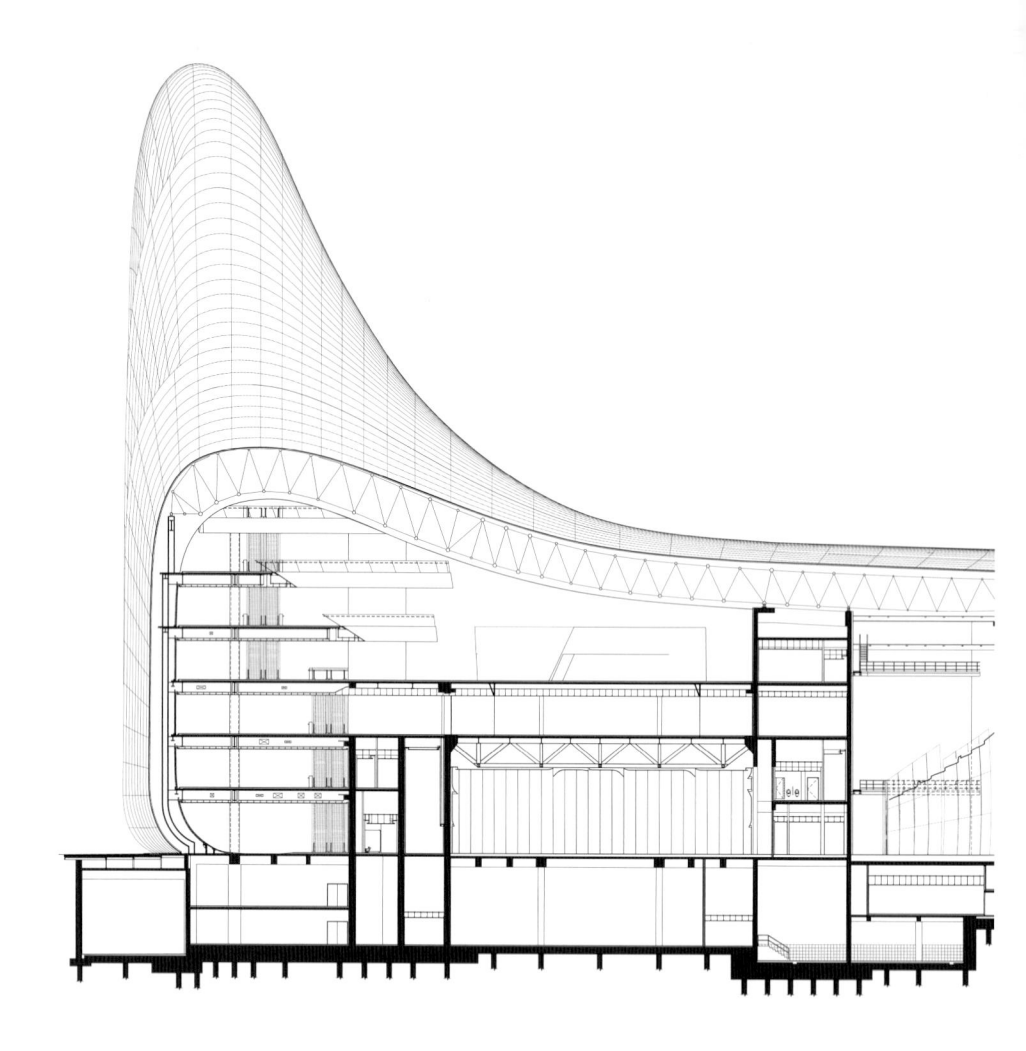

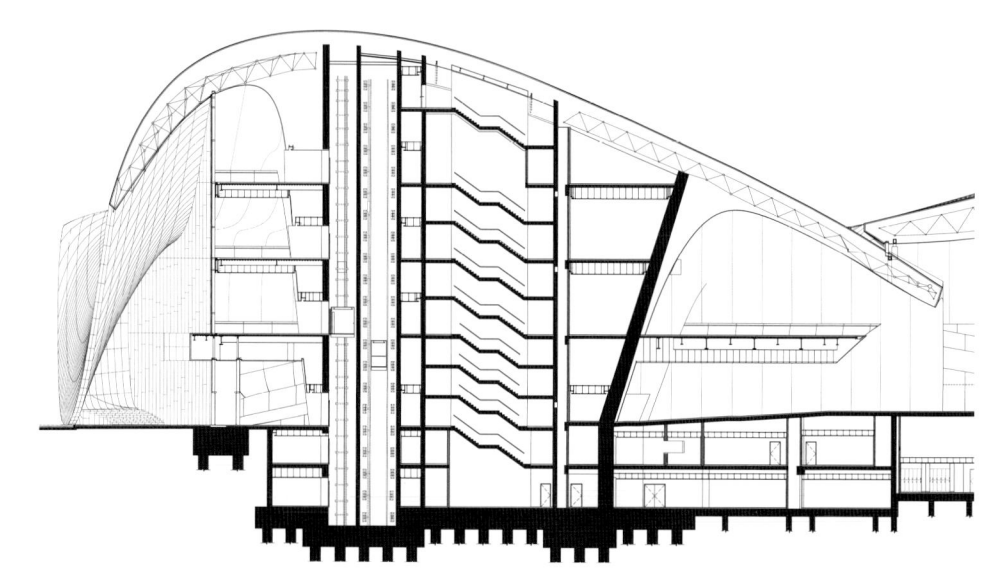

Foyer　ホワイエ　© Iwan Baan

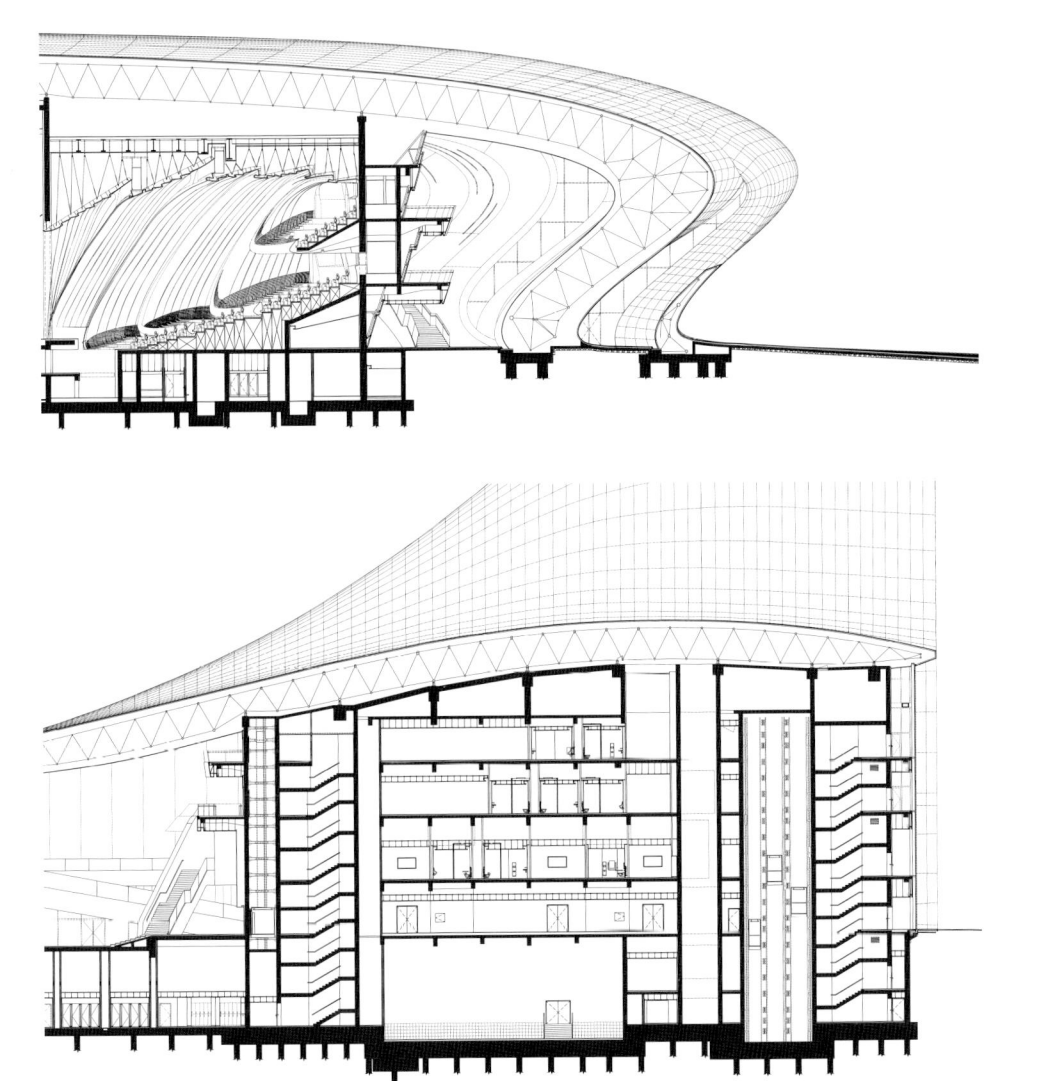

Sections　断面

形状に従ってテラス状のランドスケープをつくり、パブリック・プラザと建物、地下駐車場をつなぐ新たな通路を形成した。こうすることで地面の掘削、埋め立てをすることなく、敷地の欠点をうまくデザイン上の鍵として取り込んでいる。

形態
本プロジェクトで最も難しくかつ挑戦的なものだったのは建物の外皮である。外皮を均一でなめらかな面にしたいという我々の強い要望に対し、さまざまな機能や施工計画・技術システムが一体的に行われ、外皮に集約された。またデジタル化によって、数多くの関係者が関わる複雑な施工をスムーズにコントロールし、コミュニケーションを図ることも可能となった。
　この建物の表面を音楽に例えるとすると、パネル間の繋ぎ目はリズムと捉えることができる。合理的形状かつ建物とランドスケープの連続性も崩さないようなパネルを実現するために、建物表面のスタディが繰り返し行われた。このパネルの繋ぎ目からは本プロジェクトがいかに多様なスケールに渡って行われたかが強く読み取れる。この繋ぎ目は建物のなめらかな形の変化とその動きを強調し、さらに生産、取り扱い、輸送、組み立てといった施工における現実的な問題も効果的に解決している。また同時に座屈や外力、温度変化、地震力、風力等の動的挙動のテクニカルな課題もクリアしている。
　ヘイダル・アリエフ・センターのデザインは、敷地形状の調査・研究とセンターが果たす様々な文化芸術分野での役割をもとにつくられていった。このような明確な文脈上の関係性を拾い上げながら、アゼルバイジャンの将来的な文化的可能性を広げるようなデザインを付与していった。

Heydar Aliyev Center

2007-14
MOBILE ART -
CHANEL CONTEMPORARY ART CONTAINER
モバイル・アート－シャネル・コンテンポラリーアート・コンテナ

Hong Kong, China / Tokyo, Japan / New York, U.S.A. / Paris, France

Aerial view (Tokyo)　上空より見る（東京）

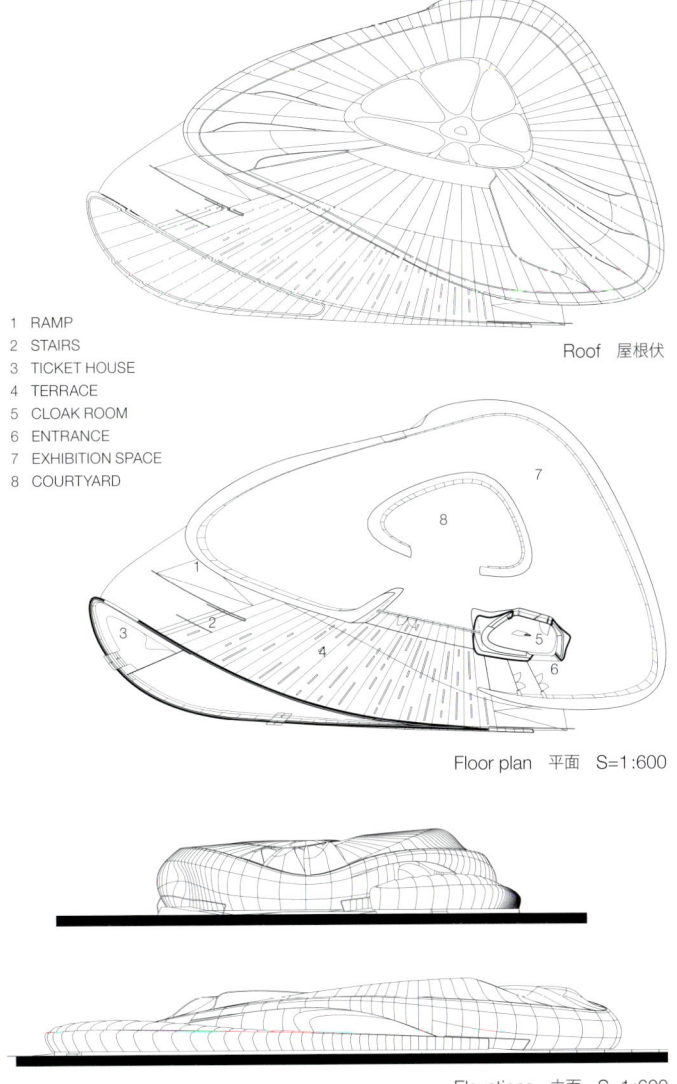

1 RAMP
2 STAIRS
3 TICKET HOUSE
4 TERRACE
5 CLOAK ROOM
6 ENTRANCE
7 EXHIBITION SPACE
8 COURTYARD

Roof 屋根伏

Floor plan 平面 S=1:600

Elevations 立面 S=1:600

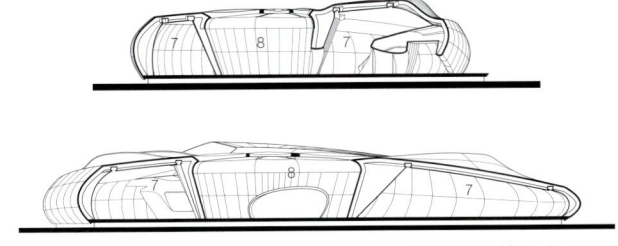

Sections 断面 S=1:600

Mobile Art - Chanel Contemporary Art Container

The form of the 700 m² Chanel Pavilion is a celebration of the iconic work of Chanel, unmistakeable for its smooth layering of exquisite details that together create an elegant, cohesive whole. The resulting functional, and versatile architectural structure of the Pavilion is a series of continuous arch-shaped elements, with a courtyard in its central space. Artificial light behind the translucent ceiling washes the walls to emphasize the "arched" structure, and assists in the creation of a new artificial landscape for art installations. A large roof light opening dramatically floods the entrance in daylight to blur the relationship between interior and exterior. In addition to the lighting and colour effects, the spatial rhythm created by the seams of each segment gives strong perspective views throughout the interior.

The 65 m² central courtyard has large transparent openings to the sky above and is designed to host events as well as provide an area for reflection after visiting the exhibition. The courtyard serves as an intermediate space between the exhibition and public area of the Pavilion. In light of the extensive shipping between cities, the steel structure has been designed to be built in under one week, which is essential for an ephemeral pavilion. With a direct visual connection to the courtyard, the 128 m² terrace continues the dialogue between the Pavilion's exterior and interior. During an event, the two spaces can be linked to become one large event zone.

Reflective materials allow the exterior skin to be illuminated with varying colours which can be tailored to the differing programmes of special events in each city. The dichotomy between the powerful sculptural mass of the Chanel Pavilion's structure and the lightness of its envelope create a bold and enigmatic element. The Pavilion's exterior develops into a rich variety of interior spaces that maximize the potential to reuse and rethink space due to the innate flexibility of its plan.

The total fluidity of the Chanel Pavilion's curvilinear geometries is an obvious continuation of Hadid's 30 years of exploration and research into systems of continuous transformations and smooth transitions. With this repertoire of morphology, Zaha Hadid is able to translate the ephemeral typology of a pavilion into the sensual forms required for this celebration of Chanel's cultural importance.

Following its acclaimed 2008 tour to Hong Kong 27 February - 5 April, Tokyo 31 May - 4 July and New York 20 October - 9 November, Chanel generously donated the pavilion to the Institut du Monde Arabe, IMA, at the end of 2010, giving Mobile Art a home in the heart of Paris until 2014. The pavilion was being used to host exhibitions in line with the centre's policy of showcasing talent from Arab countries. "Zaha Hadid, Une Architecture" 29 April - 30 October 2011, was the inaugural exhibition in the Mobile Art Pavilion at the IMA.

Containers: stacking parts of Mobile Art　コンテナ：モバイル・アートの部材が収められている

Workshop in place　現場の作業コンテナ

Members: steel frame, joint, FRP panels
部材：スティール・フレーム，ジョイント部分，FRPパネル

Assembling parts for Mobile Art　モバイル・アートを組み立てる様子

700平方メートルの広さを持つシャネル・パヴィリオンは、シャネルのアイコニックな業績を記念してつくられたもので、滑らかで精巧なディテールを持つ外皮の仕上げがエレガントさと一体的なデザインを実現している。機能的かつ多用途に利用可能なこのパヴィリオンの構造は、連続するアーチ型の部材によって構成され、パヴィリオン中央には中庭が設けられている。半透明な天井の裏の照明がアーチ型の構造を強調するように壁を照らし、アート・インスタレーションのための新たな擬似的ランドスケープを演出する。大きなトップライトからはダイナミックに光が入り込み、内部と外部の関係性を曖昧にしている。さらに照明と色の効果に加えて、壁のパネルの継ぎ目による空間のリズムが室内全体に強い視覚的なパースペクティブをもたらしている。

65平方メートルの中庭には上へと抜ける透明なトップライトが設けられ、イベントを催したり、また展示を見た後の余韻を楽しむ場所としてつくられている。中庭は展示エリアとパブリック・エリアの中間的な空間として機能する。世界中の都市を広く巡回すること、そして仮設というパヴィリオン特有の性質から、1週間以内に組み上げることのできる鉄骨の構造を考案した。中庭へと直につながる視線と128平方メートルのテラスが、パヴィリオン内外の関係を連続的なものとしている。また展示の開催期間中でも二つの空間をつないで一つの大きなイベントスペースへと変更することも可能である。

反射素材が用いられた外皮は様々な色に照らされ、各都市での特別展示プログラムに応じてその姿を変化させる。パヴィリオンの力強く彫刻的な構造体と、それを包む軽快な外皮の対照的な関係は大胆かつ不思議な物質感を醸し出している。外皮はそのまま室内へとつながり、豊かに変化する内部空間の表情をつくる。このパヴィリオン特有の柔軟な平面によって生まれる内部空間は、空間の再利用性や再考の可能性を最大限に高めている。

パヴィリオンの曲線的な形状とその流動性は、ハディドが30年に渡り探求してきた、連続的でスムーズな変形という思考の延長線上にあることは明らかである。この彼女独自の形態学的レパートリーによって、ハディドは一過性の強いパヴィリオンならではのタイポロジーを官能的な形へと翻訳し、また同時にシャネルの文化的な重要性を明示するという要求にも応えている。

2008年の巡回展—香港2月27日〜4月5日、東京5月31日〜7月4日、ニューヨーク10月20日〜11月9日—終了後、2010年末に、シャネルはパヴィリオンをパリの中心部のアラブ世界研究所（IMA）へと寄贈し、2014年までそこをこのモバイルアートの棲家とした。パヴィリオンは、アラブ諸国の優秀な才能を披露する場である研究所の展示会場として使われた。2011年4月29日〜10月30日に渡って行われた「ザハ・ハディド、一つの建築」展は、IMAに置かれたモバイル・アート・パヴィリオンでの初の展覧会となった。

Framework　骨組み

Mobile Art - Chanel Contemporary Art Container

Hong Kong (above)　香港（上）　© *Virgile S. Bertrand*
New York (middle)　ニューヨーク（中）　© *John Linden*
Paris (below)　パリ（下）　© *François Lacour*

Day view (above) 昼景（上）
Night view (below) 夜景（下）

Mobile Art - Chanel Contemporary Art Container

View from foyer toward entrance/exit　ホワイエより出入口を見る
art works: Sylvie Fleury "Crystal Custom Commando" 2008

Entrance on left, exhibition space on right (above)　左手にエントランス、右に展示スペース（上）
Exhibition room (below)　展示室（下）
art works: Michael Lin "Untitled" 2007-08 (floor), Loris Cecchini "Floating Crystals (incoherent extensive formations for my deepest vibrations)" 2007-08

Mobile Art - Chanel Contemporary Art Container

2007-14
DONGDAEMUN DESIGN PARK
東大門デザイン・パーク

Seoul, Korea

DDP has been designed as a cultural hub at the centre of one of the busiest and most historic districts of the city. It is a place for people of all ages; a catalyst for the instigation and exchange of ideas and a place for new technologies and media to be explored—presenting an ever-changing menu of exhibitions and events that feeds the cultural vitality of the city.

DDP is an architectural landscape that revolves around the ancient city wall and newly discovered cultural artefacts which form the central element of the composition linking the park and plaza together. The fluid design encourages the greatest degree of interaction between the park and the people of Seoul.

The new DDP park is a place for leisure, relaxation and refuge—a green oasis within the busy urban surroundings of Dongdaemun. The design integrates the park and plaza seamlessly as one, blurring the boundary between architecture and nature in a continuous, fluid landscape that connects the city, park and architecture together. Voids and inflections in the park's surface give visitors glimpses into the innovative world of design below, making DDP an important link between the city's contemporary culture, emerging nature and history.

DDP design is the very specific result of how the context, local culture, programmatic requirements and innovative engineering come together - allowing the architecture, city and landscape to seamlessly combine in both form and spatial experience.

The park is accessible to everyone, with folds and inflections in its surface that welcome and direct visitors through different levels of the interior. The design blurs the boundaries between architecture and urban landscape, solid and void, interior and exterior. It is an architectural landscape where concepts of spatial flow are made real—creating a whole new kind of civic space for the city.

DDP engages the community in a collective dialogue where many contributions and innovations feed into each other, allowing talents and ideas to flourish. In combination with the city's exciting public cultural programs, DDP is an important investment in the education and inspiration of future generations; further developing Korea as a center of innovation.

Aerial view　上空より見る

Dongdaemun Design Park

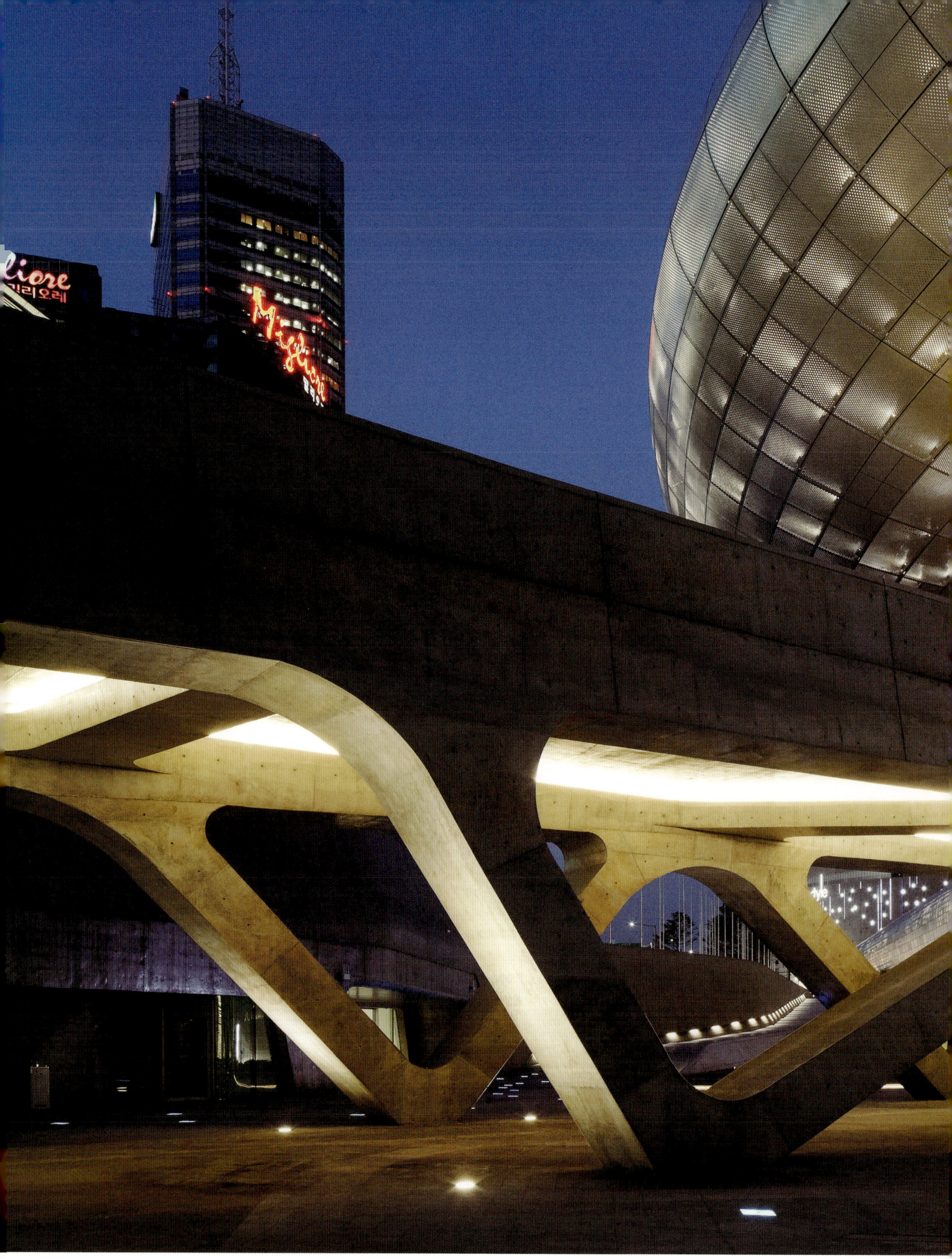

Underground plaza on second basement　地下2階の広場

東大門デザイン・パーク(DDP)は文化的なハブとして，ソウルの最も賑やかで，古い地区の中央に建っている。ここはあらゆる世代の人が集まる場所であり，様々なアイディアが誘発，刺激しあい，また新たなテクノロジーやメディアが探求される場所である。数多くの展示会やイベントによって絶えずその場が変化し，ソウルの文化的バイタリティが育まれている。

DDPはかつての古い都市の壁をぐるりと回りこむような，建築的ランドスケープとして建っているため，工事に先行して行われた調査では文化財なども発掘された。こういった歴史的な特徴が公園とプラザをつなぎあわせる中心的な要素をなしている。また流れるような外観が公園とソウル市民の相互の交流を促している。

DDPの公園は，東大門周辺の喧騒の中に佇む緑のオアシスであり，レジャーや息抜き，あるいは癒しの場所となる。公園とプラザが一体になるようになめらかにつなぎ合わせるデザインは，建築と自然の境界を曖昧にしている。また連続する流動的なランドスケープによって都市と公園，建築とを一体化している。公園の表層にある隙間や湾曲部からはその下に広がる革新的なデザインの世界を垣間見ることができ，現代の都市的

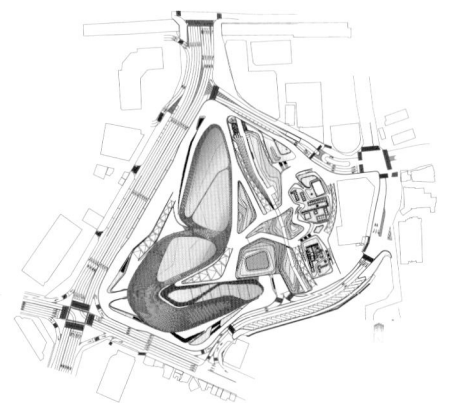

Site plan　配置　S=1:10000

Second basement　地下2階平面　S=1:5000

First floor　1階平面

1 DESIGN LIBRARY	7 CONVENTION HALL LOBBY	13 DESIGN GALLERY
2 CAFE	8 VVIP ROOM	14 PARKING / LOADING DOCK ENTRANCE
3 CHILDREN LIBRARY	9 EXHIBITION GALLERY	15 ENERGY CENTER
4 SEMINAR ROOMS	10 SPORT MEMORIAL	16 DESIGN MUSEUM
5 DDP OPERATION OFFICE	11 RELIC PARK	17 LIBRARY READING DECK
6 EXHIBITION RAMP	12 RELIC MUSEUM	18 MATERIAL LIBRARY

Partial east elevation: passageway to west side　東面：西側へ続く通路

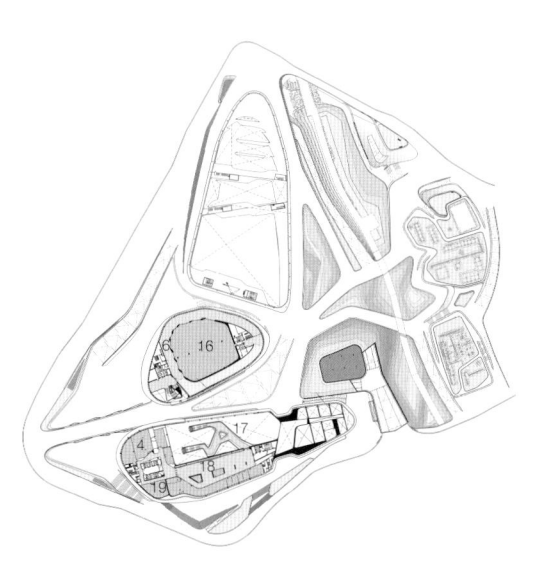

Second floor　2階平面

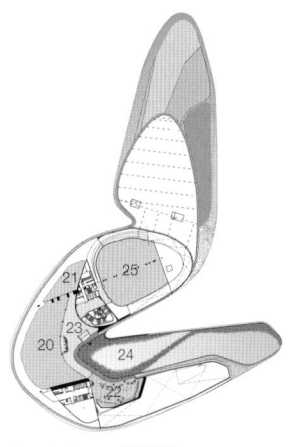

Fourth floor　4階平面

な文化と自然, 歴史を繋ぐ重要な役割を果たしている。
　DDPのデザインは土地のコンテクストや, 土着の文化, 機能的な要件, そして画期的なエンジニアリングが一体化したこの場所独自のデザインとなっている。これによって建築と街, ランドスケープが形態的にも空間体験としてもなめらかに組み合わされる。
　公園はあらゆる人に開放され, 来場者は館内のどの階からでも, 折れ曲がり湾曲した建物のサーフェスを通してダイレクトに出ることができる。このデザインは建築と都市のランドスケープ, 物体と空隙, 内部と外部の境界線を曖昧にする。これはすなわち空間の流れというコンセプトが現実化した建築的ランドスケープであり, 全く新しい都市の市民空間をつくりだしている。
　DDPは様々な貢献と革新的な活動が起こり, 両者が互いに高め合うような対話の場を用意することでコミュニティを引き合わせ, そこでは多くの才能やアイディアが育まれる。市の刺激的な文化プログラムと一体となって, DDPは韓国をイノベーションの中心地として更に発展させるであろう将来の世代のための教育とインスピレーションの重要な投資となる。

19	DESIGN ARCHIVE	25	MECHANICAL ROOM	31	INFORMATION
20	MUSEUM OF MULTITUDES	26	CONVENTION HALL	32	EVENT HALL
21	MEDIA LAB	27	PRESS ROOM	33	TICKET CENTER
22	SKY LOUNGE	28	VIP ROOM	34	UNDERGROUND PLAZA
23	LOBBY	29	RETAIL AREA	35	SUBWAY ENTRANCE
24	WALKABLE ROOF	30	PARKING FACILITIES	36	STORAGE

Dongdaemun Design Park

Lobby on fourth floor showing 'Zaha Hadid 360 Degrees' Inaugural Exhibition 21–26 March 2014 (above)
4階, ロビー：開館記念「ザハ・ハディド 360度」展 2014年3月21〜26日(上)
Staircase hall of second basement: leading to design museum, exibition area / lobby on upper floors (below)
地下2階の階段室ホール：上階のデザイン・ミュージアム, ロビー／展示スペースへ続く(下)

Downward view of staircase next to design museum　デザイン・ミュージアム横の階段室を見下ろす

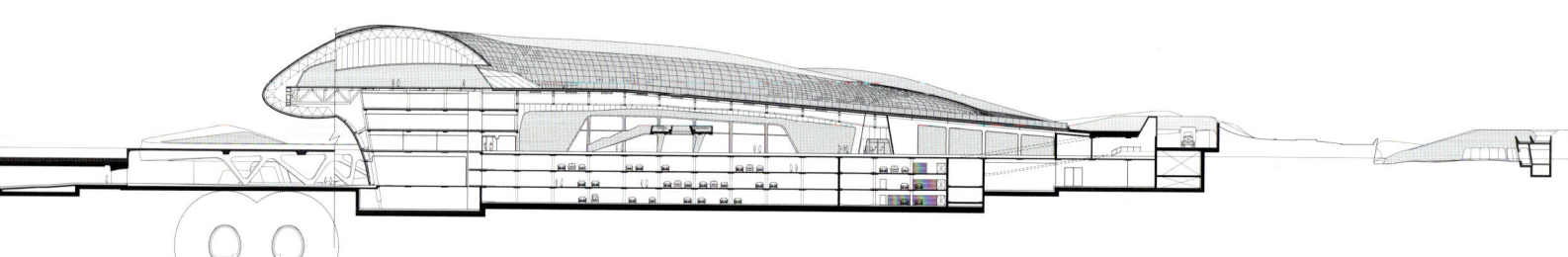

East-west section 東西断面 S=1:1600

Convention hall　コンベンション・ホール

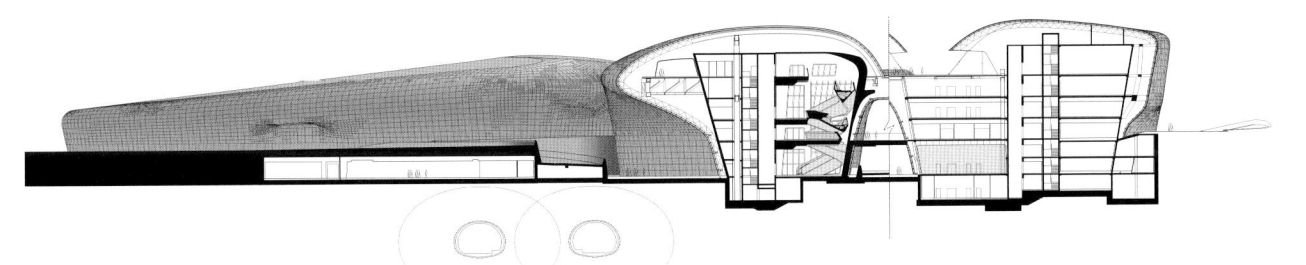

South-north section　南北断面

Dongdaemun Design Park

2007-13
JOCKEY CLUB INNOVATION TOWER, HONG KONG POLYTECHNIC UNIVERSITY

香港工科大学ジョッキー・クラブ・イノヴェーション・タワー

Hong Kong, China

View from east　東から見る　© Iwan Baan

Aerial view from southwest　南西側上空より見る　© Iwan Baan

The fluid character of the Jockey Club Innovation Tower is generated through an intrinsic composition of its landscape, floor plates and louvers, that dissolves the classic typology of the tower and podium into a seamless composition Iternal and external courtyards create new public spaces of an intimate scale which complement the large open exhibition forums and outdoor recreational facilities to promote a diversity of civic spaces.

Urbanism

The Hong Kong Polytechnic University (HK PolyU) has developed its own urban fabric by virtue of addition and growth over the last 50 years. The rich patchwork of various faculties, communities and facilities are strung together by a community of visually coherent yet very different buildings. The Jockey Club Innovation Tower is located on a very tight and irregular site on the North side of the campus. It creates and an accessible urban space which transforms how Hong Kong Polytechnic University is perceived and the way it uses its campus. The building projects a vision of possibilities for its future, as well as reflecting on the history of the HK PolyU by encapsulating in its architecture the process of change.

Architecture

The new Jockey Club Innovation Tower re-examines and address a creative, multidisciplinary environment by collecting the variety of programmes of the School of Design. Having undergone a strict process of examination of the multiple relationships amongst their unique identities, these programmes are arranged in accordance to their 'collateral flexibilities'.

Priority lies in engaging the campus staff, students and public in a welcoming new space that acts as both the building's entrance and organizer for the existing complex.

The new pedestrian level for the tower has been created as an open public foyer that channels deep into the building. The integrated pathway from Suen Chi Sun Memorial Square guides visitors to the main entrance. From here, a welcoming public space provides access to supporting facilities (shops, cafeteria, museum) through generous series of open exhibitions and 'showcase spaces' which span between the campus podium level and the ground floor.

From the entry foyer, staff, students and visitors move upwards through four levels of openly glazed studios and workshops. The many studios and workspaces accommodated within the new School of Design offer themselves as a variety of visual showcases. The route through the building becomes a transparent cascade of showcase and event spaces—allowing the student or visitor to visually connect and engage with the work and exhibits. These routes promote new opportunities of interaction between the diverse types of users. Voids bring in natural daylight, fresh air and the sense of continuity. In this way, the programmes of the tower, comprising learning clusters and central facilities, generate a dialogue between respective spatial volumes and disciplines of design.

Jockey Club Innovation Tower, Hong Kong Polytechnic University

First floor reflected ceiling　2階天井伏

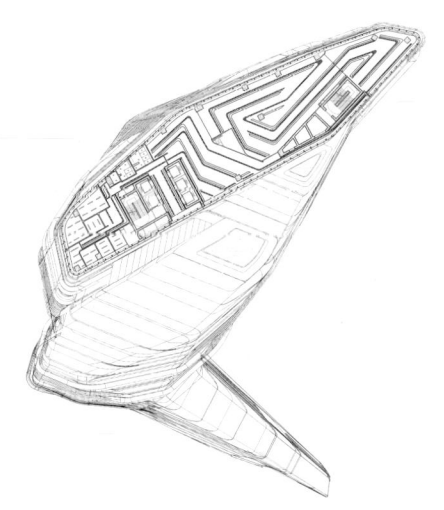

13th floor reflected ceiling　14階天井伏

First floor　2階

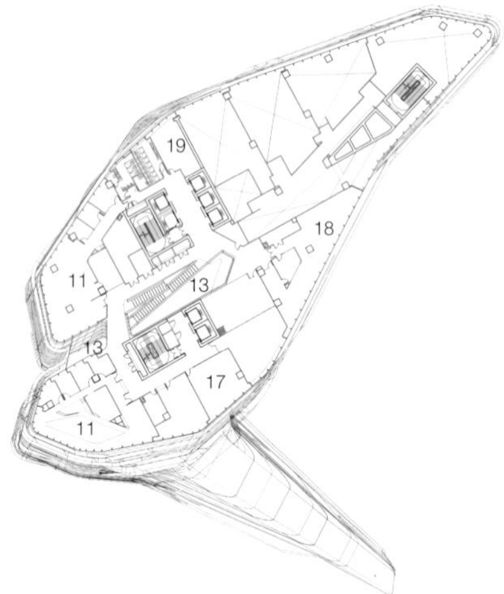

Eighth floor　9階

Ground floor　1階平面　S=1:1500

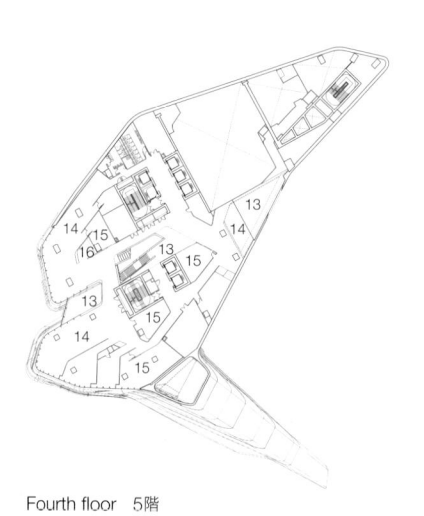

Fourth floor　5階

0m　5　15　30

1　GROUND LEVEL ENTRANCE LOBBY
2　WOOD WORKSHOP
3　METAL WORKSHOP
4　PHOTO STUDIO
5　TV PRODUCTION
6　TRANSPORTATION DESIGN LAB
7　UNDERPASS TO PHASE 8 DEVELOPMENT
8　FIRST LEVEL ENTRANCE LOBBY
9　MULTI-MEDIA WORKSHOP
10　MODEL WORKSHOP
11　OFFICE
12　OUTDOOR LANDSCAPE
13　ATRIUM
14　PROJECT SPACE
15　PROJECT ROOM
16　CAFE
17　DESIGN STUDIO
18　RESEARCH LAB
19　MEETING ROOM

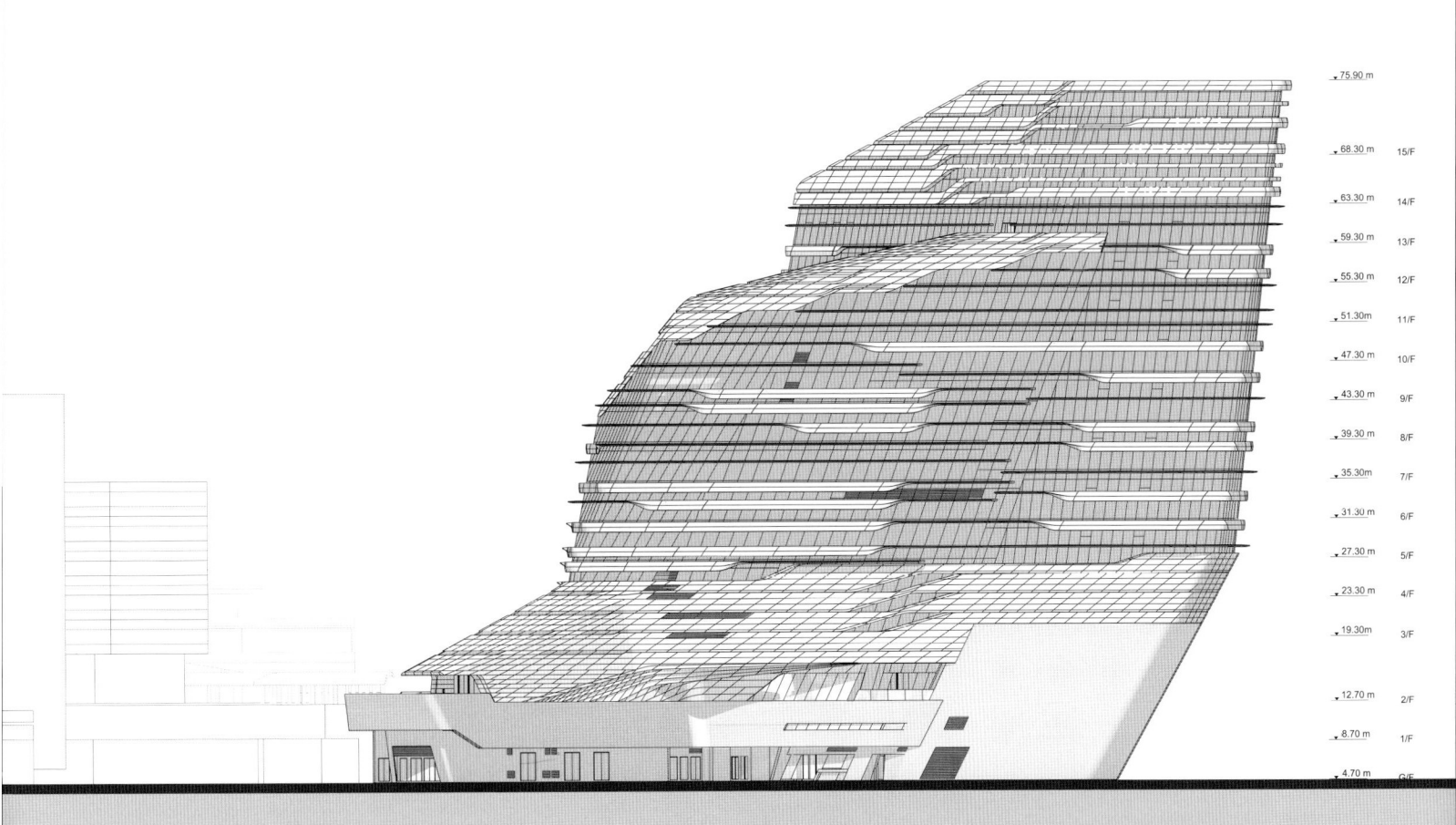

East elevation 東立面 S=1:700

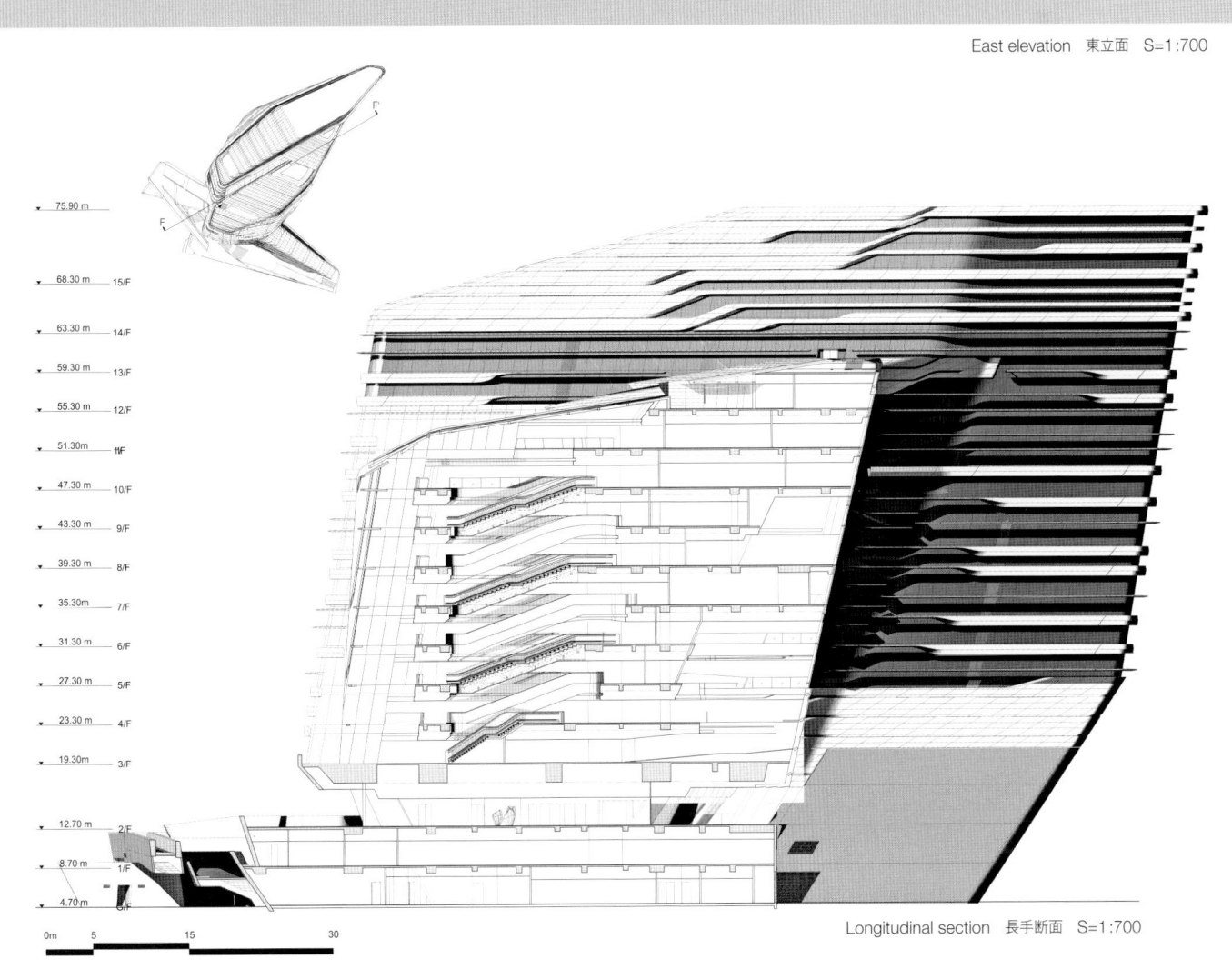

Longitudinal section 長手断面 S=1:700

Jockey Club Innovation Tower, Hong Kong Polytechnic University

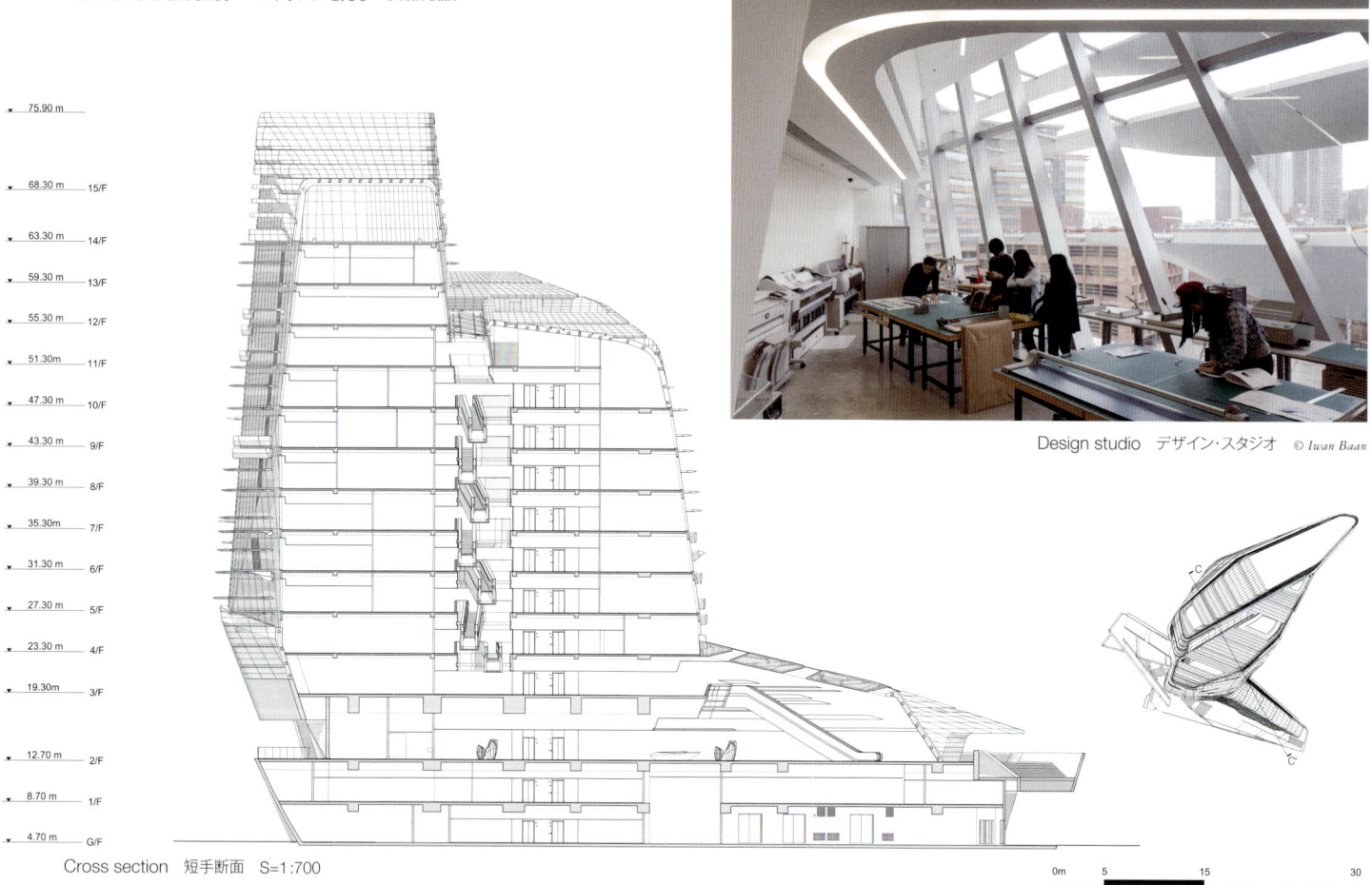

View toward entrance　エントランスを見る　© Iwan Baan

Design studio　デザイン・スタジオ　© Iwan Baan

75.90 m	
68.30 m	15/F
63.30 m	14/F
59.30 m	13/F
55.30 m	12/F
51.30 m	11/F
47.30 m	10/F
43.30 m	9/F
39.30 m	8/F
35.30 m	7/F
31.30 m	6/F
27.30 m	5/F
23.30 m	4/F
19.30 m	3/F
12.70 m	2/F
8.70 m	1/F
4.70 m	G/F

Cross section　短手断面　S=1:700

ジョッキークラブ・イノヴェーションタワーの流体のような特徴は，タワーとポディウム（基壇）の古典的なタイポロジーをシームレスな建物へと溶解する，ランドスケープ，床面，ルーバーの独特な構成から生まれている。内部と外部につくられたコートヤードは，広いエキジビション・フォーラムや野外のレクリエーション施設を補足する小規模な新しい公共空間をつくりだし，都市空間の多様化を促す。

都市化

香港工科大学（HK PolyU）はこれまでの50年間で増築と成長による都市化に努めてきた。多彩な学部，コミュニティ，そして施設の豊かなパッチワークは，視覚的に統合されているが，別々の建物によるコミュニティが繋ぎ合わされたものだ。ジョッキークラブ・イノヴェーションタワーは，大学キャンパスの北側のとても狭く変形した敷地に位置している。タワーは，大学の認識のされ方や利用のされ方を変えるような，親しみやすい都市空間をつくる。建物は，その未来の可能性へのヴィジョンを投影すると同時に，変化の過程をその建築内に包摂することでHK PolyUの歴史を反映させる。

建築

新しいイノヴェーションタワーは，大学の多様なプログラムを寄せ集めることによって創造的で総合的な環境を再検証し，取り組む。プログラムはそれぞれに固有のアイデンティティ間の，多様な関係を検証する厳格なプロセスを経て，それらに「付随するフレキシビリティ」に従って配置される。

優先事項は，建物のエントランスや既存コンプレックスの組織役としても働く新しい空間へ，大学職員，学生，一般の人を引き寄せ，喜んで迎え入れることにある。

タワーの新しいペデストリアン・レベルは開かれた公共のホワイエを構成し，建物内に深く流れ込む。Suen Chi Sun 記念広場から統合された通路が訪問者をメイン・エントランスに誘導し，ここから，人を迎え入れるパブリックな空間が，進入路をポディウムと地上レベルの間の二つのレベルを架け渡す広く開放的な展示の連続と「ショーケース」を経由して，付属的な施設（ショップ，カフェテリア，ミュージアム）へのアクセスとなる。

入口のホワイエから，職員や学生，訪問者は開放的なガラス張りのスタジオや作業場の四層を通って上へと向かう。新デザイン学部内にある多数のスタジオや作業場は，視覚に訴える多様なショーケースとして自らを提供する。

建物を貫くルートは，ショーケースやイベント空間の並ぶ，透き通る滝のような流れを構成し，学生や訪問者が学習風景や展示に注目し，興味を持つように促してくれる。これらのルートは，様々な使い手が相互交流できる新たな機会を数多くつくりだす。ヴォイドは自然光や新鮮な空気，連続感をもたらす。こうして，クラスター状に集められた教室と中央施設で構成されたタワーのプログラムは，それぞれの空間的なヴォリュームとデザインの修練との間に，対話を生みだすのである。

Atrium (above)　アトリウム（上）
Entrance lobby (below)　エントランス・ロビー（下）
© Doublespace

Jockey Club Innovation Tower, Hong Kong Polytechnic University

2009-13
THE SERPENTINE SACKLER GALLERY
サーペンタイン・サックラー・ギャラリー

West Carriage Drive, Kensington Gardens, London, U.K.

View from West Carriage Drive　ウエスト・キャリエッジ・ドライブより見る

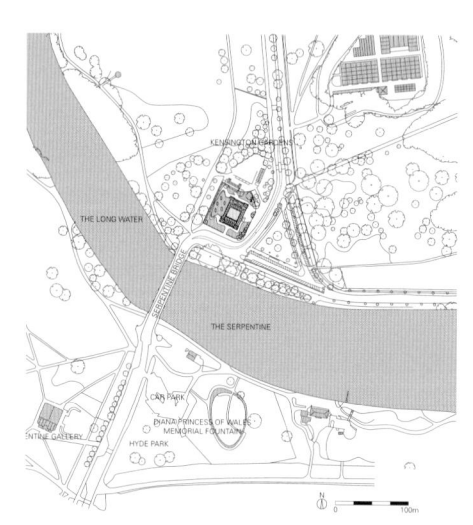

Site plan　配置　S=1:10000

The Serpentine Sackler Gallery consists of two distinct parts, namely the conversion of a classical 19th century brick structure—The Magazine—and a 21st century tensile structure. The Serpentine Sackler Gallery is thus—after MAXXI in Rome—the second art space where Zaha Hadid Architects have created a synthesis of old and new. The Magazine was designed as a Gunpowder Store in 1805. It comprises two raw brick barrel vaulted spaces (where the gunpowder was stored) and a lower square-shaped surrounding structure with a frontal colonnade. The building continued to be in military use until 1963. Since then Royal Parks used the building for storage. The Magazine thus remained underutilised until now. Over time, much amendment and alteration has occurred inside the historic building and its surroundings.

Instrumental to the transformation into a public art gallery was the decision to reinstate the historic arrangement of the Magazine building as a free standing pavilion within an enclosure, whereby the former courtyards would be covered and become internal exhibition spaces. In order to reveal the original central spaces, all nonhistoric partition walls within the former gunpowder stores were removed. The flat gauged arches over the entrances were reinstated whilst the historic timber gantry crane was maintained. Necessary services and lighting were discreetly integrated as to not interfere with "as found" quality of the

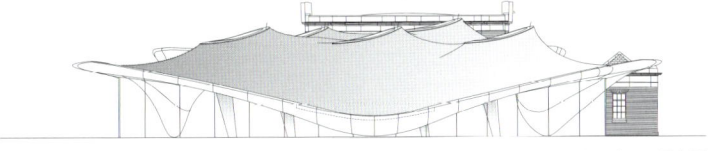

West elevation　西立面

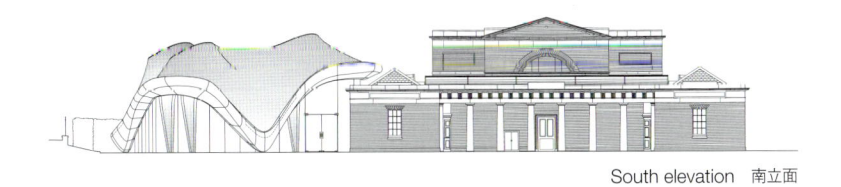

South elevation　南立面

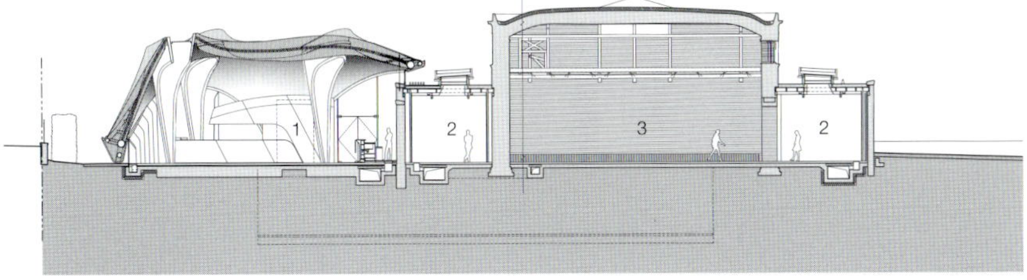

Section　断面　S=1:500

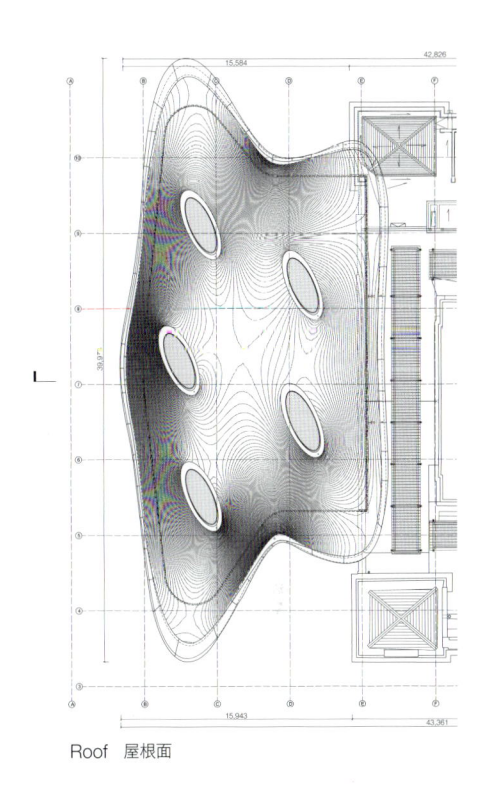

1　SOCIAL SPACE & RESTAURANT
2　GALLERY
3　POWDER ROOM
4　CONCEPT STORE
5　LIFT
6　WC
7　BABY CHANGING ROOM

Roof　屋根面

Ground floor　1階平面
S=1:500

spaces. These vaults are now part of the sequence of gallery spaces.

The surrounding structure has been clarified and rationalized to become a continuous, open sequence of exhibition spaces looping around the two central powder rooms, thus following the simplicity and clarity of Leo von Klenze's Glyptothek as an early model for a purpose built gallery.

The extension contains a generous, open social space that we expect to enliven the Serpentine Sackler Gallery as a new cultural and culinary destination. The extension has been designed to complement the calm and solid classical building with a light, transparent, dynamic and distinctly contemporary space of the 21st century. The synthesis of old and new is thus a synthesis of contrasts. The new extension feels ephemeral, like a temporary structure, although it is a fully functional permanent building. It is our first permanent tensile structure and realization of our current research into curvelinear structural surfaces.

Our aim is to create an intense aesthetic experience, an atmosphere that seems to oscillate between being an extension of the delightful beauty of the surrounding nature and of being an alluring invitation into the enigma of contemporary art.

The Serpentine Sackler Gallery

Night view toward restaurant　夜景：レストランを見る

サーペンタイン・サックラー・ギャラリーは二つの大きく異なる建物から構成され，一つはマガジンという古い19世紀のレンガ積みの建物のコンバージョンと，もう一つは21世紀的な引張構造を用いた建物である。サックラー・ギャラリーはザハ・ハディドとパトリック・シューマッハの二人による，ローマのMAXXIに続く2作目の，新旧が融合したアート・スペースである。マガジンは火薬店として1805年につくられ，未焼成レンガのヴォールト天井の空間が2部屋（火薬保管庫として使われていた）あり，正面のコロネードも含めた背の低い構造部分がそこを四角く囲んでいる。マガジンの建物は1963年まで軍事目的に使われ，その後は王立公園が倉庫として使っていたため今日まで活用されずにいた。この歴史的な建物の内部やその周囲は，長年にわたり数多くの改修や変更が繰り返されている。

公共的なアートギャラリーへの生まれ変わりを助けたのは，マガジンの建物の歴史的な流れを，独立したパヴィリオンとして再度復活させようという決断であり，これによってかつての中庭上部が覆われ，屋内展示スペースが新しく設けられた。中央のオリジナルの空間を見せるために，火薬庫内にある近年になってつくられた壁は全て取り払われた。エントランス上の水平アーチは復元され，また古い木のガントリー・クレーンはそのまま保存されている。元の空間の質を維持するために必要な機能や照明は，慎重に建物と調和され，ヴォールトの天井はギャラリー・スペースから続く連続したシークエンスの一部となっている。

建物外周の構造部分は，中央の二つの火薬庫を囲むように設けられた展示スペースの連続性と開放的なつながりを確保するためにきれいにされすっきりとした空間につくりかえられている。これはレオ・フォン・クレンツェによるギャラリー建築の初期のモデルである「グリュプトテーク」のシンプルさと明快さにならっている。

増築部分には開放的でゆったりとした社交スペースが設けられ，このサックラー・ギャラリーが新たに食事会や文化的な行事の場所として活性化することを期待している。増築部分が持つ透過性や明るさ，ダイナミックさといった21世紀的な全く異質の現代的空間が，静謐で堅いクラシカルな建物を補完している。新しいものと古いもの融合とはすなわち対照的なもの同士の融合である。増築部分はまるで短期的な仮設構造物のように感じられるが，実際は十分な機能を持った恒久的な建築物である。これは我々にとって初めての常設の引張構造物であり，また現在研究を進めているなめらかな曲面の構造体を実際の形にしたものでもある。

我々の狙いは，力強く美しい空間体験をつくることであり，それは時に周囲の自然の楽しげな美しさが拡張されたような雰囲気となり，また時に現代アートの謎へと引きこむような魅力的な雰囲気にもなりえる。

Restaurant　レストラン

The Serpentine Sackler Gallery

2010-
BEIJING CBD CORE AREA
北京中央商業地区コア・エリア

Beijing, China

Aerial view 上空より見る

Beijing CBD Core Area

179

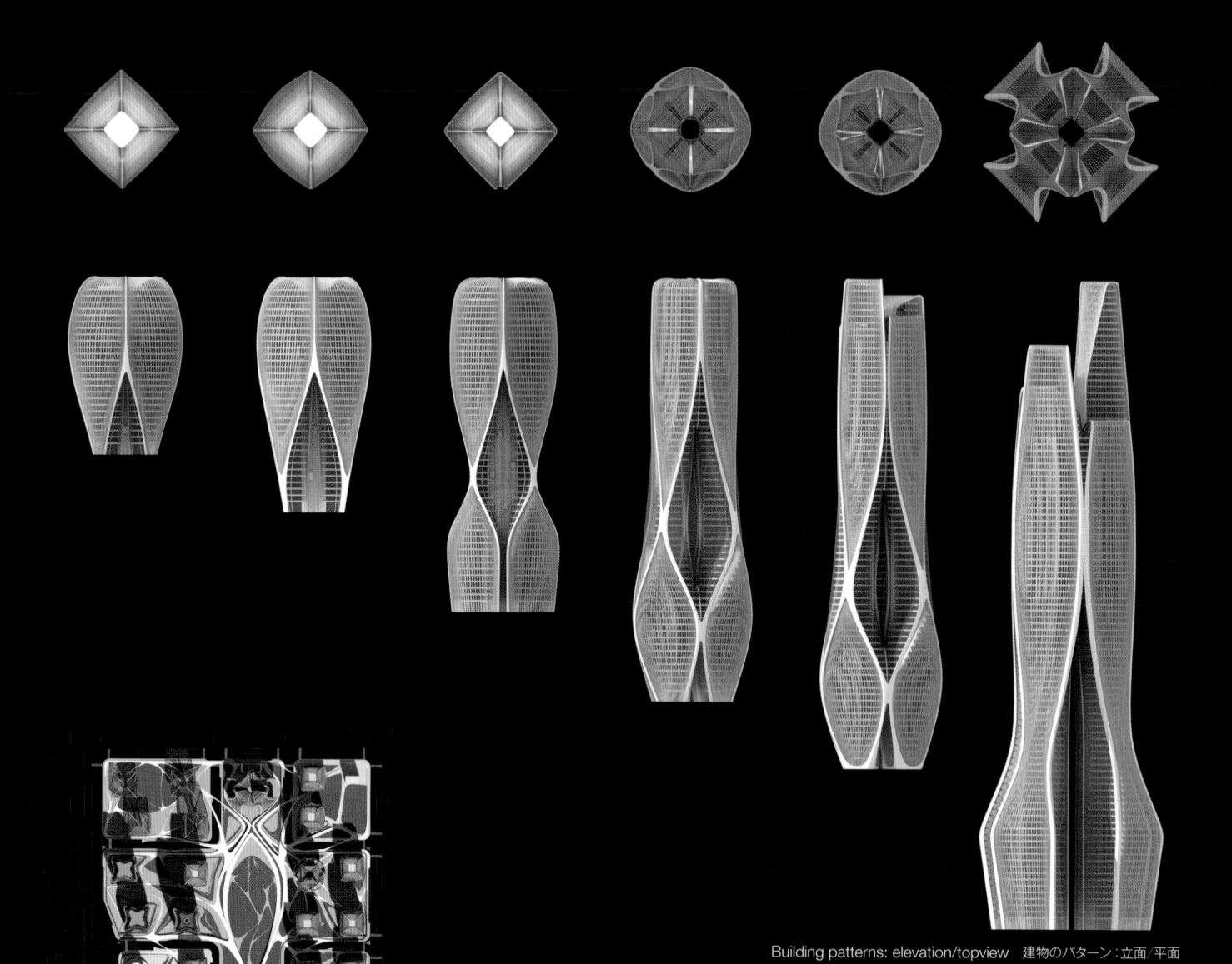

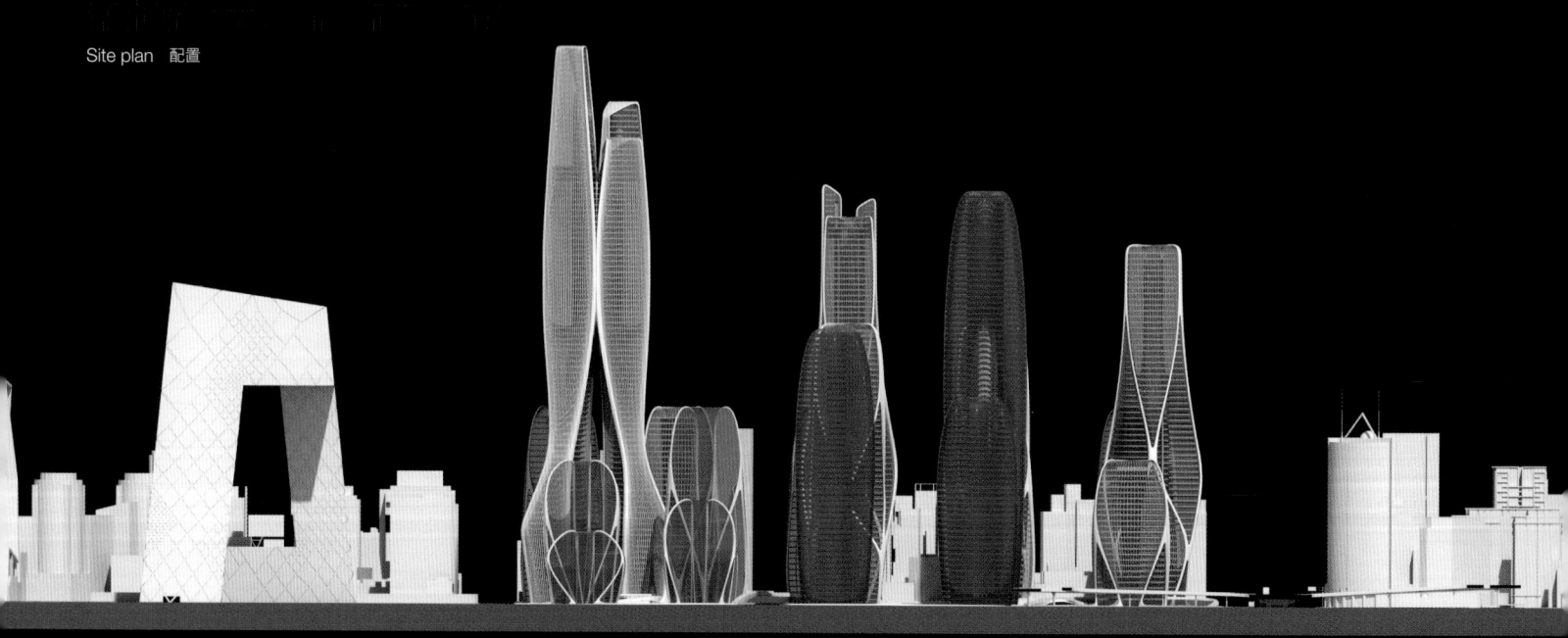

Building patterns: elevation/topview　建物のパターン：立面/平面

Site plan　配置

Site section　敷地断面

180　　　　　　　　　　1980　　　　　　1990　　　　　　2000　　　　　　2010　　　　　　2020

The Beijing CBD Core Area aspires to become one the world's premier spots for advanced, high value business. A stimulating urban environment is a critical factor in fostering a vibrant business community that provides synergies to all participants. The provision of a critical mass and density of office accommodation is merely the necessary starting point for the development of an effective urban business environment. The planned gross area fulfils this necessary precondition. The planned disposition of the tower volumes creates a variegated urban massing and lively silhouette. The axis described by the main tower together with the linear park gives a clear order and orientation to the whole urban field. However, our design goes further in its effort to establish an organic order and elegance that is akin to the beauty found in nature.

The design breaks with the typical tower and podium typology by redefining the ground as a continuous landscape that seamlessly weaves between one tower and the next. This new ground receives the existing surrounding streets and diverts its flows to the different towers and the central park. The proposed concept design doesn't work like a traditional array of adjacent buildings but rather as a cohesive network of towers that is fully integrated at ground level and coherently developed as it grows in height.

Our proposed Masterplan Concept Design for the CBD Core Area reaches far beyond the CBD, aiming at the creation of a new business and civic node for the city of Beijing that embodies values of functionality, elegance and innovation.

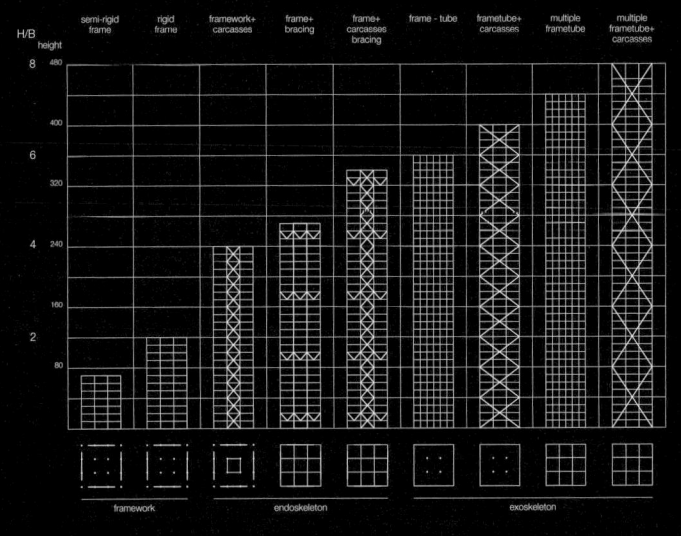

Interrelations between frame and height　フレームと高さの相関関係

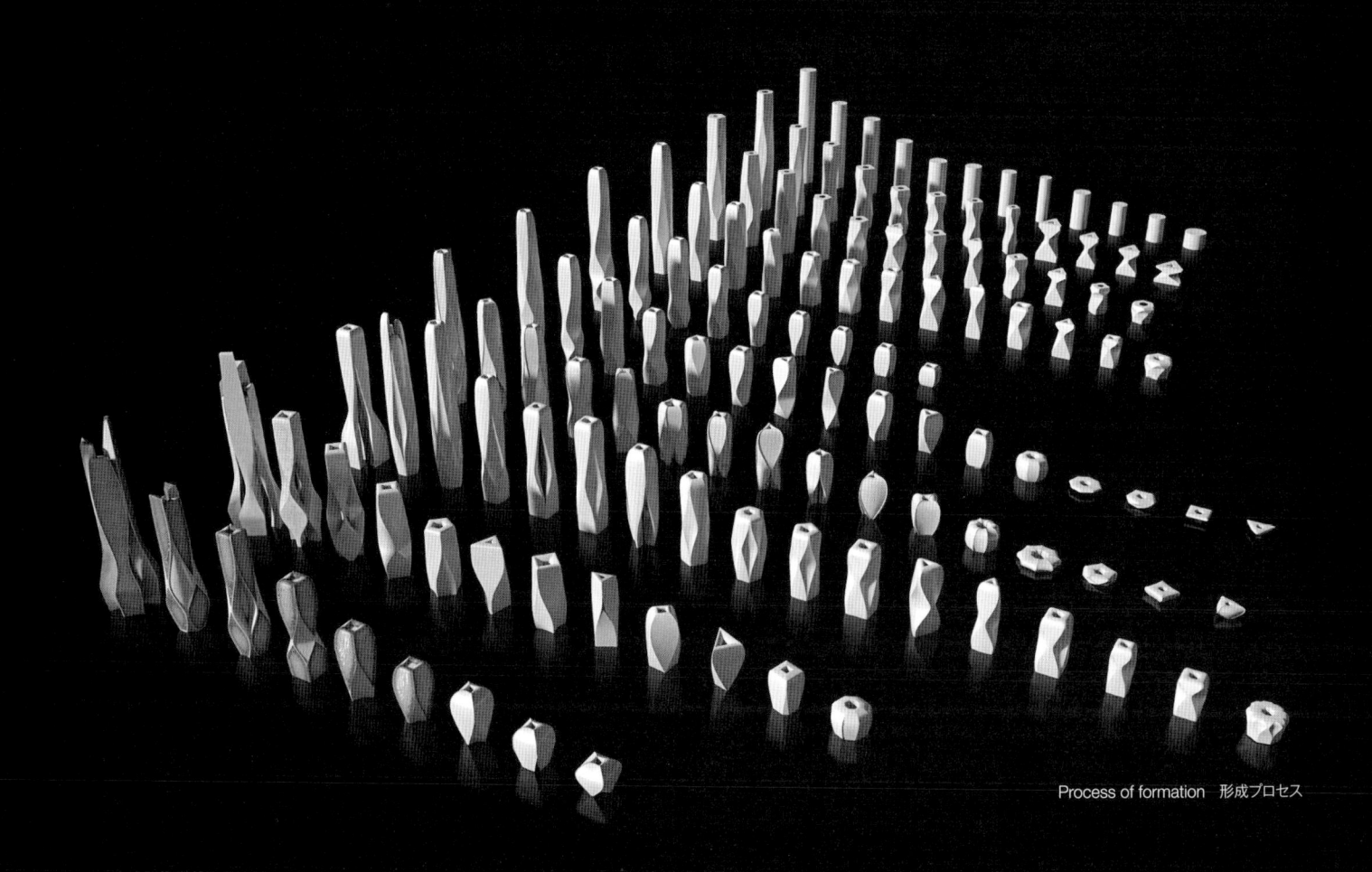

Process of formation　形成プロセス

Beijing CBD Core Area

Pedestrian views　歩行者の眺め

北京中央商業地区コア・エリアは，世界最高レベルの先進的で高価値の事業の場となることを目標とする。刺激的な都市環境は，関係する者すべてにシナジーを与える活発なビジネス・コミュニティを宿すために不可欠な要素である。絶対的な量と密度のオフィス設備を供給することは，効率的な都市商業地区の発展のスタート地点にすぎない。今回計画された敷地は，この必要条件を満たしている。計画されたタワーのヴォリューム配置は，多様な都市的集合を生み，活発なシルエットを映し出す。そして，メインタワーと直線状の公園が定義づける軸は，敷地全体に明瞭な秩序と方向性を与える。しかし，私たちのデザインはそこからさらに一歩踏み込み，自然界に見られる美しさに類する有機的な秩序とエレガンスを求めている。

このデザインは，典型的なタワーやポディウム（基壇）のタイポロジーとはかけ離れており，地面はタワーの間を縫う連続的なランドスケープとして再定義される。新たな地面は，周辺街路の交通のフローを受け入れ，他のタワーや中央の公園へと流通させる。提案されたコンセプト・デザインは，規則正しく整列された伝統的な建物のように機能することはなく，地面レベルで完全に統合され，高さ方向にも互いに連動しながらそびえ立つタワーのネットワークとして機能する。

私たちの提案するマスタープラン・コンセプトデザインは，中央商業地区コア・エリアの遥か彼方まで届き，北京という都市にとって，機能性やエレガンス，イノベーションを内包した，新たなビジネスと公共機能の中心地を創造することを目指している。

Downward view from Atrium 260 (above) アトリウム260から見下ろす（上）
Upward views of Atrium 120 (below left) / 300 (below right) アトリウム120（左下）/アトリウム300（右下）の見上げ

2012-19
NEW NATIONAL STADIUM OF JAPAN
新国立競技場

Tokyo, Japan

Site plan　配置　S=1:15000

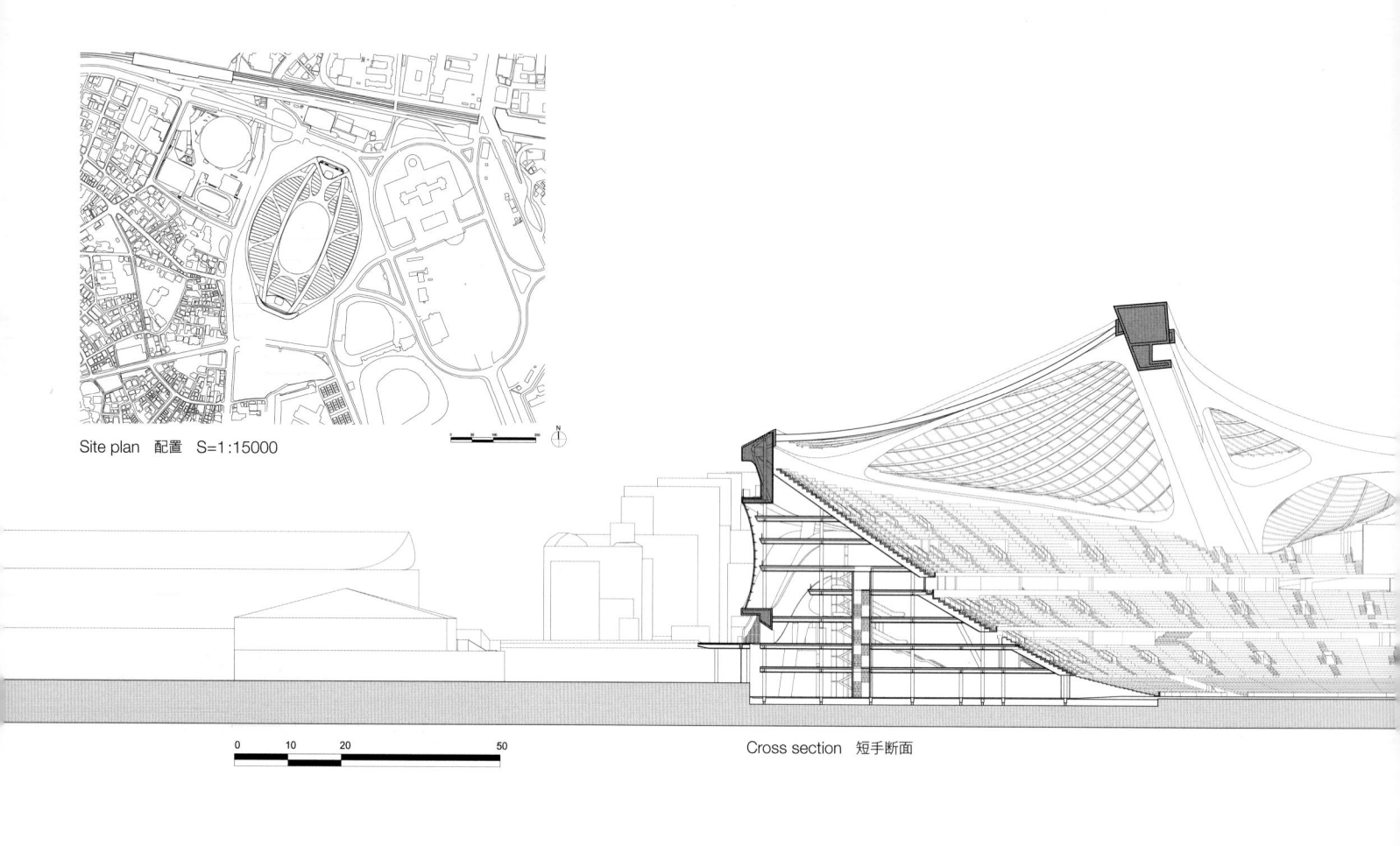

Cross section　短手断面

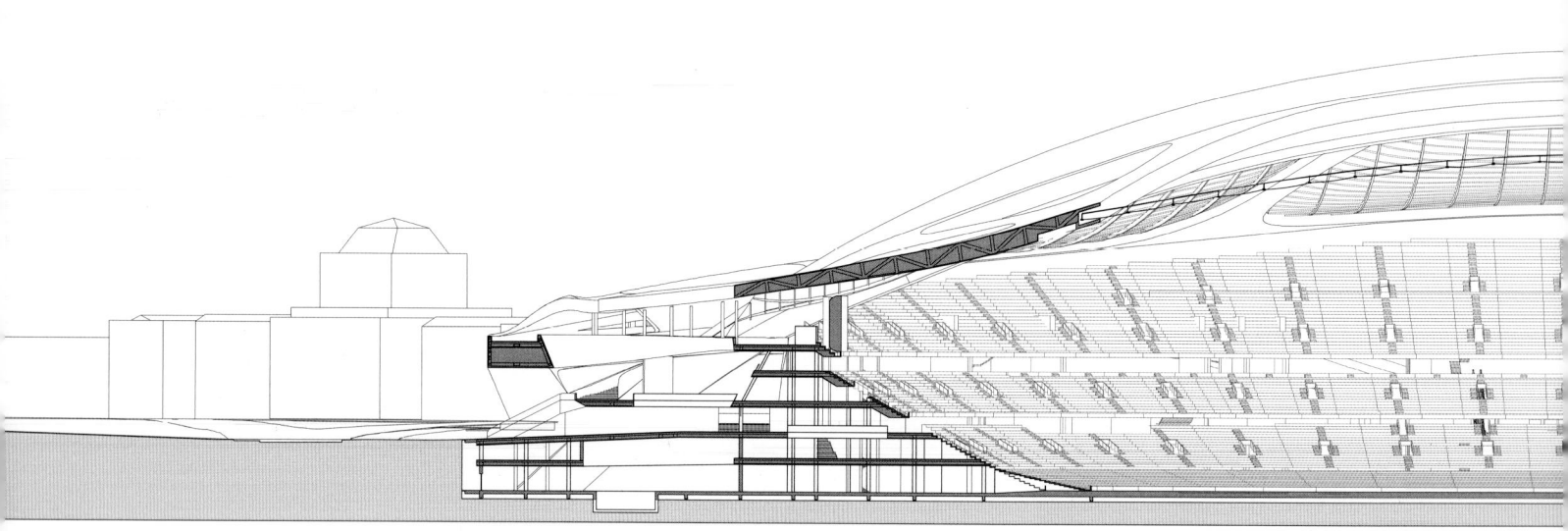

Longitudinal section　長手断面　S=1:1200

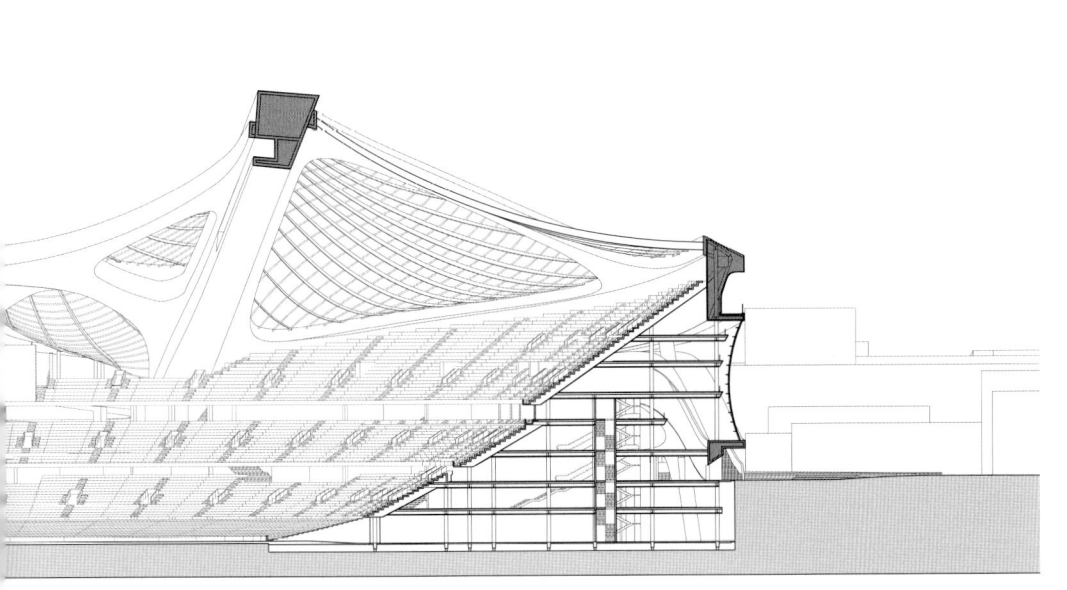

The New National Stadium of Japan is more than a large sports facility designed to the highest design specifications and functional requirements. It is a piece of the city's fabric, and urban connector which enhances and modulates people moving through the site from different directions and points of access. The elevated ground connections govern the flow of people through the site, effectively carving the geometric forms of the building.

The building volume sits gently within the urban landscape and is articulated as an assembly of stadium bowl, structural skeleton, cladding membranes and the museum, together forming an intricate structural composition that is both light and cohesive. The perimeter of the bowl structure becomes a new inhabited bridge, a continuous exhibition space that creates a new type of journey for visitors flowing along the project's north-south axis.

The stadium roof defines a silhouette that integrates gently within the cityscape around it. It is an intricate assembly of efficient long-

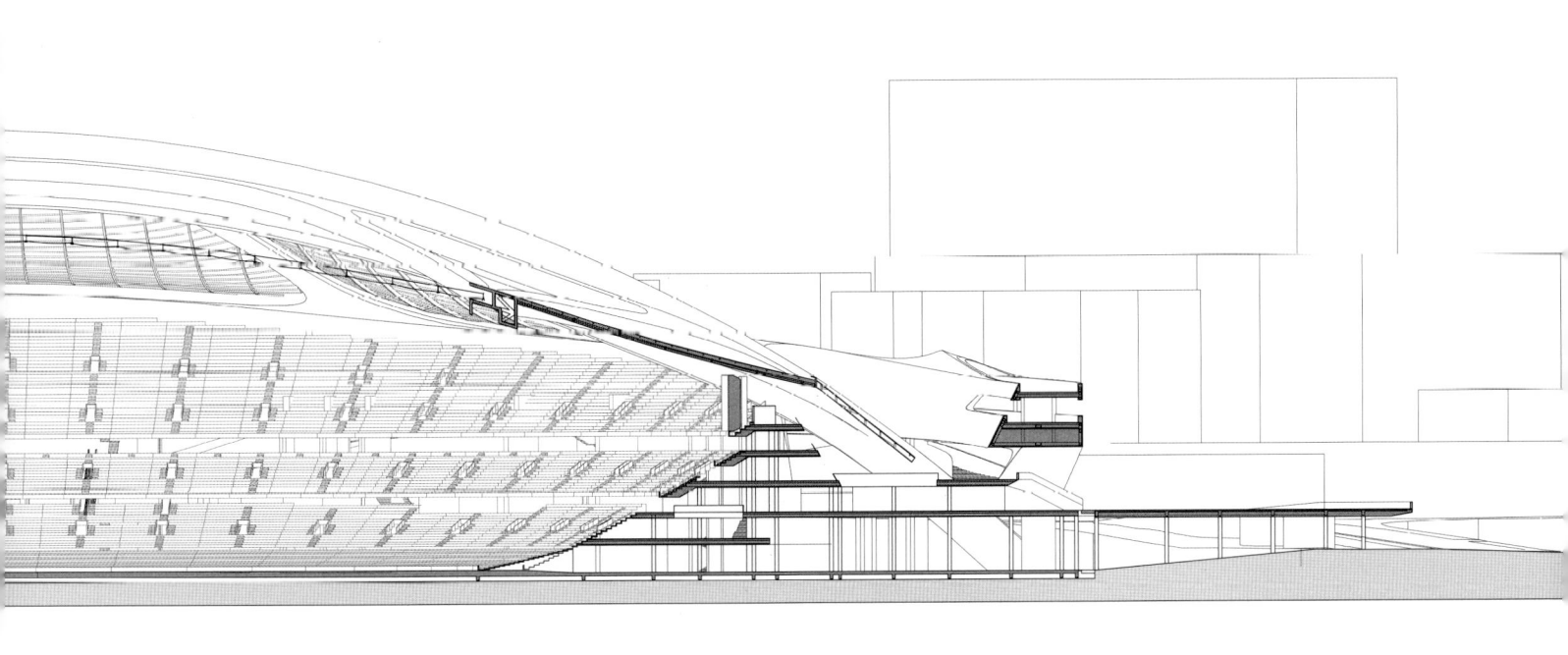

New National Stadium of Japan

spanning structural ribs which are spanned by a system of lightweight, translucent membranes. This unique structure is a lightweight solution, where the stadium elevation graciously touches the ground, defining a clear approach towards the stadium entrances. The interior of the stadium is also given a clearly identifiable identity through the strong roof structure that contrasts with the lightness of the translucent membrane tensile structures.

The New National Stadium will become the centrepiece for the 2019 Rugby World Cup and the 2020 Olympics. The New National Stadium holds a unique place in the history of stadium. With a capacity of 80,000 seats, moving roof and retractable seating, it will be the first stadium in the world custom designed to host two back to back signature world sports events.

The seating bowl has been optimized to suit both Rugby World Cup and Olympic events, with a permanent athletics track to be inserted within the stadium. The design of the bowl will bring spectators as close as possible to the athletics track and jumps, and will not compromise the viewing experience of spectators during football or rugby events.

The seating bowl is adaptable, and has been designed to allow for the scale of the stadium to remain compact. Following the Olympics it is proposed that flexible areas of seating are adapted to enhance the commercial revenue that can be generated by the facility in legacy mode.

The form of the stadium has been driven in response to the functional planning requirements of the stadium and responded closely to the volumetric constraints imposed on this building by the local planning authority requirements. The site is narrow, and bounded by trunk roads which constrain the natural proportions of an 80,000 seat stadium footprint. The roof design and vertical circulation strategy respond to this through the creation of cascade stairs that move people from the centre of the stadium (best viewing locations) to the "arrival plaza" locations to the north and south of the stadium.

Aerial view　上空より見る

New National Stadium of Japan

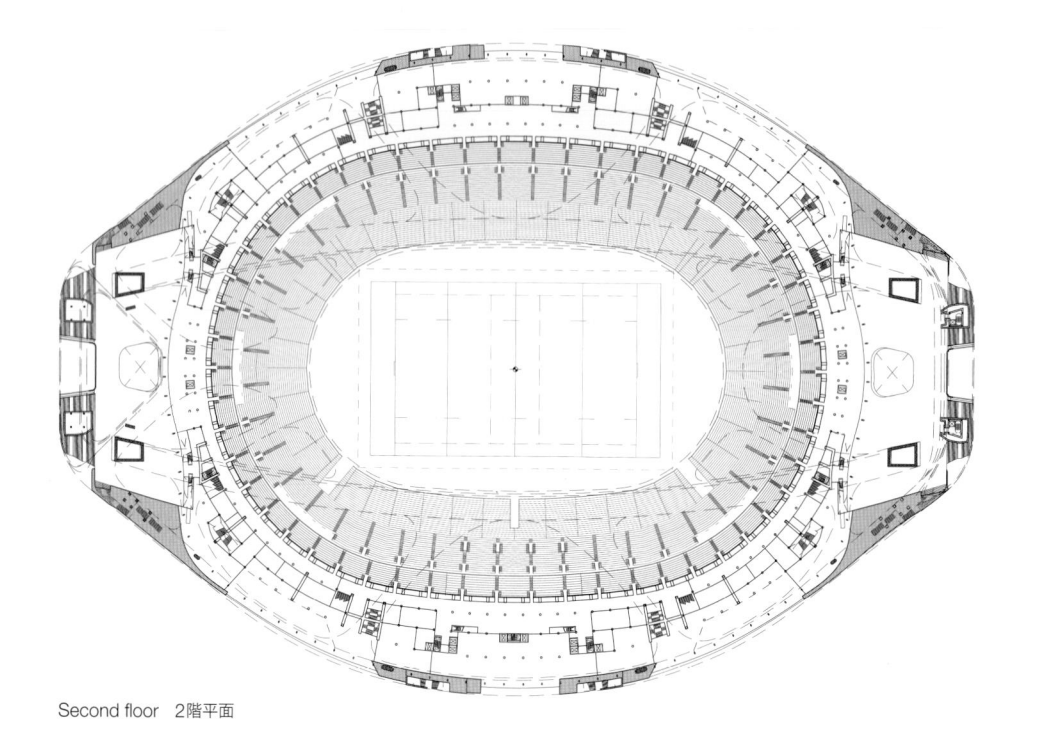

Second floor　2階平面

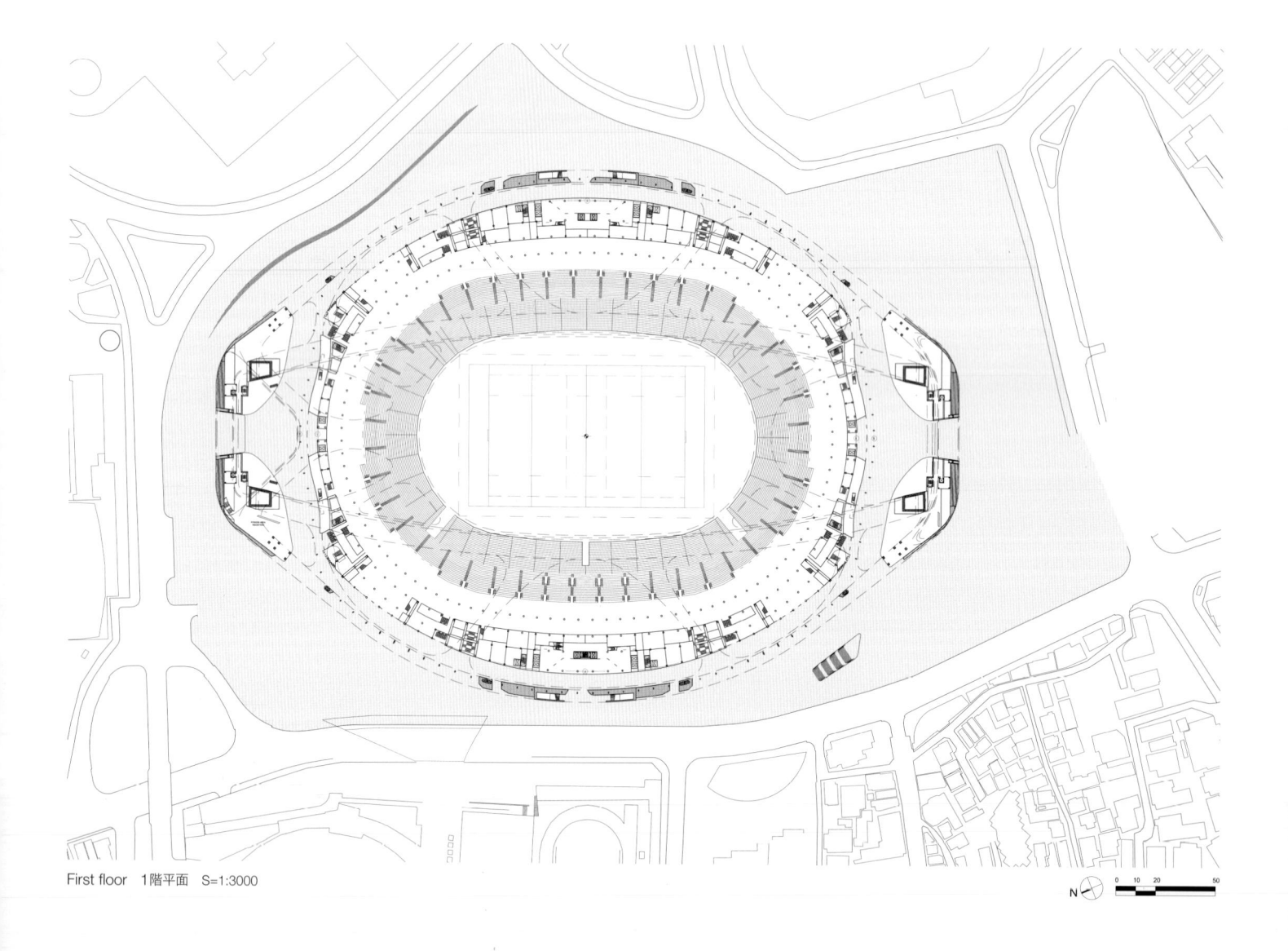

First floor　1階平面　S=1:3000

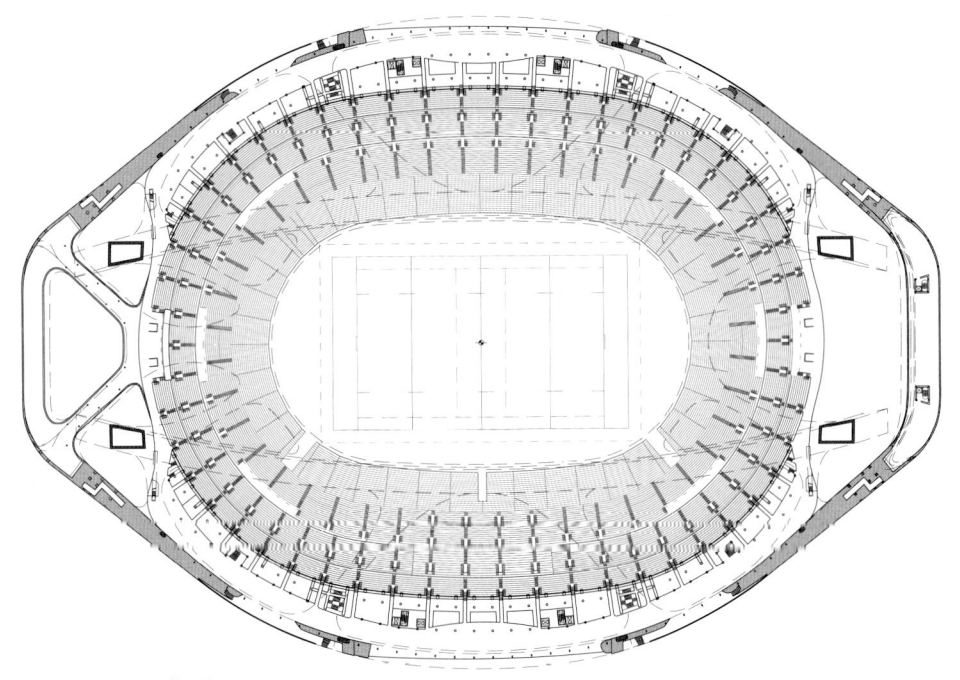

Fourth floor　4階平面

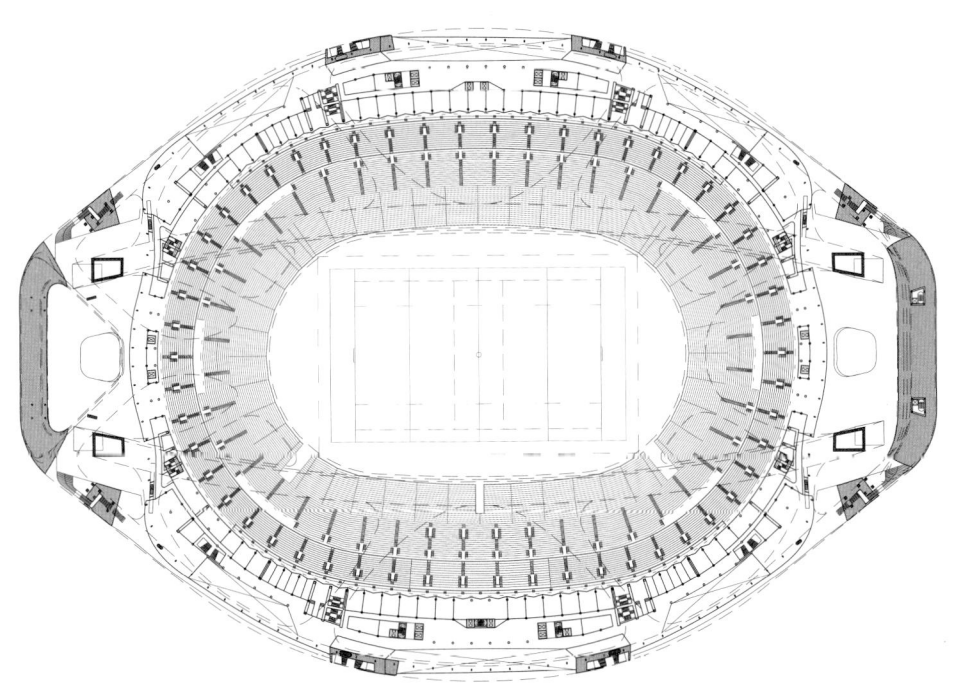

Third floor　3階平面

日本の新国立競技場は、最高の仕様や機能与件に応えるようデザインされた大規模スポーツ施設であるが、それだけの存在ではない。都市構造を織りなすピースの一片であり、様々な方向、アクセスポイントから敷地を貫いていく人々の動きを、調整、加速していくアーバン・コネクターなのだ。建物の形は、地形のように効果的に切り出され、持ち上げられた地面のつながりが、人の動きを決定づける。

建築ヴォリュームは、都市景観を尊重して配置され、スタジアムのお椀状のスタンドと構造的骨格、被覆する膜、そしてミュージアムの集合体は、分節されながらも、複雑な構成を、軽やかで、かつまとまりのあるものとして形づくっている。スタンドの外周部は、人々のために新たにこの敷地に掛けられたブリッジであり、プロジェクトの南北軸に沿って、人々にこれまでにない体験をもたらす、ひとつながりの展示スペースとなっている。

スタジアムの屋根は、周囲の街の風景にゆるやかに合うようなシルエットをつくり出す。それは大スパンを半透過の軽量な膜で掛け渡すための構造リブを、複雑でありながら効率良く組み立てた結果である。今回のプロジェクト特有の軽やかな構造的解決によって、スタジアムのエレベーションは地面とゆるやかに接し、エントランスへの明快なアプローチを生み出している。インテリアにおいても、軽く半透明な膜の張力構造と対比的な力強い屋根架構によって、はっきりとこの建物とわかるイメージが与えられる。

新国立競技場は、2019年のラグビー・ワールドカップと2020年の東京オリンピックのメイン会場となる予定だ。この競技場は、スタジアムの歴史の中でも特別な位置を占める。8万人の収容人数に、可動開閉屋根、収納可能な客席を備え、連続して行われる二つの世界レベルの大きなスポーツ・イベントに対応すべく設計された、世界初のスタジアムになるはずだ。

客席スタンドは、ラグビー・ワールドカップとオリンピックの両方に最適化され、常設の陸上トラックを取り囲んでいる。スタンドのデザインによって、観客は競技するトラックやフィールドに可能な限り近づけるようになっているが、サッカーやラグビーの観戦経験においても妥協はしていない。

スタンドは変形可能だが、スタジアムのスケールをコンパクトなままにしておけるようになっている。オリンピック開催後には、客席の可変性を活かして従来型の使い方にも対応することで、収益性を高めようとしている。

スタジアムの形態は、計画された機能的な与件に対応するように生み出されており、自治体が求める容積率の制約に厳密に応えている。敷地は狭く、幹線道路に囲まれているので、8万人規模のスタジアムに本来適したフットプリントの大きさを収めるのが難しい。この問題には、屋根のデザインと垂直動線の計画によって対応する。具体的には、カスケード状の階段をつくり、人々がスタジアムのただ中（観戦/鑑賞にベストな場所）から、スタジアムの北側と南側に設けられた「到着プラザ」にスムーズに移動できるようになっている。

New National Stadium of Japan

Stadium　スタジアム

New National Stadium of Japan

Aerial view (above) 上空より見る(上)
View from Meijijingu gaien (below) 明治神宮外苑より見る(下)

192

PRODUCT

2005/2011, 2010
CREVASSE VASE & NICHE
クレヴァス・ベース&ニッチ

Alessi

CREVASSE VASE

The two vases are cut from a single block, and scored along two diagonal lines, creating a warped, inverted surface. They can be assembled together in alternative configurations, creating solid forms, or they can stand alone as distinct objects. The playful nature of the set means that the configurations can be altered to make a variety of different shapes, and the user can build a family of objects, like an endlessly mutating jigsaw puzzle.

NICHE

The fragmentary geometry and the fluid forms of Zaha Hadid's designs are again to be seen in this modular centerpiece made up of five components, which can be assembled or used separately in different ways. Designed for Alessi, this product in black melamine with opaque finish is a sculptural volume whose sinuous form is comparable to that of a swallow's tail.

クレヴァス・ベース

二つの花瓶が2本の斜線に沿って一つの塊から切り取られ、捩じれた逆転曲面が生み出される。組み合わせてソリッドな形態にしたり、単体で自立させることもできる。遊び心に満ちたこのセットは、組み合わせを変えて様々な形態にすることができ、常に変化し続けるジグソーパズルのように、一群のオブジェをつくることができる。

ニッチ

ザハ・ハディドのデザインに見られる断片化したジオメトリと流動的な形態が、この五つの構成部分からなるモジュール式のセンターピースにも現れている。組み合わせて一つにすることもできるし、様々なかたちで個別に使うこともできる。アレッシィのためにデザインされたこのプロダクトは、ブラック・メラミンのオパーク仕上げとなっており、曲がりくねった形態がツバメの尾にも似た彫塑的なヴォリュームである。

Architects: Zaha Hadid Architects—
Zaha Hadid, Patrik Schumacher, design;
Woody Yao, Thomas Vietzke, design team
Client: Alessi, Italy
Program: vase
Dimensions: L60 x D80 x H420 mm
Materials: 18/10 mirror polished, stainless steel
Finish: silver, gun metal, bronze metal, blue, black

Architects: Zaha Hadid Architects—
Zaha Hadid, Patrik Schumacher, design;
Woody Yao, Melodie Leung, design team
Client: Alessi
Program: centrepiece
Dimensions: L600 x D300 x H70 mm
Materials: melamine with opaque finish

above: © Victoria Nightingale
below: © Alessi

Crevasse Vase & Niche

195

2007
WMF CUTLERY
WMFカトラリー

WMF

This unique cutlery set derives from the creative tension between the formal architectural research of the studio and its explorations into industrial design. Every piece has a unique expression, yet the set is conceived as a harmonious single entity—this is achieved by evoking a sense of continuity in the sculpted surfaces and fine detailing.

The use of accelerated curves, a technique more frequently employed in car design, gives the set a dynamic sense of motion—an effect complemented by the sleek, mirrored finish of the highly polished stainless steel. Giving careful consideration to the intimacy of the relationship between cutlery and user, the thickness of the material has been extruded and refined to ensure that every piece is ergonomically well balanced and pleasurable to use.

このユニークなカトラリー・セットは，建築形態の追求とインダストリアル・デザインの探求の創造的緊張から生まれた。各アイテムは特有の表現をしているが，連続性を持つ曲面と繊細なディテールにより，セットで一つの調和した全体を構成する。

カー・デザインで頻繁に用いられる技法である加速曲線を使うことによって，躍動感が生み出され，高度に研磨されたステンレス・スティールの光沢のある鏡面仕上げによってそれは一層引き立てられる。カトラリーとユーザーとの密接な関係について慎重に考慮した結果，厚みが増し，それぞれのアイテムが人間工学的にバランスがよく，使う楽しみを得られるよう洗練されたものになった。

Architects: Zaha Hadid Architects—
Zaha Hadid, Patrik Schumacher, design;
Jens Borstelmann, project designer
Client: WMF-AG
Program: cutlery
Materials: stainless steel, mirror-polished
Dimensions: small fork 1(65 x 21 mm), fork (223 x 35 mm), knife (165 x 21 mm), spoon (227 x 42 mm), small spoon (140 x 31 mm)

© David Grandorge

WMF Cutlery

2008
MELISSA SHOES
メリッサ・シューズ

Melissa

The collaboration between Zaha Hadid and Brazilian shoe brand, Melissa was an opportunity to work directly with the fashion industry to explore the possibilities of a new media. To express the studio's characteristic sense of fluidity, the natural starting point was the organic contours of the body—this inspired the idea of the shoe in flux, coming to life when worn rather than conceived as a static object in a window display. The shoes emerge from the ground and climb asymmetrically up the foot and leg in a sweeping, elegant motion. They adhere like a second skin, with a lightness of touch that blurs the boundary between body and object.

To develop the product and successfully translate the design to the production line, the studio used advanced digital modelling techniques. The ergonomic qualities of the shoes were refined through rapid prototyping and the fluidity of the design lent itself well to Melissa's plastic injection mould technology. To make the experience for the user seamless and consistent, the packaging and branding of the shoes shares the same fluidity and seamless expression as the design.

ザハ・ハディドとブラジルのシューズ・ブランド，メリッサとのコラボレーションは，ファッション産業とダイレクトに協力し，新しい表現手段の可能性を探る機会となった。われわれのスタジオの特徴である流動感を表現するため，身体の有機的な輪郭を出発点とするのはごく自然なことであった。このことから，ショーウィンドウの中の静止したオブジェではなく，履いた時に生命を吹き込まれるような，流動するシューズというアイデアに繋がった。シューズが地面から立ち上がり，滑らかで優美な動きによって脚を非対称に登る。第2の皮膚のように密着し，身体と物体との境界を曖昧にする軽やかさを備えている。

商品を開発し，デザインを生産ラインにうまく乗せるため，先端的なデジタルモデリング技術を用いた。シューズの人間工学的な質はラピッド・プロトタイピングによって向上し，流動感あるデザインは，メリッサのもつプラスチック射出成形技術に適していた。シームレスで一貫した感覚をユーザーに提供するため，パッケージングやブランディングにもデザインと同様の流動的で滑らかな表現を用いている。

Architects: Zaha Hadid Architects—
Zaha Hadid, Patrik Schumacher, design;
Ana M Cajiao, project director;
Maria Araya, Muthahar Khan, design team
Client: Grendene S/A Melissa, Brazil
Program: shoes
Materials: mould injected plastic

Melissa Shoes

© David Grandorge

2008
ORCHIS
オルキス

The Orchis stools were developed using the mathematical principle of non-oriented surfaces—the idea that an object does not possess a distinct inner or outer edge. As the curvature of the surface twists and bends, it defines an elegant composition of seat, backrest and legs. Each stool can seat one to three people and, designed for use outside, can cohere as a single object or scatter to form a field of related shapes. The products stem from the studio's advanced knowledge of material technologies and CNC milling and combine EPS foam with a reinforced fibreglass shell.

A new version in Carrara marble was produced in occasion of the 14th International Sculpture Biennale of Carrara in 2010.

オルキス・スツールは，不可符号曲面という，表とうらの区別がない物体という数学的原理を用いて開発された。曲面がねじれ，シート，背もたれ，脚を優美に構成している。各スツールは1人から3人掛けとなっており，外部での使用のために考案されているため，まとめて単一のオブジェとすることができる一方で，関連した形が散らばる場を形成することもできる。このプロダクトは，材料に関する技術とCNCフライス加工に関してスタジオがもつ先端知識に基づくものであり，EPSフォームと強化ガラス繊維のシェルを組み合わせている。

カラーラ大理石を用いた新しいバージョンが2010年の第14回カラーラ国際彫刻ビエンナーレの際に制作された。

Architects: Zaha Hadid Architects—
Zaha Hadid, Patrik Schumacher, design;
Johannes Schafelner, project designer;
Judith Schafelner, Andres Schenker, design team
Program: seating sculpture
Size: Orchis 1 (1,300 x 730 mm), Orchis 2 (1,520 x 750 mm), Orchis 3 (1,035 x 520 mm), Orchis 4 (1,750 x 830 mm)
Materials: carrara marble

© Antonio Sanz, courtesy of Ivorypress

Orchis

2009
GLACE COLLECTION
グレース・コレクション

Atelier Swarovski

This enigmatic new collection by Zaha Hadid celebrates a powerful dichotomy between the purity of Swarovski's precision cut crystals and the subtle, organic forms that envelop them.

Each piece within the collection has evolved as an abstraction of the sinuous forms evident in nature, revealing Hadid's desire for experimentation and invention throughout every stage of design and realization.

Every miniature crystal describes a unique moment in time, captured in suspension, exhibiting the tension between fluid biomorphic forms juxtaposing with the exacting, angular regularity of crystal. As the curvature of the surface of each piece flawlessly twists and turns, dynamic form and ergonomic considerations are seamlessly integrated. An asymmetrical elegance conveys an innate sense of movement that seductively encases the embedded crystalline particles.

The lightweight organic pieces translate the brilliance and refraction of light from the crystal. Hadid has aligned these particles in dynamic swooping arrangements specifically to enhance their elegant formal composition. These signature gestures define this symbiotic association. They are not so much an abstract exercise for embellishment of the human figure, but Hadid's personal investigation onto the inherent contextual relationships of her work.

This personal nature of the collection—rhythmic, seamless and articulated—gives a truly unique glimpse into Hadid's process and experimentation. Each piece intricately suspends its counterparts of crystal in gentle undulations and folds that relate directly to their organic inspirations. These concave and convex forms are never arbitrary, alluding to the ergonomic and crystalline properties that define every element of the design.

ザハ・ハディドによるこの謎めいた新しいコレクションは，スワロフスキーの精密にカットされたクリスタルの純度と，それを覆う繊細で有機的な形態との力強い対比を讃えるものである。

コレクションの各アイテムは，自然界に存在する曲がりくねった形態の抽象化であり，デザインと具現化の各段階を通じたハディドの実験と発明への欲求を示している。

小さなクリスタルは，それぞれ静止した状態で捉えられた無二の瞬間を描写しており，流動的で有機的な形態と，クリスタルの厳密でシャープな規則性との緊張感を示している。各アイテムの曲面は徹底して曲折しているため，ダイナミックな形態と人間工学的配慮が完全に融合している。非対称の優美な形態は，埋め込まれたクリスタルの粒子を魅惑的に包み込む動きの感覚を本質的に伝えている。

この軽量で有機的なアイテムは，クリスタルの光の輝きと屈折を変化させている。ハディドは，とりわけ形態上の構成の優美さを高めるために，これらの粒子をダイナミックに配置する。これらの特徴的ジェスチャーにより，この共生的結合が明確になる。それらは，人物を装飾するための抽象的な行為というよりも，むしろ，ハディドの作品が本質的にもつ文脈上の関連性についての探求の一環である。

律動的で，途切れなく，明快であるという，コレクションのこの私的な性質により，ハディドのデザイン・プロセスや実験の中に実にユニークな瞬間を垣間見ることができる。それぞれのアイテムは，緩やかにうねり，折れ曲がるクリスタルの部分は複雑にぶら下がり，有機的な発想源をダイレクトに物語る。曲がりくねった形態は決して恣意的なものではなく，デザインの全ての要素を規定する人間工学とクリスタルの特性を示唆している。

Architects: Zaha Hadid Architects—Zaha Hadid, Patrik Schumacher, design; Swati Sharma, Maria Araya, design team
Client: Atelier Swarovski
Program: jewellery
Dimensions: Necklace (L220 x D140 mm), Cuff 1 (L105 x D50 mm), Cuff 2 (L110 x D50 mm), Ring 1 (L45 x D49 mm), Ring2 (L70 x D35 mm), Pendant (L150 x D110 mm)
Materials: coloured resin and swarovski crystals in jet, opal, crystal, padpardascha and black diamond

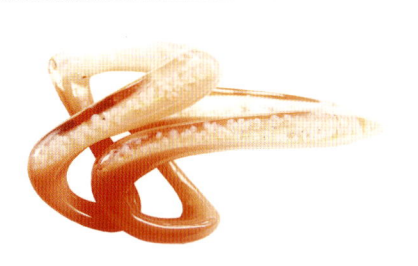

Glace Collection

203

2009
LACOSTE SHOES
ラコステ・シューズ

Lacoste, Pentland

Zaha Hadid's footwear collaboration with LACOSTE began with a digitalized interpretation of surfaces with repeated patterns. The design expression behind the collaboration with LACOSTE footwear allows the evolution of dynamic fluid grids. When wrapped around the shape of a foot, these expand and contract to negotiate and adapt to the body ergonomically. In doing so a landscape emerges, undulating and radiating as it merges seamlessly with the body.

The digital landscape is translated into a tactile landscape by a series of metal plates depicting the desired wave pattern. These plates were subsequently utilised to apply a combination of heat embossing and debossing techniques to the calf leather, thus rendering the topography in relief. This resulting topography gradually emerges on the uppers as it curves around the top and exterior fascia of each shoe, and fades across the straps. A 2D plan drawing of the 3D pattern is replicated on the sole of the shoe.

The continuity and fluidity in the design are enhanced by the minimum depth of the sole and the seamless strap closure system. The limited edition closure system features a bi-stable snapping metal band encased in the leather strap at the upper-most end. This responsive band gently wraps and secures itself at ankle height in the men's limited edition and at knee height in the women's limited edition. The unique Zaha Hadid for LACOSTE logo appears on the side of the heel and on the in-sock. The women's boots are available in black and purple, while the men's come in black and navy.

ザハ・ハディドとラコステとのフットウェアのコラボレーションは，反復的なパターンをもつサーフェスをデジタルに解釈することから始まった。ラコステとのコラボレーションの背後にあるデザイン上の表現は，ダイナミックに流動するグリッドの進化を可能にした。脚の形に巻き付いた時，これらは伸縮して，人間工学的に身体に適応する。そうして，身体と途切れなく融合した，うねり，放射するランドスケープが現れる。

デジタルなランドスケープは，望ましい波形を描いた一連の金属板によって立体のランドスケープに変換される。さらに，これらの板は，エンボス加工とデボス加工を組み合わせてカーフ・レザーに施すために使われ，トポグラフィを浮き彫りにする。この立体的な地形は，シューズの先端と外側に沿って曲がりながら徐々に上の方へ上がっていき，留めバンドにかかって消えていく。3次元パターンを平面化したプランはソールに複製される。

デザインの連続性と流動性は，最小限の奥行きのソールとシームレスな留めバンドによって強調される。限定版の留め方は，レザーのストラップの上端に内包された金属バンドの留め具が特徴となっている。このバンドはしなやかに巻き付き，男性用では足首の高さで，女性用では膝の高さで固定される。「Zaha Hadid for LACOSTE」の特別なロゴがヒールの側面とインソックに施される。女性用のブーツは黒と紫の2色，男性用は黒と紺の2色が用意されている。

Architects: Zaha Hadid Architects—
Zaha Hadid, Patrik Schumacher, design;
Woody Yao, Maria Araya, Danilo Arsic,
Margarita Valova, Maha Kutay, Nick Armitage,
Dylan Davies, design team
Client: Lacoste, Pentland
Program: shoes
Materials: leather and rubber

Lacoste Shoes

2012
LIQUID GLACIAL
リキッド・グレイシャル

David Gill Galleries

The Liquid Glacial design embeds surface complexity and refraction within a powerful fluid dynamic. The elementary geometry of the flat table top appears transformed from static to fluid by the subtle waves and ripples evident below the surface, while the table's legs seem to pour from the horizontal in an intense vortex of water frozen in time. The transparent acrylic material amplifies this perception; adding depth and complexity through a flawless display of infinite kaleidoscopic refractions. The result generates a wonderful surface dynamic that inherits a myriad of colours from its context and continually adapts with the observer's changing viewpoint. The form is of its creator; a design that does not compromise functionality or ergonomic requirements and a coherent evolution of her architectural narrative exploring movement through space.

リキッド・グレイシャルのデザインは，表面の複雑性と屈折を，動的な流動性の中に埋め込んでいる。平坦なテーブルトップの単純なジオメトリが，テーブル下の微細なさざ波によって静的なものから流動的なものへ変化しているように見える一方で，水平面から生じた激しい水の渦が静止してテーブルの脚となったようにも見える。透明なアクリル素材がこうした知覚を増幅させており，万華鏡のような無限の屈折によって奥行きと複雑さが加えられている。その結果，見事にダイナミックな表面が生じており，周囲からの無数の色を取り込み，見る人の視点の移動に応じて連続的に変化する。形態はそのクリエイター特有のものである。そのデザインは機能性あるいは人間工学的要件を損なうことなく，空間を通して動きを探求するザハ・ハディドの建築的物語は一貫して展開してゆく。

Architects: Zaha Hadid Architects—
Zaha Hadid, Patrik Schumacher, design;
Fulvio Wirz, Mariagrazia Lanza,
Maha Kutay, Woody Yao, design team
Client: David Gill Galleries
Program: dining & coffee table
Dimensions: liquid glacial dining table (section 1: L2,515 x D1402 x H75 mm / section 2: L2,827 x D1,405 x H750 mm), liquid glacial coffee table (L2,500 x D870 x H400 mm)
Materials: polished plexiglas clear

© Jacopo Spilimbergo

Liquid Glacial 207

2013
ARIA & AVIA LAMPS
アリア&アヴィア・ランプ

Slamp

ARIA
A suspended centrepiece which gently illuminates its environment with light dramatically cast through its sculptural fins. An elegant embodiment of the seamless fluidity of movement.

AVIA
A dramatic sweeping motion lifts the soft billowing cloud, simultaneously drawn towards ceiling and ground.
  Movement and light ripple across this delicately layered interplay of solid and void, constantly evolving, compressing and contracting, from each varied perspective.

アリア
吊り下げられたセンターピースが，彫刻的なフィンを通した劇的な光で周囲を優しく照らす。シームレスな流動性の優美な具現化である。

アヴィア
柔らかい不定形の雲が劇的な動きで持ち上がり，天井と地面に向かって同時に引き寄せられる。
  運動と光が，この繊細に重ねられたソリッドとヴォイドの相互作用に，波紋のように広がり，視点に応じて絶えず発達したり収縮したりする。

Architects: Zaha Hadid Design—
Zaha Hadid, Patrik Schumacher, design;
Melodie Leung, Swati Sharma, Maha Kutay, design team
Client: Slamp
Program: lighting
–
Avia
Materials: 52 layers of Opalflex®
Colour: black or white
–
Aria
Materials: 50 layers Cristalflex®
Colour: transparent with black or white print

Aria & Avia Lamps

2013
ZEPHYR SOFA
ゼファ・ソファ

The sinuous shape of the Zephyr sofa has been inspired by natural rock formations shaped by erosion: the application of subtractive processes that carve solid matter. The resulting formal language gives the Zephyr sofa increased ergonomic properties without compromising the design's fluidity or proportion; translating into a concept that allows for multiple seating layouts. The carved profile incorporates deep backrests and generous undercuts for unrivalled comfort. A lacquered finish applied to Zephyr's structural elements highlights every subtle nuance of its composition, and is contrasted by the tactile qualities of its bespoke upholstery and cushioning.

Zephyr showcases Cassina Contract's unrivalled technical experience and long-standing tradition of artisan excellence.

ゼファ・ソファの曲がりくねった形は，浸食によって形成された自然の岩石層から発想を得ている。つまり，ソリッドな物質を彫る，引き算的方法の適用である。結果として生じる形態により，ゼファ・ソファのデザインの流動性あるいはプロポーションが損なわれることなく，人間工学的な特性が向上しており，多様な座席配置を可能にするコンセプトに繋がっている。彫り出された外形は，深い背もたれと大きなアンダーカットが一体となり，無類の快適さをもたらす。構造部材に用いられたラッカー仕上げによって，構成の微妙なニュアンスが強調され，特注の生地とクッションがもつ触覚的な質との対比を生み出している。

ゼファは，カッシーナ・コントラクトの比類のない技術と経験，卓越した職人の長い伝統を反映している。

Architects: Zaha Hadid Design—
Zaha Hadid, Patrik Schumacher, design;
Fulvio Wirz, Mariagrazia Lanza,
Maha Kutay, design team
Program: seating
Consultant: Cassina Contract, manufacturer
Dimensions: 3,200 x 3,020 x 730 mm
Materials: wool upholstered foam with fibre glass base

Zephyr Sofa

© *Jacopo Spilimbergo*

2013
MERCURIC TABLE COLLECTION
マーキュリック・テーブル・コレクション

Citco

In the past, artists carved. Today the designer, working with artisan skills and the technological innovation, can impress form, function and vision upon marble. Hadid in collaboration with Citco has reinterpreted marble in her unmistakable idiom.

過去，芸術家たちは彫刻した。今日ではデザイナーは，職人技能と技術革新を備えて，形態，機能，そしてヴィジョンを大理石に刻むことができる。ハディドは，シトコとのコラボレーションにおいて，大理石を再解釈し，彼女特有の表現に落とし込んだ。

Architects: Zaha Hadid Design—
Zaha Hadid, Patrik Schumacher, design;
Fulvio Wirz, Filipa Gomes, Mariagrazia Lanza, Maha Kutay, design team
Client: Citco
Program: set of tables
Mercuric I (limited edition: edition of 12 + 2AP per colour)
Dimensions: L 870 x W700 x H400 mm
Materials: nero marquina bianco di covelano vena oro
Colour: black or white
Mercuric II (limited edition: edition of 12 +2AP per colour)
Dimensions: L1,400 x W 900 x H400 mm
Materials: nero marquina bianco di covelano vena oro
Colour: black or white
Mercuric III (limited edition: edition of 12 +2AP per colour)
Dimensions: L1,700 x W950 x H400 mm
Materials: nero marquina bianco di covelano vena oro
Colour: black or white

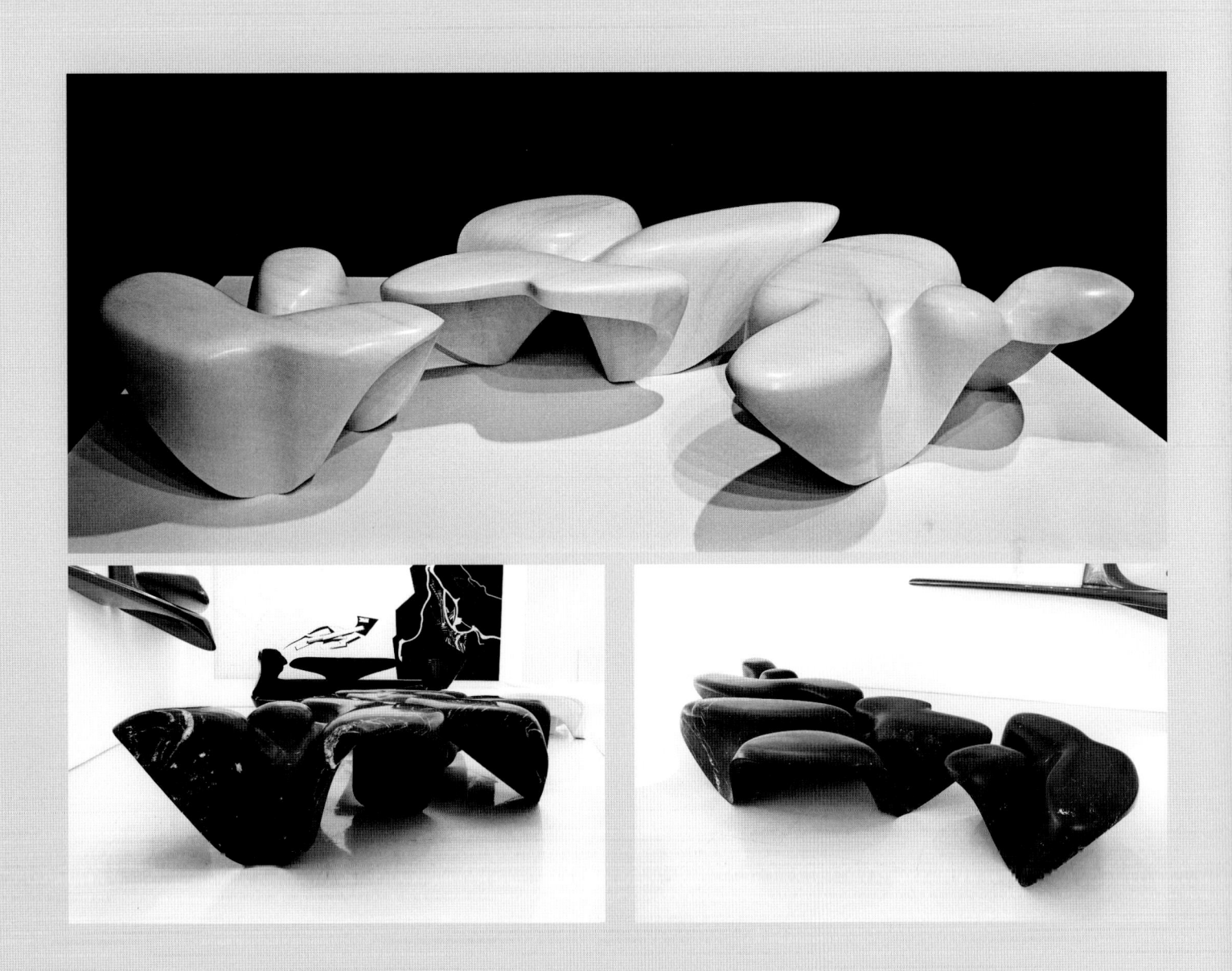

© *Jacopo Spilimbergo (above)*

Mercuric Table Collection

2013
SKEIN COLLECTION
スケイン・コレクション

Caspita

Zaha Hadid Architects have collaborated with Swiss goldsmiths Caspita on a collection that combine innovative design technologies and the highest level of craftsmanship. These multi-faceted lattice pieces explore the intricate yet extremely strong cellular structures within nature. Each piece has been further shaped by ergonomic considerations in a dialogue that defines the formal language of the collection and expresses the exciting new possibilities and potential for working to the finest detail in gold.

The Skein collection includes finely crafted rings and bracelets in 18 carat gold, some inlaid with precious stones within the delicate latticework structure, and launched at the Zaha Hadid Design Gallery in London on November 28th, 2013 during the Caspita pop-up store.

ザハ・ハディド・アーキテクツは，スイスの金細工ブランドであるカスピタとコラボレーションして，革新的なデザイン技術と最高度の熟練技能を組み合わせたコレクションを制作した。これらの多角形の格子からなるアイテムは，自然界にある複雑だが極めて強固な細胞構造を追求して生まれた。それぞれのアイテムは人間工学的な配慮に基づいてさらに形づくられ，コレクションに共通する形態的特徴が明確になり，ゴールドの繊細なディテールに刺激的な新しい可能性をもたらしている。

スケイン・コレクションには，18カラットゴールドの精巧につくられたリングとブレスレットが含まれ，一部には繊細な格子細工に宝石がはめ込まれている。コレクションの立ち上げは2013年11月28日にロンドンのザハ・ハディド・デザイン・ギャラリーのカスピタ・ポップアップ・ストアで行われた。

Architects: Zaha Hadid Architects—
Zaha Hadid, Patrik Schumacher, design;
Maha Kutay, Melodie Leung,
Evgeniya Yatsyuk, Melissa Woolford,
Michael Grau, Hussam Chakouf, design team
Client: Caspita
Program: jewellery
Size: cuff (L 16.8 x W 8.55 x H 8.65 cm), ring (L 4.7 x W 2.7 x H 2.8 cm), ring with diamond (L 4.7 x W 2.7 x H 2.8 cm)
Materials: 18 carat gold, diamond
Finish: cuff and ring (white gold, yellow gold, rose gold, black gold), ring with diamond (white gold with white diamonds, yellow gold with white diamonds, rose gold with white diamonds, black gold with white or black diamonds)

© Jörg Brockmann

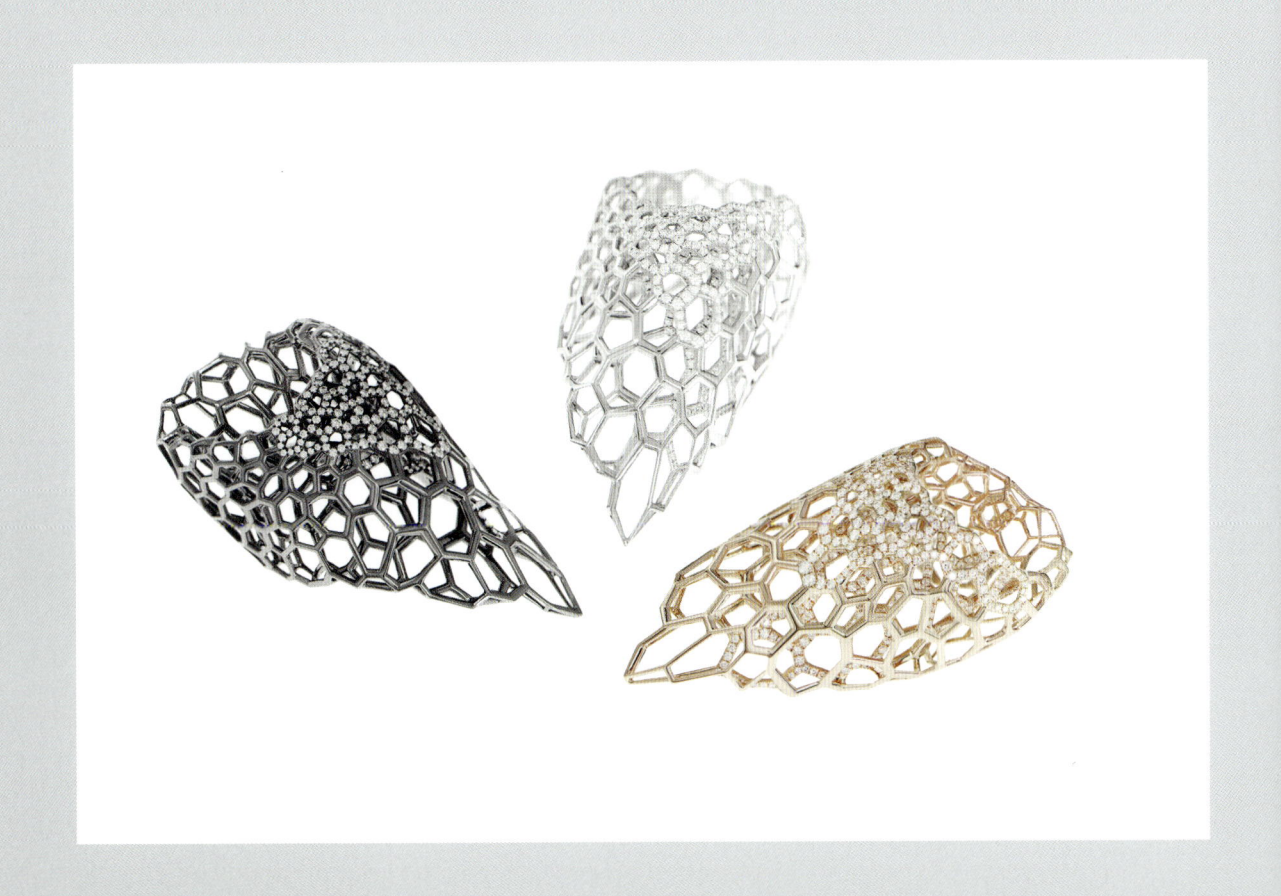

Skein Collection

215

2013
NOVA SHOES
ノヴァ・シューズ

United Nude

The revolutionary design of the NOVA shoe combines innovative materialization and ergonomic considerations with the dynamism of Hadid's unmistakable architectural language to convey an inherent sense of movement; revealing the experimentation and invention of Hadid's process through every stage of design and construction.

"United Nude's collections are provocative yet sensual. Rem D Koolhaas' unrelenting experimentation at the cutting edge of fashion never fails to capture our imagination." explains Hadid. "I have always appreciated those who dare to experiment with materials and proportions. Our collaboration with United Nude reinterprets the classic shoe typology; pushing the boundaries of what is possible without compromising integrity."

The NOVA design incorporates intricate striations juxtaposed with dramatic realignments, establishing a direct formal relationship with the shoe's primary structure and expressing the dynamic forces applied by every step of the wearer.

ノヴァの画期的なデザインは，革新的な技術と人間工学的配慮を，ハディド特有の建築言語がもつ力強さと組み合わせ，本質的な運動の感覚を伝えており，デザインと具現化の各段階を通じたハディドの実験性と創造性を明らかにしている。

「ユナイテッド・ヌードのコレクションは挑発的だが官能的でもある。ファッションの最先端におけるレム・D・コールハースの不断の実験的試みは，常に私たちの想像力を刺激する」とハディドは説明する。「マテリアルとプロポーションで大胆な試みを行う人々を私は常に評価してきた。ユナイテッド・ヌードとのコラボレーションは，古典的な靴のタイポロジーに再解釈を加えるものであり，一貫性を損なうことなく可能性の限界を押し広げる試みである」。

ノヴァのデザインは，複雑な縞を劇的に再配置しており，靴の主要構造と形態的に直接結びついて，履く人の動きによって生じるダイナミックな力学を表現する。

Architects: Zaha Hadid Architects—
Zaha Hadid, Patrik Schumacher, design;
Maren Klasing, Maha Kutay, Woody Yao,
design team
Client: United Nude
Program: shoes
Colours: black chrome, rosegold chrome, silver chrome
Sizes: 35-40
Materials: fibreglass, vinyl, chrome, leather, rubber

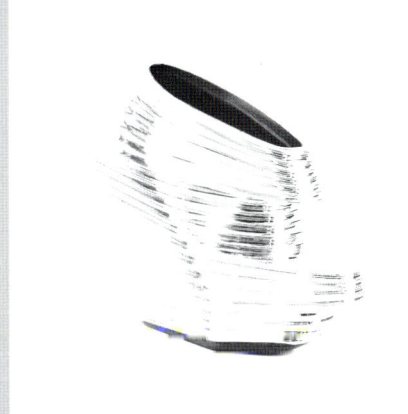

© United Nude

NOVA Shoes 217

2014
DESIGN COLLECTION
デザイン・コレクション

Zaha Hadid Design

During a career spanning thirty years, Zaha Hadid has created some of the world's most iconic buildings, as well as having worked on numerous product collaborations with some of the most admired international brands. Now for the first time, she has developed her own capsule collection of exceptional pieces for the home, inspired by the forms of her architectural work.

The collection features gift items and home accessories that have been designed using state of the art techniques and crafted by artisans from across Europe, including platters, trays, vessels, candles and candelabras, stools and a chess set.

Contrast is key throughout the collection, both in terms of materials and colours. Traditional bone china and ceramic are offset against modern resins and acrylics, while neon pops of lime and fuchsia provide a stark contrast to pared back pieces in off-white or black. What remains consistent throughout, is the use of Zaha Hadid's signature aesthetic: shapes are fluid, forms are free and each piece is unmistakably Zaha Hadid.

Standout pieces include the Field of Towers chess set, which features beautiful playing pieces in polished black resin. The board itself is muted and black, but conceals a vivid green interior for storing the pieces. Over time, new playing pieces will be released in limited edition colours and finishes, allowing owners to collect a set that is unique to them.

Also of note is the Aqua Platter, which will be made to order. Its namesake is the London 2012 Olympic Games Aquatics Centre, designed by Zaha Hadid. A truly fluid shape, the platter comprises four pieces which can each be used individually or arranged together to create one dramatic display.

ザハ・ハディドの30年にわたるキャリアにおいて、彼女は、世界で最もアイコニックな建築をいくつも生み出してきた。世界有数のインターナショナル・ブランドと共に、数多くのプロダクト・デザインも同様に手掛けている。しかし今回初めて、ザハ自身のコレクションとして、自らの建築の形態からインスピレーションを受けた、小さなホームウェア・セットが展開される。

コレクションは、ギフト向けや家庭用品が中心で、高度な芸術的技法でデザインされ、ヨーロッパ中の職人によってつくり出される。ラインナップには、大皿や盛り皿、各種の器、ロウソクや燭台、スツールやチェスセットが含まれている。

素材と色のコントラストがこのコレクションのキーポイントである。伝統的な陶磁器が現代的なアクリルなどの樹脂と重ね合わされ、光沢のあるポップな黄緑や赤紫が、ぴったり合わさった外側のオフホワイトや黒と、完全なるコントラストをつくり出す。どこまでも変わらないのは、ザハ・ハディドの名そのものである美学に貫かれていることだ。形は流麗で、構成は自由自在。しかし、一つひとつはまぎれもなくザハである。

特に際だっているものの一つが、チェスセット「フィールド・オブ・タワーズ」で、美しく磨き上げられた黒い樹脂のチェス駒が特徴である。チェス盤自体はとてもシックな黒であるが、内側には駒をしまう鮮やかな緑のスペースが隠されている。

「アクア」にも言及しなくてはならない。この大皿はオーダーメイドでつくられ、ザハ・ハディド設計の2012年ロンドン五輪の「アクアティック・センター」と同じ名前を持つ。非常に流体的な形の4枚のピースからなり、別々としても使えるが、一つのものとしてアレンジしてドラマティックに見せることもできる。

Design: Zaha Hadid, Patrik Schumacher
—
Field of Towers (chess set)
Design team: Woody Yao, Maha Kutay, Steven Blaess, Carine Posner
—
Aqua (platters)
Design team: Woody Yao, Maha Kutay, Steven Blaess, Swati Sharma, Thomas Jensen, Melodie Leung
—
Aqua (table mat)
Design team: Woody Yao, Maha Kutay, Steven Blaess, Thomas Jensen
—
Rim (vessels)
Design team: Woody Yao, Maha Kutay, Steven Blaess, Wandy Mulia
—
Braid (candle holder & candelabra)
Design team: Woody Yao, Maha Kutay, Steven Blaess, Johanna Huang
—
Prime (scented candles)
Design team: Woody Yao, Maha Kutay, Melodie Leung, Steven Blaess, Evgeniya Yatsyuk
—
Radia (stool & side table)
Design team: Woody Yao, Maha Kutay, Steven Blaess, Wandy Mulia

AQUA / Numbered Edition Platters
アクア／プラッター（限定版）

BRAID / Single Candle Holder
ブレイド／ろうそく台（1本用）

BRAID / Double Candelabra
ブレイド／ろうそく台（2本用）

AQUA / Table Mat
アクア／テーブル・マット

RIM / Vessels
リム／器

PRIME / Scented Candles
プライム／アロマ・キャンドル

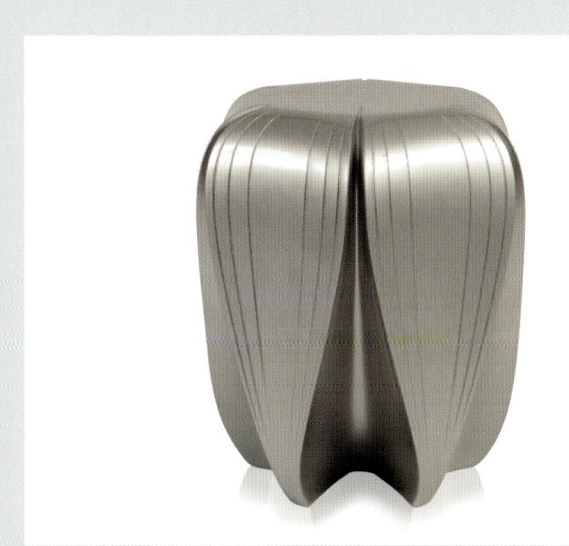

RADIA / Stool & Side Table
ラディア／スツール＆サイドテーブル

FIELD OF TOWERS / Numbered Edition Chess Set
フィールド・オブ・タワーズ／チェスセット（限定版）

Design Collection

THE INSTRUMENTALITY OF APPEARANCES IN THE PURSUIT OF A LEGIBLE URBAN ORDER
PATRIK SCHUMACHER, 2014

判読可能な都市秩序の追求手段としての外観
パトリック・シューマッハ

Introduction:
The fundamental question of architecture's purpose

The most striking feature of the work of Zaha Hadid and Zaha Hadid Architects is its unusual, intense, memorable appearance, often referred to as "iconic". Our work is certainly visually stimulating, inspires curiosity, and seems to radiate an enigmatic beauty. But is this all? Can this be its raison d'être? How can we justify the pursuit of beauty? Architecture and urban design surely should not be treated as a visual art delivering a mere visual feast or attention grabbing spectacle! Is this intense and costly investment in the spectacular visual appearance of the built environment not an unjustifiable indulgence? Is our work really this superficial? Where is the concern for function here? How does the intense appearance of our work relate to the fundamental social purposes the built environment is meant to serve?

It is the first general goal of this essay to explain why appearances and aesthetic values matter and how they function to facilitate the most profound societal purposes of the built environment. A second, more specific goal is to explain why our work looks the way it looks and how and why the visual, formal-aesthetic expression of our work—our style—evolved during the 30 years covered in this exhibition. This second goal will involve a discussion of the transition from Deconstructivism to Parametricism.

The Meaning of Beauty:
The Hidden Efficacy of Aesthetic Values

The concept of beauty is shrouded in mystery. Architectural theory should not only lift the veil of mystery but explain why this sense of mystery exists. The first point to make here is the pervasiveness of aesthetic judgments—intuitive judgement on the basis of appearance—in our daily lives. We navigate our physical and social environment largely on the basis of intuitive appeal and repulsion.

What is beautiful? Whatever appeals at first sight. Being impressed by beauty is a gut reaction. However, this immediate gut reaction operates according to an underlying rationality. Aesthetic responses—including the aesthetic responses to cities and buildings—are a form of instant, intuitive evaluation. The recognition of beauty within a built environment is the recognition of the vitality of this environment, on the basis of its mere appearance, prior to a more in-depth experience and verification of its vitality or functionality. Aesthetic responses have specific advantages and disadvantages in comparison with evaluations based on careful examination and analysis. Aesthetic responses are less reliable but much faster than knowledge based responses. Aesthetic values, internalized as 'tastes', perform acts of discrimination or classification, without requiring explicit knowledge. They are totalizing rather than differentiating, i.e., they operate via global impressions rather than via the isolation of factors. Aesthetic judgements are rational inasmuch as they provide an intuitive appreciation of

序論：建築の目的に関する根本的な問題

ザハ・ハディドおよびザハ・ハディド・アーキテクツの一連の作品が持つ最も際立った特徴とは，非凡かつ強烈で記憶に残り「アイコニック」と表されることの多いその外観である。確かに我々の作品は視覚に刺激的で好奇心をかき立て謎めいた美しさを発している。しかしそれだけなのだろうか？ それがレゾン・デートルなのか？ 美の追求をいかに正当化できるだろうか？ 建築と都市デザインは，単に目を楽しませたり注目を鷲掴みにし，スペクタクルを供するヴィジュアル・アートとして扱われるべきではないことは当然のこと！ この建築環境の，目を見張るような外観に対する強烈で高価な投資は，弁解の余地もないただの道楽なのか？ 我々の作品は本当にそこまで表面的なものなのか？ そこに機能性への配慮はないのか？ 本来，建築環境が満たさなければならない根本的な社会目的に，この強烈な外観がどのように関連してくるのか？

このエッセイの目標は第1に，なぜ外観と美的価値は重要であり，それらがいかに建築環境の最も深遠な社会目的の実現に寄与しているかを説明することにある。第2に，より具体的な目標として，なぜ我々の作品があのような見た目をしているのか，そしてなぜその視覚的で表面上の美的表現──我々のスタイル──がこのエキシビジョンがカバーする30年の間に進化してきたのかを説明したいと思っている。後者については，脱構築主義からパラメトリシズムへの転換についての考察も含める予定である。

美の意味：美的価値の隠された効率性

美の概念は謎に包まれている。建築理論は，神秘のベールをめくるだけでなく，なぜそれが謎めいた感じがするのかも解明できなければならない。ここでまず重視しておきたいのは，私たちの日常生活の中における美的判断──見た目から直感的に判断すること──の浸透性の高さである。私たちは，身体的そして社会的環境の中を，主に直感的なアピールと拒否反応をもとに渡り歩いている。

美とは何か？ それは一目見て感じるアピール全般のことだ。美に感銘を受けるのは本能的なリアクションである。しかしこの即座の本能的リアクションは合理性に裏打ちされたものだ。審美的反応──町並みや建物に対する審美的反応を含む──は，即時的で本能的な評価の一つの形である。建築環境の中に美を見出すことは，そこに実際に足を踏み入れ活気や機能性を確かめる前

The Instrumentality of Appearances in the Pursuit of a Legible Urban Order

performativity, short-circuiting extended experience or analysis. Aesthetic judgement thus represents an economical substitute for judgement based on investigation.

Aesthetic valuation has a deeply rooted biological function. Organisms are attracted to what sustains life and repulsed by what threatens life. The biological function of aesthetic appeal is thus to orient the organism towards what performs well for it. Aesthetic responses are conditioned responses, based on the universal biological 'learning' mechanism of conditioning. The discrimination of the beautiful versus the ugly is thus a culturally over-determined instantiation of the fundamental biological mechanism of conditioned attraction versus repulsion. This basic function should still underlie the most artificial and culturally mediated forms of aesthetic evaluation. The correlation between the beautiful and the well performing is still obvious in the widespread aesthetic appreciation of young, healthy women or male athletic bodies. The biological basis of aesthetic values is thus a factor to be reckoned with. However, the fact that aesthetic values are socially over-determined and thus culturally and historically relative is equally indisputable.

There is no contradiction between these two facts, the fact of the biological function of aesthetic values and the fact of their cultural relativity. The capacity to respond aesthetically has been subjected to the adaptive rationality of the ongoing cultural evolution. The rationality of aesthetic values—the relationship of beauty to performativity—is in principle maintained, albeit continuously updated with regard to the evolving life processes of society. Aesthetic evaluations evolve historically but, at any stage, function quasi-instinctively.

Aesthetic values encapsulate condensed, collective experiences within useful dogmas. However, as society evolves what was once vital might have become dysfunctional and new vital, functional societal processes might be unduly constrained by the established canons of beauty. The phenomena they bring forth appear ugly. Their aesthetic rejection becomes a fetter on further progress. A contradiction develops that can only be solved by an aesthetic revolution. Aesthetic sensibilities have to be adapted via aesthetic revolutions.

The latest aesthetic revolution is being delivered by Parametricism via the transitional episodes of Postmodernism and Deconstructivism. Postmodernism and Deconstructivism started to aesthetisize the new urban diversity, irregularity and chaotic, collage-like complexity of the spontaneous, market-driven urbanisation processes that had escaped the strictures of the modernist canon of urban planning and design. Parametricism aims is to go beyond this aesthetization of spontaneous maverick developments in its pursuit of radically new ordering principles and aesthetic values that are congenial to the workings of Postfordist Network Society, projecting once more a total make-over of the organisation and physiognomy (appearance) of the built environment of the 21st century, just like Modernism had delivered for the 20th century.

に，見た目だけを頼りにその環境の生命力を認識することである。審美的反応は，入念な調査と分析に根ざした評価と比較すると，はっきりしたメリットとデメリットを持つ。審美的反応は信頼性が乏しいが，知識に基づく反応よりもはるかに速い。美的価値は「嗜好」として内面化され，明示的な知識を必要とすることなく識別や分類を行う。分化するのではなく要約するもの，つまり要素を分離する方向ではなく，全体的な印象を通して働く。審美的判断は，長期の経験や分析を短絡し，遂行性に対する本能的な評価を供する限りは合理的である。すなわち，審美的判断とは，調査に基づく判断に対する節約的な代用品なのだ。審美的評価は根深い生物学的機能を有している。有機体は生命を維持するものに惹かれ，生命を脅かすものに拒否感を抱く。美的アピールの生物学上の機能は，つまり有機体が自身のためになる性能へと関心を向けることだ。審美的反応とは，普遍的な生物学的条件付けの「学習」メカニズムに基づき条件付けられた反応である。美しいと醜いの区別は，つまり条件付けられた魅了と拒否の根本的な生物学的メカニズムにおいて，文化的に決定されつくしてきた例示なのだ。この基本的機能は，ほぼすべての人工的で文化を媒介とする審美的評価の形の基礎となるものである。「美しい」と「高性能」の関係性は，若く健康的な女性や男性の鍛えられた体に対する審美的評価が広く受け入れられている現状にもはっきりと表れている。つまり美的価値の生物学的論拠は，無視のできない要素なのだ。ただし，美的価値が社会的に決定し尽くされており，文化や歴史に関連しているという事実も同様に議論の余地のないものである。

美的価値の生物学上の機能という事実と，それらの文化的関連性という二つの事実の間に矛盾は無い。美に反応する能力は，今なお進む文化的発展に適応する合理性に従うものである。社会の進化する生活プロセスに合わせ絶え間なくアップデートされているにもかかわらず，美的価値の合理性——美の遂行性に対する関係——は原則維持されている。審美的評価は歴史とともに進化するが，どの段階においてもほぼ本能的に機能する。

美的価値は，有用な定説に含まれる集団的経験の凝縮を要約するものである。ただし社会が進化するにつれ，以前は不可欠だったものが機能不全となり，新しく不可欠で機能的な社会のプロセスが既存の美的基準によって不当に押し込められてしまう，という状況もあり得る。結果，もたらされる現象は醜く見えるかもしれない。そういった審美的拒絶は将来的な進歩への足かせとなる。

Beauty and the evolution of concepts of order

Above we established the functionality of beauty—whatever works well will eventually become validated as beautiful—and we established the historical relativity of aesthetic values, i.e. sensibilities need to be (periodically) brought in line with the morphological conditions of the historically most vital social life-processes. Beauty keeps changing its physiognomy. Aesthetic regimes are transitory.

But is the category of beauty really devoid of any features that persist across its different, concrete historical manifestations? Contemporary architects recognize the beauty of past eras (although they would not find it appropriate to use any of these older styles to frame contemporary institutions). Is it possible to identify an invariant characteristic, a universally applicable condition that must be met by all environments (and even by all phenomena) recognized as beautiful?

Yes, I believe there is an invariant aspect that guides all discriminations of beauty versus ugliness: the sensation of beauty is always bound to a sense of order as distinct from chaos. Order as the universal and invariant aspect of beauty has been alluded to by many classical definitions of beauty. For instance Leon Battista Alberti's famous definition reads as follows:

> *'Beauty is that reasoned harmony of all the parts within a body, so that nothing may be added, taken away, or altered, but for the worse.'* [i]

The positive principle of harmony/order is emphasized by reference to an 'integral body' and contrasted with a mere agglomeration:

> *'The harmony is such that the building appears a single, integral, and well-composed body, rather than a collection of extraneous and unrelated parts.'* [ii]

The same point is further explicated by negating its opposite which might thus be taken as the implicit definition of the ugly: a composition should be

> *'neither jumpy, nor confused, nor disorganized, nor disconnected, nor composed of incongruous elements, … nor too disjointed or distant from the rest of the body.'* [iii]

Alberti references order via the phrase 'harmony of all the parts'. This can be accepted as a very general, abstract formula. However, his insistence on completeness, i.e., that nothing may be added, taken away or altered, is specific to Classical architecture and can no longer be considered a universal and invariant feature of beauty. Alberti's concept of an organic whole, with symmetry and strict rules of proportion, with a state of completeness or perfection that tolerates neither additions nor subtractions, describes a general ideal of beauty that remained in force from the Renaissance until the Historicism of the 19th century. The restrictions of symmetry, proportion and wholeness/completeness were abandoned within 20th-century Modernism. Instead, order was maintained via the order of the module, the grid and via the order of dynamic equilibrium. In addition features like simplicity and lightness were pursued, further specifying the Modernist sense of beauty. The formal heuristics of Parametricism call for order via lawful differentiation and

---

そこに生じる矛盾は美的改革によってのみ解消される。美的改革を通じて新しい美的感覚に順応してゆくしかない。

この直近の美的改革は，ポストモダニズムと脱構築主義という過渡的エピソードを経てもたらされている。ポストモダニズムと脱構築主義は，新しい都市の多様性，変則性，そしてモダニズムの都市計画とデザインの規範の拘束から逃れ得た，自然発生的で市場主導型なプロセスの混沌としてコラージュのような複雑さを美化し始めた。パラメトリシズムが目指すのは，この自然発生的で異端児的な発達の美化にとどまることなく，ポスト・フォーディズム的ネットワーク社会の動き方に合った，急進的で新しい美的価値観や秩序原理を追求し，モダニズムが20世紀にそうしたように，21世紀の建築環境の構成とフィジオノミー(外観)の大々的なイメージチェンジを再度計画することである。

秩序概念の進化と美

ここまで，美の機能性——うまく行くものでさえあればいずれ美しいというお墨付きを得る——について立証してきた。また美的価値観の歴史的な相関性，つまり美的感覚は，歴史的に見て，最も不可欠な社会的生活プロセスの形態学的条件と(定期的に)調和させなければならない点についても立証した。美はそのフィジオノミーを変化させ続ける。美的レジームは束の間のものだ。

しかし，様々な歴史的徴候を貫き持続する特徴を，美のカテゴリーは本当に持ち得ないのだろうか？　現代の建築家たちは過去の時代の美を認めている(ただし，現代の公共施設をそういった昔のスタイルの容れ物に収めるのは不適切だと看做している)。美しいと認められた，すべての環境に(そしてすべての現象にさえ)当てはまるような，普遍的に適用可能な条件や不変的性質というものを見つけ出すのは可能なのだろうか？

そう，私はあらゆる美と醜の区別を導くような不変的側面が存在すると信じている。美の感覚はいつでも，混沌とは明らかに異なる秩序の感覚と結びついている。美の普遍的かつ不変的側面としての秩序は，これまでにも多くの古典的な美の定義の中ではのめかされてきた。例えばレオン・バッティスタ・アルベルティの有名な定義においてはこのように記されている。

> 「美とは身体のすべてのパーツの間にある筋のとおった調和であり，そこに何かを加えたり差し引いたり変化を加えたりすれば悪い方にしか向かわない」。[i]

correlation. These concepts are implemented via rule-based (algorithmic) design processes. A sense of order as distinct from chaos is maintained in all historical concretizations of the concept of beauty. Order vs chaos is thus the invariant criterion of beauty.

Chaos, the absence of any perceived order, is disorienting and thus threatening, especially if the whole environment lacks order. The effort to give order to the built environment has been a constant feature of the process of civilization.

To be navigable at all the built environment needs to be rule-based, ordered.[iv] This is a crucial aspect of its functionality. A disordered, random agglomeration of buildings and spaces cannot be navigated. Thus, in the final analysis, the hypothesis that order vs chaos is a historically invariant criterion of beauty (at least with respect to built environments) is consistent with the general insight about the nature of aesthetic values, namely that they are means for the rapid, intuitive/perceptual recognition of functionality, and as such an indispensable aspect of our cognitive constitution.

Architecture and the Societal Efficacy of the Built Environment

Now we can start to appreciate that the appearance of the built environment means something and indicates something about its functional quality. While adherence to aesthetic criteria is no guarantee of functionality, it at least gives a first indication, sufficient to justify its further approach and exploration under the presumption (hypothesis) of its functionality. In contrast, a building or urban field that fails to meet the specific aesthetic criteria (ordering principles) of its time is at least raising suspicions about its functionality. This applies to both technical and social functionality. However, architecture—in distinction to engineering—is primarily concerned with social functionality. This social functionality of the built environment is not only indicated and revealed by its appearance but crucially depends upon its legible appearance. This is so because appearances do not only work via beauty vs ugly (indicating functional vs dysfunctional), but the appearance might also relate (more or less) vital information about which specific function types and interaction scenarios might be encountered within an urban field and within the spaces and buildings that come into view. However, this is not a trivial matter that can be taken for granted.

'Social functionality' of the built environment here means its fitness for purpose, i.e. the efficient facilitation of social processes, the efficient hosting of satisfying and productive social interaction events. This requires more than efficient spatial organisation, i.e. room sizes and adjacency relations. The social functionality of the built environment requires first of all that the potential, relevant participants of all the different specific interaction events can find each other in specific locations and can self-sort into constellations conducive to the event pattern in question. In order for this to happen potential participants need to be able to orient them-

調和/秩序の肯定的な原則は「完全無欠な身体」を参照することにより強調され，単なる集塊状態と対比されている。

「調和とは建物が異質で関連性の無いパーツの寄せ集めではなく，一つの良い構図の完全な躯体として立ち現れることである」。[ii]

これはさらに醜の暗黙の定義ととれる，その反対の否定として説明されている。構成とは，

「飛び飛びだったり混乱していたり乱雑であったり一貫性整合性がなかったり，不調和な要素で構成されていてはならない（……）身体の他の部分とバラバラであったり，離れすぎていてはいけないものである」。[iii]

アルベルティは「あらゆるパーツの調和」という言い方で，秩序について言及する。これは非常に大雑把で抽象的な公式として容認することができる。ただ，彼の完全であることへのこだわり，つまり何も加えたり差し引いたり変えたりしてはならないという主張は古典主義建築特有のもので，美の普遍的かつ不変的特徴であるとはもはや言い難い。プロポーションに関する厳格なルールとシンメトリー，そして加えることも差し引くことも許さない，完全で完璧な状態を持つアルベルティの有機的な統一体という概念は，ルネッサンス期から19世紀の歴史主義までの間に勢力を保っていた一般的な美の理想型を表すものである。シンメトリーやプロポーション，完全性/完璧性の制限は20世紀モダニズムの間に捨て去られた。その代わりにモジュールの秩序，グリッド，そして動的な平衡によって秩序は維持された。加えてシンプルさや軽さといった特性が追求され，モダニズムの美的感覚をさらに明確にしていった。パラメトリシズムの形式的なヒューリスティクスは，規則に適った差異化や相関性というかたちで秩序を求めた。こういった概念は，規則に基づく（アルゴリズム的な）デザイン過程によって実行される。混沌とは全く異なる秩序の感覚が，すべての歴史的な美の概念の具体化において維持されている。秩序vs混沌とは，すなわち美の不変的な基準である。

混沌，知覚できる秩序の欠如は混乱を招き，特に環境全体が秩序に欠ける場合は脅威となる。建築環境に秩序を与えようとする努力は，文明の過程から一度も姿を消すことがなかった。

まずもって操縦可能であるために，建築環境は，規則に基づいたもの，秩序あるものでなければならない。[iv] それは機能性の極めて重要な側面である。建物や空間の無秩序でランダムな凝集は舵取りすることができない。従って，最終的な分析としては，秩序vsカオスが歴史的に不変な美の基準であるとする仮説（少な

selves successfully and efficiently within the built environment. A key criterion for this is the visual articulation and legibility of the built environment. This insight leads us to reject the common place opposition between appearance and performance or representation and operation. Instead we arrive at the formula performance through appearance or operation through representation. This also motivates my thesis: all design is communication design.

The built environment, with its complex matrix of territorial distinctions, is a giant, navigable, information-rich interface of communication. Society can only exist and evolve with the simultaneous ordering of space. There is no and never has been a human society without a built, artificial habitat, just as their does not exist a human society without language. Both are required to make social cooperation possible. The elaboration of a built environment (however haphazard, precarious, and initially based on accident rather than purpose and intention) seems to be a necessary condition for the build-up of any stable social order. The gradual build-up of larger, structured social groups must go hand in hand with the gradual build-up of an artificial spatial order; social order requires spatial order. The social process needs the built environment as a plane of inscription where it can leave traces that then serve to build-up and stabilize social structures, which in turn allow the further elaboration of more complex social processes. The spatial order of the human habitat is both an immediate physical organizing apparatus that separates and connects social actors and their activities, and a material substrate for the inscription of an external "societal memory." These "inscriptions" might at first be an unintended side effect of the various activities. Spatial arrangements are functionally adapted and elaborated. They are then marked and underlined by ornaments, which make them more conspicuous. The result is the gradual build-up of a spatio-morphological system of signification. Thus, a semantically charged built environment emerges that provides a differentiated system of settings to help social actors orient themselves with respect to the different communicative situations constituting the social life-process of society. Only on this basis, with this new material substrate upon which the evolutionary mechanisms of mutation, selection, and reproduction could operate, was the evolution of mankind out of the animal kingdom, and all further cultural evolution, possible. Thus, the built environment, as the cross-generationally stable, material substrate of the cultural evolution, acts functionally equivalent to the DNA as the material substrate of the biological evolution.

The importance of the built environment for ordering and framing society remains undiminished. However, what, in former times, was left to the slow evolutionary process of trial and error has, since the Renaissance, become more and more the domain of competency and responsibility of the specialized discourse and profession of the discipline of architecture. During the Renaissance a consciously innovative theory-led design discipline equipped with a compelling system of drawings (including perspective) displaced the

---

くとも建築環境に関して)は，美的価値の性質についての一般的な見識，すなわちそれが即時的で直感/知覚的認識の手段であり，それ自体が人の認知構成に不可欠な側面であることと矛盾しない。

建築と建築環境の社会的効率

私たちはようやく，建築環境の外観はなにがしかの意味を持ち，その機能の質について示唆するものだと評価することができる。美的基準の遵守が機能性を保証するものではないにしろ，少なくとも最初の兆候を見せ，その機能性という前提(仮定)の元での更なるアプローチと探求を正当化するに十分である。対照的に，同時代の特定の美的基準(秩序のための原則)を満たさない建物や都市的領域は，少なくともその機能性についての疑念をもたらす。これは技術的・社会的な機能性についても同様である。しかし，建築土木と区別して——は本来社会的機能性と関係しているものである。この建築環境の社会的機能性は，単にその外観によって示唆され解明されるだけでなく，その判読可能な外観に極めて多くを依存している。というのも，外観とは，単に美vs醜(機能的vs機能不全を示す)という問題にとどまらないからだ。外観は，都市領域内で視界に入る空間や建物の中で，どのタイプの機能や相関シナリオに遭遇するのかという極めて重要な情報にも(大なり小なり)関係する。そしてこれを些細で当たり前のことと思ってはいけない。

ここでの建築環境の「社会的機能性」とは，いかにそれが目的に適ったものであるか，つまり社会的プロセスを効率良く円滑にし，生産的かつ満足のいく社会的相互作用イベントを効率的に主催するという意味であり，部屋のサイズや近接関係といった効率的な空間構成以上のものを必要とする。建築環境の社会的機能性が必要とするのは何よりもまず，すべての様々な特定相互作用イベントに関連する参加者たちがそれぞれ特定の場所で出会い，該当イベントに貢献するような集合体へと自発的に分かれていくことである。そのためには参加者たちは，建築環境内においてうまく効率よく自分で動ける必要がある。そこで鍵となるのが，建築環境の判読可能な視覚的明瞭さである。この本質を見抜くことで，私たちは，外観と性能あるいは表現と実務というありがちな対比を捨て去ることになる代わりに「外観による性能」あるいは「表現による実務」という公式に辿り着く。またこれは私の論題「すべてのデザインはコミュニケーションのデザインである」の原動力となるものでもある。

former tradition-bound building. I call this the big bang of architecture. I consider the Gothic era effecting the transition from tradition bound building to architecture proper. Since then an accelerating succession of architectural styles—Renaissance, Mannerism, Baroque, Rococo, Neo-classicism, Historicism, Eccleticism, Art Noveau, Modernism, Postmodernism, Deconstructivism, Parametricism—has taken charge of the innovation of the built environment in its adaptive coevolution with the historical transformations of European and then World society. In the most general abstract terms the evolutionary trajectory of world civilisation has been an increase in the overall level of societal differentiation or complexity. Each major historical (epochal) transformation implied adaptive transformations in the morphology of the built environment which in turn required aesthetic revolutions, the relearning of the aesthetic sensibilities and values of both designers and end-users.

Parametricism—
Candidate Epochal Style for the 21st Century??
Many have come to believe that the pluralism of styles and perspectives that emerged in the 1970s and 1980s—Postmodernism, High-Tech modernism, Deconstructivism, Neo-historicism, Minimalism—is an inherent and inevitable characteristic of our epoch, and that a globally shared architectural agenda analogous to the modern movement is no longer possible. Against this stands the fact that a global convergence of design research efforts has gathered sufficient momentum within the architectural avant-garde over the last 15 years to make the emergence of a new unified paradigm and agenda in analogy to modernism plausible today. Six years ago I proposed a name for this movement—parametricism—and started my attempts to summarize its novel features, methodologies, and values. As a committed participant I also tried to explicate its rationality, advantages, and preliminary achievements in the light of the current 'historical' condition: the globalized, knowledge- and network society. Due to the 2008 financial crisis and its economic aftermath—the great recession—the proliferation of parametricism has been much slower than one might have expected six years ago. However, further progress has been made in the movement's evolution from an (ongoing) avant-garde design research agenda to a movement with the strategic agenda of global implementation across all scales and programme categories. At least this is the author's ambition. Its viability is demonstrated by the dramatic expansion of Zaha Hadid Architects in scale, scope and global reach.[v]

Is this ambition and claim towards the global implementation of the new paradigm not contradicted by the diversity of climatic, socio-economic, and cultural conditions? My answer to this often posed question is that differentiation and local adaptation is the very essence of parametricism. The abstractness and thus open-endedness of its general principles guarantee the adaptive versatility of its solution space. While the world is more diverse and differ-

地域性の差異という複雑なマトリックスを持つ建築環境は，巨大かつナビゲーション可能な，情報豊かなコミュニケーションのインターフェイスである。同時進行的な空間の秩序化なくして社会は存在・進化できない。言語を持たない人間社会が存在しないのと同様に，人工的に建てられた居住環境を持たない人間社会など後にも先にも存在しない。どちらも社会的協調を実現するために必要なものなのだ。建築環境の整備は（いくら無計画でいい加減で，当初は目的や意図はなく偶然の産物であったとしても）安定した社会的秩序を築く上で必要な条件となる。大型で構造化された社会的集団を築き上げるには，それと連動して人工的な空間的秩序をも築き上げなければならない。社会的秩序には空間的秩序が必要なのだ。社会のプロセスは，碑文を刻む面としての建築環境を必要とする。そこに残される痕跡が社会的構造を築き，安定化させ，より複雑な社会的プロセスの更なる整備を可能とする。人間の居住環境の空間的秩序は，社会の当事者たちとその活動を結びつけたり分離させたりする，即時的な物理的組織化の装置であると同時に，外部からの「社会の記憶」を刻み付ける物質的基板である。こういった「碑文」は，最初はさまざまな活動の意図せぬ副作用に見えるだろう。機能的に適用され整備される空間の配置は，やがてそれが目立つようなマーキングやアンダーラインで飾り付けられる。その結果，意味の空間形態学的システムが徐々に構築される。このように，意味性を帯びた建築環境が立ち現れ，社会的生活プロセスを構成する様々なコミュニケーションの状況と関連して，社会の当事者たちが自分の位置を確認できるような，分化した環境システムを供する。これに基づいて，変異・淘汰・再生の進化メカニズムが可能となる新たな物質的基板のおかげで，人類が動物界を離れ，その後も進化し続けることが可能となった。つまり文化的進化において，世代を越えて安定した物質的基板としての建築環境は，生物学的進化の物質的基板であるDNAに相当する機能を有しているのだ。

社会を秩序化し組み立てる上での建築環境の重要性は揺るぎないものであるが，昔であれば試行錯誤の緩やかな進化プロセスに委ねられていたのが，ルネッサンス以降，ますます建築という分野に特化した話法や専門職の能力や責任の領域へと入り込んできている。ルネッサンス期には，説得力あるドローイングのシステム（パースペクティヴを含む）を身につけた意識的に革新的な理論先導のデザイン分野が，それまでの伝統に縛られた建築に取って代わった。私はこれを建築ビッグバンと呼んでいる。また，ゴシッ

entiated—across countries and continents as well as within its mega-cities—it also is more interconnected and integrated than ever, so that talk of a single world society becomes ever more justified. Thus no region, culture or subculture can remain secluded from the most advanced, global best practice architectural paradigm.

The key historical category that motivates and calls for parametricism's take over from modernism is 'post-fordist network society' as distinct from the prior era of fordist mass society. In *The Autopoiesis of Architecture* the author has elaborated a theory of styles within which the concept of epochal styles implies a historical alignment with societal (socio-economic) epochs. As indicated above, architecture emerged from tradition bound building as differentiated, consciously innovative, theory-led discipline in the Renaissance and advanced via the progression of epochal styles, in co-evolution with the other societal subsystems like science, the economy, politics etc. that started to be differentiated at the same time. The epochal location of parametricism can be succinctly characterized by the following table. (Postmodernism and Deconstructivism are not featured because they are transitional rather than epochal styles, transitional episodes between Modernism and Parametricism, like Art Nouveau and Expressionism were transitional styles on the way to Modernism.)[vi] *(fig.1, 2)*

Parametricism is the contemporary style that is most vigorously advancing its design agenda on the basis of computationally augmented, parametric design techniques. It is a wide-spread paradigm and global movement within con-

	Building/Architecture	Society/Socio-Economic epoch
Tradition-Bound Building	Medieval vernacular	feudalism
	Romanesque	feudalism
Transition	Gothic	feudalism + rising cities
Architectural History: Epochal Styles	Renaissance	early capitalism / city states
	Baroque	mercantilism/absolutism
	Neo-Classicism/ Historicism	bourgeois capitalism, nations-states
	Modernism	fordism/international socialism
	Parametricism	global, post-fordist network society

	建物/建築	社会/社会経済上の時代区分
伝統に縛られた建物	中世ヴァナキュラー	封建主義
	ロマネスク	封建主義
過渡期	ゴシック	封建主義+都市の台頭
建築史：時代のスタイル	ルネッサンス	初期資本主義/都市国家
	バロック	重商主義/絶対主義
	新古典主義/歴史主義	ブルジョワ資本主義, 国民国家
	モダニズム	フォード主義/国際的社会主義
	パラメトリシズム	グローバル, ポスト・フォーディズム的ネットワーク社会

fig.1 Epochal alignments of styles　時代別スタイルの位置付け

ク期が伝統に縛られた建築から真の建築への転換をもたらしたとも見ている。以来, ルネッサンス, マニエリスム, バロック, ロココ, 新古典主義, 歴史主義, 折衷主義, アールヌーヴォー, モダニズム, ポストモダニズム, 脱構築主義, パラメトリシズムといった一連の建築様式の矢継ぎ早の台頭は, ヨーロッパに続き, 世界における歴史的変遷との適応的共進化について, 建築環境の革新を担ってきたのだ。最も一般的な抽象的意味において世界文明の進化の軌跡とは, 社会的差異あるいは複雑さの全体的なレベルの底上げであった。主要(その時代において画期的)な歴史的転換はどれも, 建築環境の形態学の適応的転換と引き換えに必要となった美的改革や, デザイナーとエンドユーザーの双方による美的感覚と価値観の再学習, という意味合いを含んでいた。

パラメトリシズム——21世紀の新時代的スタイル候補として
1970年代と1980年代に出現したスタイルとパースペクティヴの多元主義——ポストモダニズム, ハイテク・モダニズム, 脱構築主義, 新歴史主義, ミニマリズム——は私たちの時代の先天的かつ不可避な特徴であり, 現代のムーブメントと類似した, 世界規模で共有される建築的アジェンダなどは, もはや不可能であると考えるようになった者は多い。これに対抗するのは, 世界規模でのまとまったデザイン研究努力が, ここ15年ほどの建築アバンギャルドにおいて今日有望と思われるモダニズムと類似する新しい統一パラダイム, ならびにアジェンダを生むほどの気運を高めたという事実である。6年前, 私はこのムーブメントをパラメトリシズムと名付けることを提案し, 今までにない特徴・方法論・価値観をまとめる試みを始めた。このムーブメントに携わる者として現在の「歴史的」条件の観点からその合理性やアドバンテージ, そして予備段階での成果, すなわちグローバル化された知識とネットワーク社会について詳説することも試みてきた。2008年の金融危機とその経済的後遺症——大規模不況——のせいでパラメトリシズムの拡散は, 6年前に期待していたよりも大幅に遅くなってしまったものの, ムーブメントの進化には, (現行の)アヴァンギャルドなデザイン研究アジェンダから全スケールおよびプログラム・カテゴリーを横断するグローバルな導入を目指す戦略的アジェンダへ, という展開が見られつつある。少なくとも, それが筆者の抱いている人望である。その実行可能性は, ザハ・ハディド・アーキテクツのスケール, 影響力そして国際性の上での劇的な拡大が証明している。[v]

The Instrumentality of Appearances in the Pursuit of a Legible Urban Order

fig.2 Parametricism: Zaha Hadid Architects,
Istanbul Masterplan, 2007
パラメトリシズム：ザハ・ハディド・アーキテクツ，
イスタンブール基本計画．2007

temporary architecture that emerged and gathered momentum during the last 15 years. The author is an active participant in the advancement of this movement via teaching arenas like the AA Design Research Lab and via the designs and buildings of Zaha Hadid Architects. The movement—the only truly innovative direction within contemporary architecture—has by now sufficiently demonstrated its capacity to credibly aspire to become the universally recognized best practice approach to architectural and urban design globally. Parametricism is ready to make an impact: to transform the physiognomy of the global built environment and the totality of the world of designed artefacts, just like modernism did in the 20th century.

From Visual Chaos
to Urban Order as Interface of Communication
Since 1980 we live in the era of a market-led post-fordist socio-economic restructuring. The re-admission of international market forces and entrepreneurship combusted with the versatile productive potentials of the micro-electronic revolution to unleash a new socio-economic dynamic: the emergence of post-fordist network society. Life-style diversification and the new diversity in products and services made economically viable by the new design and production systems engaged in mutual amplification. The diversity of new enterprises coupled with accelerating cylcles of innovation (made viable by the new technologies and expanded

　この新パラダイムの世界的導入への野望と主張は，気候や社会経済，そして文化的条件とは矛盾しないのだろうか？　投げかけられることの多いこの疑問に対する私の答えは，差別化とローカル適応化こそが，パラメトリシズムの本質そのものであるということ。その一般原則の抽象性，すなわち無制約であるさまは，解として導かれる空間の適応柔軟性を保証する。世界は今までになく多様で分化している——国や大陸間，そして巨大都市内においても——一方でより相互連携され統合もされているため，たった一つの世界社会について語ることは，今まで以上に理に適ったことになってきている。従って，いかなる地域も文化もサブカルチャーも，最先端かつ最良事例である建築パラダイムと無関係でいることはできないのだ。

　パラメトリシズムがモダニズムに取って代わるきっかけとなる歴史上のカテゴリーは，それ以前のフォード主義的マス社会の時代とははっきり異なる「ポスト・フォーディズム的ネットワーク社会」である。『建築のオートポイエーシス』の中で，筆者は，時代のスタイルという概念が社会（社会経済）の時代区分の歴史的調整という意味を含む，スタイル論について詳細に述べている。上述のように建築は，ルネッサンス期の伝統に縛られた建物から分化して意識的に革新的で理論先導の分野へと生まれ変わり，諸時代に特有なスタイルの連続を通じて，同時に分化を始めた科学，経済，政治といった他の社会の下位システムの進化と共に進歩を遂げた。以下の表は，各時代におけるパラメトリシズムの位置付けについて簡潔にまとめたものである。（ポストモダニズムと脱構築主義について触れていないのは，どちらも時代を代表するスタイルというよりも過渡的なもの，つまりアールヌーヴォーと表現主義がモダニズムへの道の途中に現れる過渡的スタイルであるのと同様に，モダニズムからパラメトリシズムに至るまでの間に起きた過渡的な出来事であるためである。[vi]）[fig.1,2参照]

　パラメトリシズムは，コンピュータを用い増強されたパラメトリックなデザイン技術を基にしたデザイン指針を，最も積極的に推し進めている現代的スタイルである。現代建築の世界においてここ15年の間に出現し，勢いを増してきた世界規模のムーブメントであり，幅広い支持を受けているパラダイムである。筆者は，AAスクールのデザイン・リサーチ・ラボといった教育の場やザハ・ハディド・アーキテクツのデザインや建築物などを通して，このムーブメントの発展に積極的に加わっている。現代建築における真に革新的な唯一の方向性といえるこのムーブメントは，これまで十分に建築と都市デザインに対する最良の実践アプローチであると，グロー

markets) engendered a much differentiated and intensified societal communication. The planned decentralization via mute, monotonous, zoned satellite settlements separating sleeping silos from industrial estates was no longer a viable recipe for societal advancement. In terms of urban development this implied the return to the historic centres with individual incisions as well as a deregulated, laissez faire sprawling beyond the bounds of emerging mega-cities.[vii] Both tendencies can be described as forms of collage, the anti-thesis of planned or designed development. The result is what I have called garbage spill urbanisation. Deconstructivism was the attempt to sublimate and aestheticize this new vital urban phenomenon. *(fig.3)*

This free-wheeling, chaotic mode of development is certainly better adapted to the new socio-economic dynamics than the bankrupt, simplistic order of modernist planning and urbanism. However, it produces a disorienting visual chaos that compromises the vital communicative capacity of the built environment. While the new diversity and open-endedness of post-fordist social phenomena is being accommodated, the unregulated agglomeration of differences produced the global effect of white noise sameness everywhere without allowing for the emergence of distinct urban identities within a legible urban order. While laissez faire development can deliver a socially (market) validated program mix and program distribution, it seems bound to produce visual chaos in the urban dimension. This visual disorder is not only ugly and distracting, it is disorienting and thus compromises the social functionality of the built environment.

The phenomenological disarticulation of the emergent organisational complexity hampers the full potential for complex social organisation and communication. The articulation of a legible spatial order—the architect's core competency—is itself a vital aspect not only of the city's liveability but also of its economic productivity. Social functionality depends as much on subjective visual accessibility as it depends on objective physical availability. Architects

fig.3 Deconstructivist sublimation of urban collage, Zaha Hadid paitings, 1983, 1986
都市コラージュの脱構築主義的昇華、ザハ・ハディド画、1983、1986

バルかつ普遍的に認められることを確実に目指すに足る能力を示してきた。パラメトリシズムは、モダニズムが20世紀にそうであったように、グローバルな建築環境と人工物のデザインの世界全般の外観を変えるほどの影響をすぐにでも及ぼすことができる。

視覚的カオスから
コミュニケーションのインターフェイスとしての都市的秩序へ

1980年以来、私たちは市場先導型のポスト・フォーディズム的社会経済の再編の時代を生きている。国際的な市場原理と起業家精神を再び受け入れたことで、マイクロエレクトロニクス革命の多彩な生産的ポテンシャルが燃え上がり、ポスト・フォーディズム的ネットワーク社会の出現という新しい社会経済の原動力を解き放った。新しいデザインと生産システムにより、経済的に実行可能となったプロダクトやサービスにおける新しい多様性とライフスタイルの多様化が、相互拡大に共に取り組むようになった。新興事業の多様性に加え、イノベーションサイクルの加速(新しい技術と市場拡大のおかげで実行可能となった)が非常に分化、そして強化された社会的コミュニケーションを生み出した。単調で変化の少ないゾーン分けされた衛星住宅地として、工業地帯とベッドタウンを隔離する分散化計画は、もはや社会の発展のレシピたりえなくなっていた。都市開発においてこれは、個別の切り口や新興メガシティの境界線を越えた無秩序で自由放任な広がり、そして歴史的な中央市街地への回帰を意味していた。[vii] どちらの傾向も計画、もしくはデザインされた開発のアンチテーゼ、つまり一種のコラージュであると言える。結果、私が「ゴミ箱からあふれた都市化」と呼ぶものだ。脱構築主義とはこの新しく活き活きとした都市的現象を昇華し美化しようとする試みであった。[fig.3参照]

この自由奔放でカオス的な発展モードが、破綻した単純すぎるモダニスト的プランニングやアーバニズムよりも新しい社会経済的ダイナミクスによほど適合しているのは確かなのだが、方向感覚を失わせるような視覚的カオスを招き、建築環境に不可欠なコミュニケーション能力を犠牲にしてしまう。ポスト・フォーディズム的社会現象の新しい多様性と制限のない自由さが受け入れられつつある一方で、無法状態の差異の凝集が、判読可能な都市秩序内にはっきりとした都市的アイデンティティが出現しないままに、どこも同じようなホワイトノイズというグローバルな効果を生んでしまう。放任主義的開発が社会的(市場的)に有効な混合プログラムとプログ

The Instrumentality of Appearances in the Pursuit of a Legible Urban Order

should recognize this instrumentality of visual appearances as a key moment of their core competency and task. Social cooperation requires that specifically relevant actors find each other and configure within specific communicative situations. This insight motivates architectural attempts to articulate a complex variegated urban order that allows for the intuitive navigation and orientation within an information-rich built environment that makes its rich offerings visually accessible. That is the design agenda of parametricism and parametric urbanism. There is no doubt that the new computational ordering devices like gradients, vector fields, and the methods of associative modelling and geometric data-field transcoding allow designers to generate intricately ordered urban morphologies with distinct identities that could in principle make a much larger amount of programmatic information perceptually tractable.

While Deconstructivism was celebrating, sublimating and aestheticizing urban chaos, Parametricism is attempting to once more transform the morphology and aesthetics of the built environment, not by trying to arrest, mute or deny the complexity of postfordist network society—as minimalism tries—but by trying to organize and articulate societal complexity via its new computationally empowered formal ordering capacities. The failure to grasp the instrumentality of the built environment's appearance has for too long hampered the architecture's proactive pursuit of formal articulation as a key competency of the discipline. The crucial work on formal/aesthetic problems which in practice takes up the larger part of the architect's design work is being denigrated or denied in the discipline's self-descriptions. Architecture is responsible for the built environments social (rather than technical engineering) functionality. Social functionality of the built environment largely depends upon its communicative capacity, which in turn is a matter of visual communication.

The city is a complex, densely layered text and a permanent broadcast. Our ambition as architects and urban designers must be to spatially unfold more simultaneous choices of communicative situations in dense, perceptually palpable, and legible arrangements. The visual field must be rich in interaction opportunities and information about what lies behind the immediate field of vision. *(fig.4)*

fig.4 Zaha Hadid Architects, Gallaxy SOHO, Beijing China, 2012
ザハ・ハディド・アーキテクツ, 銀河SOHO, 中国, 北京, 2012

ラム分布をもたらすことができる一方で, 都市的ディメンションにおける視覚的カオスを生んでしまう運命にもあるようだ。この視覚的無秩序は醜く目をそらしたくなるだけでなく, 方向感覚を失わせるため, 建築環境の社会的機能を犠牲にしてしまうことになる。

そこに発生した組織化する複雑性の現象学的離断は, 複雑な社会的組織とコミュニケーションへの可能性を全面的に妨害する。判読可能な空間的秩序の明確さ——建築家において核となる職能——はそれ自体, 都市の居住性だけでなく経済的生産性にとっても不可欠なものである。社会の機能は主体の視覚的アクセシビリティと同じくらい客観的な物理的利用可能性にも左右される。建築家は視覚的外観という手段が自らの核となる職能と課題にとって, 最も重要な局面にあるということを認識せねばならない。社会的協調には, 特に関連ある当事者たちが互いに出会うことができ, 特定のコミュニケーション状況の中に構成される必要がある。この本質の理解が, 建築環境内で, 提供された情報量の豊かさを視覚的にアクセス可能とする直感的なナビゲーションと方向付けを見越した, 複雑で変化に富んだ秩序を明確にする建築的試行の意欲をかき立てるのだ。それがパラメトリックなアーバニズムとパラメトリシズムのデザイン指針である。疑いの余地もなく, グラデーションやベクトル場といったコンピュータによる新しい秩序化装置や, 結合モデリングの方法と幾何学的データフィールドのトランスコーディングによって, デザイナーは, 原理上では遥かに多くのプログラム情報を知覚的に扱い易くすることのできる明確なアイデンティティを持ち, 複雑に秩序化された都市的形態学を生成することができるのだ。

脱構築主義が都市的カオスを祝い, 昇華し, 美化している間にも, パラメトリシズムは, ポスト・フォーディスム的ネットワーク社会の複雑性を阻んだり, 弱めたり, 否定しよう——ミニマリズムがそうしようとしているように——とするのではなく, コンピュータが後押しするその新しい形式的秩序化能力を通して社会の複雑性を組織し明確にしようとすることで, 建築環境の形態学と美学を今再び変換させようと試みている。建築環境の外観が持つ媒介としての力を把握し損ねたことで, あまりに長きに渡り, 建築の分野における最も重要な職能としての形式的明確さの先見的な追求が阻まれてきた。建築家のデザイン実務の大部分を占める形式的/美的問題についての極めて重要な仕事は, この分野の自己記述性において中傷, あるいは否定されてきている。建築は建築環境の社会的機能性についての責任を負う。建築環境の社会的機能

The simultaneous enhancement of freedom and order: inversion of architecture's entropy law

My thesis is that the built environment should be conceived and designed as a three-dimensional, 360 degree, layered interface of communication. It can communicate the more the more becomes simultaneously visible. But that is not enough. Its communicative capacity depends on the coherency of its internal order so that what is visible allows for inferences about what is invisible or not yet visible. This depends on the consistency of its form-function correlations, so that a positional or morphological distinction or differ-

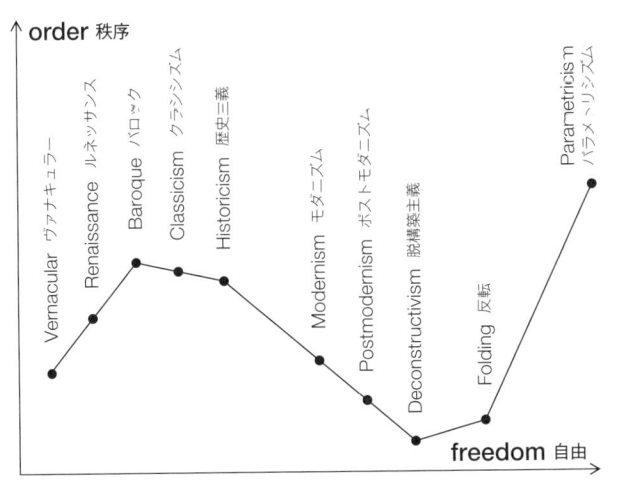

fig.5 The simultaneous enhancement of freedom and order: inversion of architecture's entropy law
自由と秩序の同時充実：建築のエントロピー法則の逆転

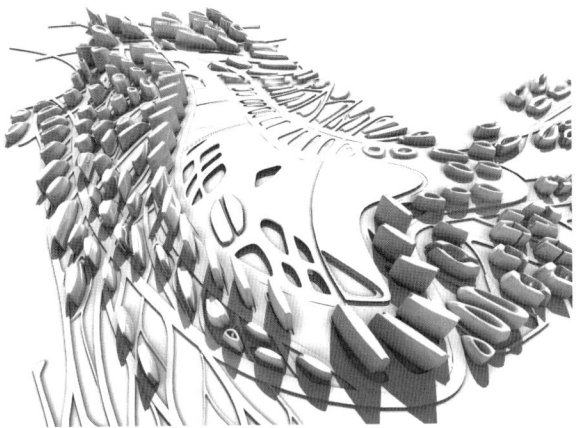

fig.6 Parametricism: Energy Research Campus, Ryad (above), Zaha Hadid Architects Masterplans for Appur (below)
パラメトリシズム：エネルギー・リサーチ・キャンパス、リヤド（上）、ザハ・ハディド・アーキテクツ イスタンブール基本計画、アップール（下）

性は、その多くをそのコミュニケーション能力に依っており、それはまた視覚的コミュニケーションの問題でもある。

都市とは複雑で何層にも重なったテクストであり、永続的な発信源である。建築家、そして都市デザイナーとしての我々の大望は、高密度で知覚的に明白かつ判読可能な配置の中に、より多くのコミュニケーション状況の同時選択肢を空間的に展開することであるに違いない。視覚的フィールドには豊富な相互交流の機会と、目の前の視野の裏に控えている情報が豊富に揃えられていなければならない。[fig.4参照]

自由と秩序の同時充実：建築のエントロピーの法則の反転
私が提唱するのは、建築環境がコミュニケーションの3次元的・全方向的階層のインターフェイスとして考案され設計されるべきであるという命題である。同時に視覚化されればされるほど、より多くをコミュニケートできるのだが、それでは十分ではない。そのコミュニケーション能力は、目に見えるものが、目に見えないものあるいはまだ不可視なものの推測を許すよう、内的秩序の整合性に左右される。これはフォルムと機能間の相関関係の一貫性に依る

ところであり、位置あるいは形態の区別や違いが、期待される社会的相互作用パターンあるいは社会的機能という意味で予想可能な差異を生む。

パラメトリシズムは自由と秩序を同時に充実させるものである。そこで、現在進行中の建築とアーバニズムのエントロピー増大の反転について、つまり、この300年間、建築の秩序立てる能力が衰退してきた軌跡の逆転についてそろそろ述べることにしよう。[fig.5参照]

脱構築主義を、「あふれたゴミ箱」というコラージュの都市プロセスの美的イデオロギーとして見ることもできる。古典的建築からモダニズムへの移行と同様に、モダニズムから脱構築主義とコラージュへの移行は、自由と汎用性の度合いの拡大（より複雑な社会を提供するべく）をもたらすと同時に、構成ルール、すなわち秩序化の手段の緩和あるいは棄却、その結果として視覚的秩序の衰退という対価を支払った。パラメトリシズムは連携、勾配、連想論理といった新しい構成ルールを通して、その秩序化能力の同時向上と連動したさらなる自由度と汎用性をもたらす初めてのスタイルである。原理上では、現在あらゆるデザイン動向はルールに基づくものであり、従って視覚的秩序、つまり高まる複雑さに直面した建築

ence makes a predictable difference in terms of expected social interaction pattern or social function. *(fig.5)*

Parametricism delivers the simultaneous enhancement of freedom and order. We might speak of the inversion of architecture and urbanism's ongoing entropy, i.e. the inversion of architecture's 300 year trajectory of the degeneration of its ordering capacity.

Deconstructivism can be looked at as the aesthetic ideology of this urban process of "garbage spill" collage. Like the move from classical architecture to modernism, the move from modernism to deconstructivism and collage delivered an expansion of degrees of freedom and versatility (to accommodate a more complex society) that was paid for by a relaxation or rejection of rules of composition, i.e. of means of ordering, and thus a resultant degeneration of the visual order. Parametricism is the first style that delivers further degrees of freedom and versatility in conjunction with a simultaneous increase in its ordering capacity via new compositional rules like affiliations, gradients and associative logics. In principle all design moves are now rule based and thus with the potential to enhance the visual order and thus legibility of the built environment in the face of an increased complexity. *(fig.6)*

If we look at the historical progression of styles we find that the last 300 years established architecture's entropy law: all gains in terms of design freedom and versatility have been achieved at the expense of urban and architectural order, i.e. increases in versatility had to be bought by a progressive degeneration of architecture's ordering capacity. The increase of degrees of freedom established via the enrichment of architecture's formal-compositional repertoire was the paramount criterion of progress in architecture's pursuit of matching the requisite variety of societal complexity. Order was progressively eroded. This long trend of a negative correlation of freedom and order can be reversed under the auspices of parametricism. Parametricism offers the simultaneous increase in freedom and order and thus inaugurates a new phase of architectural neg-entropy. Parametricism's radical ontological and methodological innovation translates into a massive leap in both dimensions of architectural progress considered here, i.e. it entails an unprecedented expansion of architecture's compositional freedom and versatility and an unprecedented leap in architecture's ordering capacity through the deployment of algorithms and associative logics. This reversal of architecture's entropy law, this new ordering capacity or architectural neg-entropy is the critical factor in architecture's potential to halt the ongoing urban disarticulation of the world's built environments. However, this factor can only come into play if parametricism achieves hegemony as the unified, epochal style of the 21st century.

Neither a hegemonic Postmodernism, nor a hegemonic Deconstructivism could overcome the visual chaos that allows the proliferation of differences to collapse into global sameness (white noise). Both Postmodernism and Deconstructivism operate via collage, i.e. via the unconstrained

---

環境の判読可能性を高める潜在能力を秘めている。[fig.6参照]

スタイルの発展の歴史を見てみると，ここ300年の間に建築のエントロピーの法則が確立されたことがわかる。すなわち，デザインの自由さと汎用性という側面で得られたものはすべて，都市的そして建築的秩序の負担によるもの，つまり汎用性の向上は，建築の秩序化能力が衰退していくことと引き換えに得られたものであった。建築の形式／構成レパートリーの強化による自由度の向上は，建築が社会的複雑性の多様化という要件を満たすことを追求する中で最も優先される基準であった。秩序は段々と浸食されていった。パラメトリシズムの仲介により，この長きにわたった自由と秩序のネガティブな相関関係の傾向を覆すことが可能となる。パラメトリシズムは自由と秩序の同時充実をもたらし，建築的な負のエントロピーの新たなフェーズを開く。パラメトリシズムの急進的で存在論的かつ方法論的な革新は，ここで論じられる建築的発展の両側面における大きな飛躍へと変換される。すなわち，アルゴリズムや連想論理の配備により，建築の構成的自由と，汎用性の前例のない拡張と，建築の秩序化能力における前例のない飛躍を引き起こすのだ。この建築のエントロピーの法則の逆転，新しい秩序化能力あるいは建築的な負のエントロピーは，世界における現在進行中の建築環境の都市的離断を，建築が止めるという可能性にとって重大な因子である。しかし，この因子が力を発揮できるのはパラメトリシズムが21世紀の時代を代表する統一スタイルとしてヘゲモニーを確立する場合だけだ。

覇権主義的ポストモダニズムも覇権主義的脱構築主義も，差異の増殖がグローバルな類似（ホワイトノイズ）に倒れ込むのを許すような視覚的カオスを打開することができなかった。ポストモダニズムと脱構築主義はどちらもコラージュによって，すなわち制約のない差異の凝集によって運用されている。パラメトリシズムだけが，多重システムの相関関係と規則に沿った分化の原則による複雑性の増大と，秩序の同時向上を組み合わせる能力を有している。パラメトリシズムは，放任主義的都市化が至る所で生み出している視覚的カオスとの類似というホワイトノイズを打開することができるのだ。パラメトリシズムはボトムアップなプロセスで，つまり政治的あるいは官僚的な権力に頼ることなく新興の秩序とローカルなアイデンティティを産出する新しいアーバニズムへの可能性を残すものである。パラメトリシズムの判断基準と方法論的原則は，先行する状態に依存し，ローカルな性質の自己増幅を生み出す傾向がある。この文脈的連携と，連続性を確立，強化するという活力のエートスは，

agglomeration of differences. Only Parametricism has the capacity to combine an increase in complexity with a simultaneous increase in order, via the principles of lawful differentiation and multi-system correlation. Parametricism can overcome the visual chaos and white noise sameness that laissez faire urbanisation produces everywhere. Parametricism holds out the possibility of a new urbanism that produces an emergent order and local identity in a bottom up process, i.e. without relying on political or bureaucratic power. The values and methodological principles of parametricism are prone to produce path-dependent, self-amplifying local identities. Its ethos of contextual affiliation and ambition to establish or reinforce continuities allows for the development of unique urban identities on the basis of local contexts, topography, climate etc. Parametricist order does not rely on the uniform repetition of patterns as Modernist urbanism does. In contrast to Baroque or Beaux Arts master-plans, Parametricist compositions are inherently open ended (incomplete) compositions. Their order is relational rather than geometric. They establish order and orientation via the lawful differentiation of fields, via vectors of transformation, as well as via contextual affiliations and sub-system correlations. This neither requires the completion of a figure, nor—in contrast to Modernist master-plans—the uniform repetition of a pattern. There are always many (in principle infinitely many) creative ways to transform, to affiliate, to correlate. Parametricism thus holds out the prospect of a post-fordist urban order.

ローカルな文脈，地形，気候などに基づく固有の都市アイデンティティを生み出すことを可能にする。パラメトリシズム的秩序はモダニズム的アーバニズムとは異なり，同じようなパターンの繰り返しに依存しない。バロックやボザールの基本計画とは対照的に，パラメトリシズム的構成は本質的に終わりのない（不完全な）構成である。それらの秩序は幾何学的というよりも相関的で，諸分野の規則に沿った差異化により変換のベクトルや文脈上の連携とサブシステムの関連性を通して秩序と方向性を決めるものである。これは，形状の完成も同じようなパターンの繰り返し——モダニズムの基本計画とは対照的に——も必要としない。そこには常に多くの（原理上では無限に多くの）変換，連携，相関についてのクリエイティブなやり方がある。パラメトリシズムは，ポスト・フォーディズム的都市的秩序の可能性を提供するものである。

i. Leon Battista Alberti, *On the Art of Building in Ten Books*, translated by Joseph Rykwert, Neil Leach & Robert Tavernor, MIT Press (Cambridge, MA/London), 1988, p.156
ii. Ibid, p.24
iii. Ibid, p.163
iv. For patterns to be recognized and deciphered, patterns need to exist.
v. Zaha Hadid started in 1980. After 20 years, in 2000, Zaha Hadid Architects had only completed 3 small buildings and was employing 20 people. Currently ZHA is employing 450 people, working on about 80 projects world-wide, across all programme categories, including many large scale projects over 100,000 sqm and several above 300,000.
vi. For a more elaborate theory of styles see: Patrik Schumacher, The Autopoiesis of Architecture, Volume 1, John Wiley & Sons Ltd., London 2010.
vii. For a more elaborate account of Parametricism as Epochal Style for the 21st Century see: Patrik Schumacher, The Autopoiesis of Architecture, Volume 2, John Wiley & Sons Ltd., London 2012

i. レオン・バティスタ・アルベルティ著，『建築論』，(ジョセフ・リクワート，ニール・リーチ，ロバート・タヴァナー訳，マサチューセッツ工科大学出版局，マサチューセッツ州ケンブリッジ/ロンドン 1988年)，156頁
ii. 同上24頁
iii. 同上163頁
iv. パターンが認識され解読されるためには，まず存在する必要がある。
v. ザハ・ハディドが1980年から仕事を始めて20年後の2000年，ザハ・ハディド・アーキテクツ(ZHA)はわずか3つの建物を竣工させるだけの，20人ほどが働く事務所だった。現在，ZHAは450人が，世界中の80もの，あらゆるプログラムを横断するプロジェクトに携わっている。その中には，10万m²から30万m²に及ぶ巨大スケールのプロジェクトも含まれている。
vi. より精巧な様式理論を知るために，以下参照。パトリック・シューマッハ著『建築のオートポイエーシス(第1巻)』，(ジョン・ワイリー&ソンズ社，ロンドン，2010年) ※日本語未翻訳
vii. 同じく21世紀の画期的な様式としてのパラメトリシズムについては，パトリック・シューマッハ著，『建築のオートポイエーシス(第2巻)』，(ジョン・ワイリー&ソンズ社，ロンドン，2012年) ※日本語未翻訳

PATRIK SCHUMACHER
Born in Bonn, Germany in 1961.
　He joined Zaha Hadid Architects in 1988. He is a partner and senior designer of the practice, as well co-author of a series of major projects.
　He studied architecture at University of Stuttgart and at Southbank University in London. Completed architectural diploma and received degree Dipl.Ing. from Stuttgart University in 1990. He also studied philosophy in Bonn and London. In 1999 he received doctoral degree Dr. Phil. at Institute for Cultural Sciences at University of Klagenfurt.
　In 1996 he co-founded "Design Research Laboratory" at Architectural Association. He has taught a series of post-graduate option studios with Zaha Hadid at University of Illinois, Columbia University and at Graduate School of Design at Harvard University. Currently, he is a tenured Professor at Institute for Experimental Architecture, Innsbruck University and guest professor at University of Applied Arts in Vienna.

パトリック・シューマッハ
1961年，ドイツ・ボン生まれ。1988年にザハ・ハディド・アーキテクツに入所。事務所の共同経営者，主任デザイナーであるだけでなく，一連の主要なプロジェクトの共同設計者でもある。シュトゥットガルト大学，サウスバンク大学(ロンドン)で建築を学ぶ。1990年，シュトゥットガルト大学にて工学修士を取得。さらにボンとロンドンにて哲学を学び，クラーゲンフルト大学文化科学研究所にて哲学博士を取得。1996年，AAスクールに「デザイン・リサーチ・ラボ」を共同設立。イリノイ大学，コロンビア大学，ハーバード大学デザイン大学院にてザハ・ハディドと共に選択科目のスタジオで教鞭を執る。現在，インスブルック大学建築研究所(オーストリア)の終身教授，ウィーン応用芸術大学の教授を務める。

The Instrumentality of Appearances in the Pursuit of a Legible Urban Order

PROJECT DATA
作品データ

THE PEAK (p.22-)
Architects: Zaha Hadid Architects—Zaha Hadid, design; Michael Wolfson, Jonathon Dunn, Marianne van der Waals, N. Ayoubi, design team; Michael Wolfson, Alistair Standing, Nan Lee, Wendy Galway, presentation
Consultants: Ove Arup and Partners—David Thomlinson, structural
Program: proposal for leisure club

THE WORLD (89 DEGREES) (p.34-)
Painting

GRAND BUILDINGS, TRAFALGAR SQUARE (p.36-)
Architects: Zaha Hadid Architects—Zaha Hadid, Brian Ma Siy, design; Michael Woldson, Marianne Palme, Kar Hwa Ho, Piers Smerin, competition
Program: mixed use development

TOMIGAYA BUILDING (p.40-)
Architects: Zaha Hadid Architects—Zaha Hadid, Michael Wolfson, design; Satoshi Ohashi, project architect; Brenda MacKneson, Alistair Standing, Signy Svalastoga, Paul Brislin, Nicola Cousins, David Gomersal, Edgar Gonzalez, Erik Hemingway, Simon Koumijan, Palvi Jaaskelainen, Patrik Schumacher, design team; Daniel Chadwick, Tim Price, models
Co-architect: Hisashi Kobayashi & Associates
Client: K-One Corporation
Consultant: Ove Arup & Partners—Peter Rice, Yasuo Tamura, structural
Program: office building
Size: 238 m²

AZABU JYUBAN BUILDING (p.44-)
Architects: Zaha Hadid Architects—Zaha Hadid, Michael Wolfson, David Gomersall, Piers Smerin, David Winslow, Paivi Jaaskelainen, design; Daniel Chadwick, Tim Price, models; Satoshi Ohashi, project architect (Japan)
Project Team: Hisashi Kobayashi & Associates
Consultants: Ove Arup and Partners
Client: K-One Corporation
Program: mixed-use office building

BERLIN 2000 (p.48-)
Painting

VICTORIA CITY AERIAL (p.50-)
Architects: Zaha Hadid Architects—Zaha Hadid, design; Michael Wolfson, Nicholas Boyarski, Patrik Schumacher, Edgar Gonzalez, Paul Brislin, Nicola Cousins, Signy Svalastoga, C.J. Lim, Kim Lee Chai, Israel Nurnes, Matthew Wells, Simon Koumijan, competition team; Daniel Chadwick, model

Consultant: Ove Arup and Partners with Peter Rice, Matthew Wells, structural
Program: mixed-use development
Total floor area: approx. 75,000 m² (15 floors)

HAFENSTRASSE OFFICE & RESIDENTIAL DEVELOPMENT (p.52-)
Architects: Zaha Hadid Architects—Zaha Hadid, design; Claudia Busch, Edgar Gonzalez, Brian Langlands, Philippa Makin, Patrik Schumacher, Signy Svalastoga, Nicola Cousins, Mario Gooden, Ursula Gonsior, Vincent Marol, design team; Daniel Chadwick, model
Co architect: Mirjane Markivic Hamburg
Client: The Free Hansestadt Hamburg
Consultant: Ove Arup & Partners with Peter Rice
Program: mixed-use development
Total floor area: 871 m², corner building (8 Floors); c.2800 m², middle site building (10 floors)

KMR, ART AND MEDIA PARK (p.54-)
Architects: Zaha Hadid Architects—Zaha Hadid, design; Brett Steele, Brian Ma Siy, Paul Brislin, Cathleen Chua, John Comparelli, Elden Croy, Craig Kiner, Graeme Little, Yousif Albustani, Patrik Schumacher, Daniel Oakley, Alistair Standing, Tuta Barbosa, David Gomersall, C.J. Lim, project team; Michael Wolfson, Anthony Owen, Signy Svalastoga, Edgar Gonzales, Graig Kiner, Patrik Schumacher, Ursula Gonsinor, Bryan Langland, Ed Gaskin, Yuko Moriyama, Graeme Little, Cristrina Verissimo, Maria Rossi, Youisif Albustani, competition team; Ademir Volic, Daniel Chadwick, Richard Threadgill, models
Consultant architect: Roland Mayer Germany
Client: Kunst-und Medienzentrum Rheinhafen GmbH, Germany
Consultant: Ove Arup and Partners UK, Boll und Partner, structural; Ove Arup and Partners UK, Mornhinweg and Partner, services; Tillyard GmbH, cost consultants
Program: site development

MOON SOON (p.58-)
Archtiects: Zaha Hadid Architects—Zaha Hadid, Patrik Schumacher, design; Bill Goodwin, Shin Egashira, Kar Hwa Ho, Edgar Gonzalez, Brian Langlands, Ed Gaskin, Yuko Moriyama, Urit Luden, Craig Kiner, Dianne Hunter-Gorman, project team
Consultants: Michael Wolfson, Satoshi Ohashi, David Gomersall
Program: restaurant and bar interior design

VITRA FIRE STATION (p.68-)
Architects: Zaha Hadid Architects—Zaha Hadid, design; Patrik Schumacher, design/project architect; Simon Koumijan, Edgar Gonzalez, Kar Wha Ho, Voon Yee-Wong, Craig Kiner, Cristina Verissimo, Maria Rossi, Daniel R. Oakley, Nicola Cousins, David Gomersall, Olaf Weishaupt, design team
Local Architect: Roland Mayer
Client: Vitra International AG
Program: private firestation
Size: 852 m²

CARDIFF BAY OPERA HOUSE (p.78-)
Architects: Zaha Hadid Architects—Zaha Hadid, design; Brian Ma Siy, project architect; Patrik Schumacher, Ljiljana Blagojevic, Graham Modlen, Paul Brislin, Edgar Gonzalez, Paul Karakusevic, David Gomersall, Tomás Amat Guarinos, Wendy Ing, Paola Sanguinetti, Nunu Luan, Douglas Grieco, Woody K.T. Yao, Voon Yee-Wong, Anne Save de Beaurecueil, Simon Koumjian, Bijan Ganjei, Nicola Cousins, project team; Ademir Volic, Michael Kennedy, James Wink, model makers
Client: Cardiff Bay Opera Trust
Consultant: Ove arup and Partners UK, structural, services and acoustics; Percy Thomas Partnership, model consultant; Projects, theatre; Brett Butler-Tillyard, costing
Construction: Bovis Lehrer McGovern—Alan Lansdell
Program: proposal for opera house
Size: 25,000 m²

ROSENTHAL CENTER FOR CONTEMPORARY ART (p.82-)
Architects: Zaha Hadid Architects—Markus Dochantschi, project architect; Ed Gaskin, assistant project architect; Ana Sotrel, Jan Hübener, David Gerber, Christos Passas, Sonia Villaseca, James Lim, Jee-Eun Lee, Oliver Domeisen, Helmut Kinzler, Patrik Schumacher, Michael Wolfson, David Gomersall, project team; Shumon Basar, Oliver Domeisen, Jee-Eun Lee, Terence Koh, Marco Guarnieri, Stéphane Hof, Woody K.T. Yao, Ivan Pajares, Wassim Halabi, Nan Atichapong, Graham Modlen, competition team
Local architects: KZF incorporated
Client: The Contemporary Arts Center
Construction Manager: Turner Construction Company
Consultant: THP Limited, Jane Wernick, structural; Ove Arup & Partners, acoustics; Heapy Engineering, services; Steven R. Keller & Associates, security; Charles Cosler Theatre Design Inc., theatre; Office for Visual Interaction Inc., lighting
Program: museum
Size: 8,500 m²

MAXXI: MUSEUM OF XXI CENTURY ARTS (p.94-)
Architects: Zaha Hadid Architects—Zaha Hadid, Patrik Schumacher, design; Gianluca Racana, project architect; Anja Simons, Paolo Matteuzzi, Mario Mattia, site supervision team; Anja Simons, Paolo Matteuzzi, Fabio Ceci, Mario Mattia, Maurizio Meossi, Paolo Zilli, Luca Peralta, Maria Velceva, Matteo Grimal, Amin Taha, Caroline Voet, Gianluca Ruggeri, Luca Segarelli, design team; Ali Mangera, Oliver Domeisen, Christos Passas, Sonia Villaseca, Jee-Eun Lee, James Lim, Julia Hansel, Sara Klomps, Shumon Basar, Bergendy Cooke, Jorge Ortega, Stephane Hof, Marcus Dochantschi, Woody Yao, Graham Modlen, Jim Heverin, Barbara Kuit, Ana Sotrel, Hemendra Kothari, Zahira El Nazel, Florian Migsch, Kathy Wright, Jin Wananabe, Helmut Kinzler, competition team
Client: Italian Ministry of Culture
Consultant: ABT srl, planning; Anthony Hunt Associates, OK Design Group, structural/M&E; Max Fordham and Partners ; Equation Lighting, lighting; Paul Gilleron Acoustic, acoustic
Program: museum
Size: 30,000 m²

PHAENO SCIENCE CENTER (p.110-)
Architects: Zaha Hadid Architects—Zaha Hadid, architectural design; Christos Passas, project architect; Sara Klomps, assistant project architect; Sara Klomps, Gernot Finselbach, David Salazar, Helmut Kinzler, project team; Janne Westermann, Chris Dopheide, Stanley Lau, Eddie Can, Yoash Oster, Jan Hubener, Caroline Voet, competition team; Patrik Schumacher, special contribuor; Silvia Forlati, Guenter Barczik, Lida Charsouli, Marcus Liermann, Kenneth Bostock, Enrico Kleinke, Constanze Stinnes, Liam Young, Chris Dopheide, Barbara Kuit, Niki Neerpasch, Markus Dochantschi, contributors
Local architects: Mayer Baehrle Freie Architekten BDA—Rene Keuter, Tim Oldenburg, project architects; Sylvia Chiarappa, Stefan Hoppe, Andreas Gaiser, Roman Bockermühl, Annette Finke, Stefanie Lippardt, Marcus Liermann, Jens Hecht, Christoph Volkmar, project team
Client: Neulandgesellschaft mbH on behalf of the City of Wolfsburg
Consultants: Adams Kara Taylor, Tokarz Freirichs Leipold, structural; NEK, Buro Happold, services; Hanscomb GmbH, cost consultant; Fahlke & Dettmer, Interaction Office for Visual, lighting
Program: mixed-use centre for science
Size: 27,000 m²

LONDON AQUATICS CENTRE (p.122-)
Architects: Zaha Hadid Architects—Zaha Hadid, Patrik Schumacher, design; Jim Heverin, project director; Glenn Moorley, Sara Klomps, project architects; Alex Bilton, Alex Marcoulides, Barbara Bochnak, Carlos Garijo, Clay Shorthall, Ertu Erbay, George King, Giorgia Cannici, Hannes Schafelner, Hee Seung Lee, Kasia Townend, Nannette Jackowski, Nicolas Gdalewitch,

Seth Handley, Thomas Soo, Tom Locke, Torsten Broeder, Tristan Job, Yamac Korfali, Yeena Yoon, project team; Saffet Kaya Bekiroglu, competition architect; Agnes Koltay, Feng Chen, Gemma Douglas, Kakakrai Suthadarat, Karim Muallem, Marco Vanucci, Mariana Ibanez, Sujit Nair, competition team
Sports Architects: S+P Architects
Client: Olympic Delivery Authority
Consultants: Ove Arup & Partners, structural/services; Arup Fire, fire safety; Arup Acoustics, acoustics; Robert-Ian Van Santen Associates, facade; Arup Lighting, lighting; Winton Nightingal, kitchen design; Reef, maintenance access; Edwin Shirley Staging, temporary construction; Arup Security, security; Mark Johnson Consultants, AV+IT; Access = Design, access; Total CDM Solutions, CDM co-ordinator; Southfacing, BREEAM; CLM, quantity surveyor/project manager
Contractors: Balfour Beatty, main contractor; Finnforest Merk GmbH, timber sub-contractor; Morrisroe, concrete sub-contractor
Program: aquatics centre
Size/Area: 36,875 m^2
Total Floor Area: 29,030 m^2 (legacy mode: 3,725 m^2, basement; 15,137 m^2, ground floor; 10,168 m^2, first floor), 42,866 m^2 (olympic mode: 3,725 m^2, basement; 15,402 m^2, ground floor; 16,387 m^2, first floor; 7,352 m^2, seating area)
Footprint Area: 15,950 m^2 (legacy mode), 21,897 m^2 (olympic mode)

HEYDAR ALIYEV CENTER (p.142-)
Architects: Zaha Hadid Architects—
Zaha Hadid, Patrik Schumacher, design;
Saffet Kaya Bekiroglu, project designer/architect; Sara Sheikh Akbari, Shiqi Li, Phil Soo Kim, Marc Boles, Yelda Gin, Liat Muller, Deniz Manisali, Lillie Liu, Jose Lemos, Simone Fuchs, Jose Ramon, Tramoyeres, Yu Du, Tahmina Parvin, Erhan Patat, Fadi Mansour, Jaime Bartolome, Josef Glas, Michael Grau, Deepti Zachariah, Ceyhun Baskin, Daniel Widrig, Murat Mutlu, project team; special thanks to Charles Walker
Client: The Republic of Azerbaijan
Main contractor/architect of record: DiA Holding
Consultants: Tuncel Engineering AKT, structural; GMD Project, mechanical; HB Engineering, electrical; Werner Sobek, facade;
Etik Fire Consultancy, fire; Mezzo Stüdyo, acoustic; Enar Engineering, geotechnical;
Sigal, infrastructure; MBLD, lighting
Subcontractors and manufacturers: MERO, steel space frame; Bilim Makina, installation of space frame; Doka, formwork; Arabian Profile, external cladding panels; Lindner, internal skin cladding; Sanset İkoor, auditorium wooden cladding; Quinette, auditorium seats; Zumtobel, lighting fixtures; Baswa, special acoustic ceilings; Astas, installation of ceilings; Solarlux, multipurpose hall facade door; Bolidt, polyurethane floor finish;
Kone Elevators + Ikma, installation of elevators; MM Mühendisler Mermer, marble cladding works; HRN Dizayn, landscape LED installation;

Thyssen Group, escalator; Remak Makina, fire doors/concrete-cladded doors; Tema, gypsum panel works; MIM Mühendislik, structural steel; Elekon Enerji Sistemleri, main building lighting control system; NIS Epoksi Kaplama Sistemleri, epoxy works; Projects Group, lighting fixtures light; Limit Insaat, external skin insulations + structure; Design-build, procurement
Program: mixed-use cultural center
Auditorium capacity: 1,000
Materials: 13,000 unique fiberglass reinforced polyester panels (40,000 m^2), 3,150 fiberglass reinforced concrete panels (10,000 m^2), max 70 fiberglass reinforced polyester panels production per day, space frames (12,569 members/3,266 nodes, museum; 17,269 members/4,513 nodes, auditorium), 70,000 internal skin fixing plates, Total surface space frame area: approx. 33,000 m^2
Surface area of inner skin: over 22,000 m^2
Total length: 10,092 m (metal deck roof purlins at tender stage 3,607)
Site area: 111,292 m^2
Total area: 26,853 m^2 (metal roof deck trays at tender stage 3,936)
Roof area 39,000 m^2

**MOBILE ART -
CHANEL CONTEMPORARY ART CONTAINER** (p.150-)
Architect: Zaha Hadid Architects—
Zaha Hadid, Patrik Schumacher, design;
Thomas Vietzke, Jens Borstelmann, project architects; Helen Lee, Claudia Wulf, Erhan Patat, Tetsuya Yamasaki, Daniel Fiser, project team
Client: Chanel
Consultants: Arup, engineering; Davis Langdon, cost consultant; ES Projects, main contractor/tour operator; Stage One Creative Services Ltd., FRP manufacturing
Program: traveling exhibition pavilion designed for CHANEL
Major materials: fibre re-inforced plastic (facade cladding), PVC, ETFE roof lights (roof), steel 74 t (primary structure: 69 t pavilion and 5 t ticket office), aluminum extrusions (secondary structure), 1,752 different steel connections
Size: 700 m^2

DONGDAEMUN DESIGN PARK (p.158-)
Architects: Zaha Hadid Architects—
Zaha Hadid, Patrik Schumacher, design;
Eddie Can Chiu-Fai, project leader; Craig Kiner, Charles Walker project managers;
Kaloyan Erevinov, Martin Self, Hooman Talebi, Carlos S. Martinez, Camiel Weijenberg, Florian Goscheff, Maaike Hawinkels, Aditya Chandra, Andy Chang, Arianna Russo, Ayat Fadaifard, Josias Hamid, Shuojiong Zhang, Natalie Koerner, Jae Yoon Lee, Federico Rossi, John Klein, Chikara Inamura, Alan Lu, project team; Kaloyan Erevinov, Paloma Gormley, Hee Seung Lee, Kelly Lee, Andres Madrid, Deniz Manisali, Kevin McClellan, Claus Voigtmann,

Maurits Fennis, competition team
Client: Seoul Metropolitan Government, Seoul Design Foundation
Consultants: ARUP, structural/M.E.P.F. services engineer/lighting/acoustics; Gross Max, landscape; Group 5F, facade; Evolute, geometry; Davis Langdon & Everest, quantity surveyor
Local architects: Samoo Architects
Local consultants: Mechanical Samoo Mechanical Consulting (SMC), structural;
Samoo TEC, electrical/telecom; M&C, facade; Saegil Engineering & Consulting, civil;
Dong Sim Won, landscape;
Korean Fire Protection, fire
Program: art/exhibition halls, conference hall, design museum/design labs, design market

JOCKEY CLUB INNOVATION TOWER, HONG KONG POLYTECHNIC UNIVERSITY (p.168-)
Architects: Zaha Hadid Architects—Zaha Hadid, Patrik Schumacher, design; Woody K.T. Yao, project director; Simon Yu, project leader;
Hinki Kong, Jinqi Huang, Juan Liu, Bianca Cheung, Charles Kwan, Zhenjiang Guo, Junkai Jian, Uli Blum, project team; Hinki Kwong, Melodie Leung, Long Jiang, Zhenjiang Guo, Yang Jingwen, Miron Mutyaba, Pavlos Xanthopoulus, Margarita Yordanova Valova, competition team
Local architects: AGC Design Ltd., AD+RG (competion stage)
Client: Hong Kong Polytechnic University
Consultants: Ove Arup & Partners Hong Kong Ltd., geotechnical/structure/MEP/facade;
Team 73 Hong Kong Ltd., landscape;
Westwood Hong & Associates Ltd., acoustic
Program: school of design development
Net occupied floor area: 15,000 m^2

THE SERPENTINE SACKLER GALLERY (p.174-)
Architects: Zaha Hadid Architects—
Zaha Hadid, Patrik Schumacher, design;
Charles Walker, project director; Ceyhun Baskin, Inanc Eray, project leaders (phase 1);
Thomas Vietzke, Jens Borstelmann, project leaders (phase 2) Fabian Hecker, project leader (phase 3); Torsten Broeder, Timothy Schreiber, Laymon Thaung, David Campos, Suryansh Chandra, Matthew Hardcastle, Dillon Lin, Marina Duran Sancho, Jianghai Shen, project team (phase 2); Torsten Broeder, Anat Stern, Timothy Schreiber, Marcela Spadaro, Inanc Eray, Ceyhun Baskin, Elke Presser, Claudia Wulf, project team (phase 3);
Melodie Leung, Maha Kutay, Claudia Glas-Dorner, Evgeniya Yatsyuk, Kevin Sheppard, Carine Posner, Maria Leni Popovici, Loulwa Bohsali, Karine Yassine, Steve Blaess, restaurant mise en scene & gift shop
Conservation architects: Liam O'Connor Architects
Client: The Serpentine Trust
Consultants: Isometrix, lighting; ARUP, structural/services/fire; Sefton Horn Winch, kitchen; DP9,

planning consultants; Rise, project management; Gleeds, cost consultants/contract administrator
Program: art gallery and restaurant
Gross internal area: 1,566 m^2
Internal area (usable): 1,355 m^2
Building footprint: 1,328 m^2

BEIJING CBD CORE AREA (p.178-)
Architects: Zaha Hadid Architects—
Zaha Hadid, Patrik Schumacher, design;
Tiago Correia, project director;
Victor Orive, Danilo Arsic, project architects;
Paulo Flores, Thomas Buseck, Mostafa El Sayed, Yevgeniya Pozigun, Tobi Adamolekun, Ines Fontoura, Fabiano Continanza, Alejandro Diaz, Rafael Gonzalez, Ines Fontoura, Shajay Bhooshan, Maria Tsironi, Spyridon Kaprinis, Xiaosheng Li, Rafael Contreras, Andrea B. Caste, Giuseppe Morando, Edgar Payan, Maren Klasing, Seda Zirek, Yuxi Fu, Torsten Broeder, Kaloyan Erevinov, project team
Program: masterplan and tower design

NEW NATIONAL STADIUM OF JAPAN (p.184-)
Architects: Zaha Hadid Architects—Zaha Hadid, Patrik Schumacher, design; Jim Heverin, project director; Paulo Flores, Yoshi Uchiyama, project architects; Irene Guerra, Junyi Wang, Takehiko Iseki, Dillon Lin, Alberto Barba, Ai Sato, Ben Kikkawa, Tetsuya Yamasaki, Carlos Michel-Medina, Antonio Monserrat, Fernando Poucell, Rafael Contreras, Karoly Markos, Cristiano Ceccato, project team
Sports architects: Arup Associates—
Clive Lewis, Nick Birmingham
Designers: Nikken Sekkei + Azusa Sekkei + Nihon Sekkei + Arup Japan JV
Client: Japan Sports Council
Program: athletics stadium

**EXHIBITION "ZAHA HADID"
TOKYO OPERA CITY ART GALLERY**
Exhibition design: Zaha Hadid Architects—
Zaha Hadid, Patrik Schumacher, design;
Woody Yao, exhibition co-curator/design;
Maha Kutay, Margarita Valova, Yoshi Uchiyama, Olga Yatsyuk, Johanna Huang, Zhenjiang Guo, Paulo Flores, Alia Faisal Zayani, Claudia Fruianu, project team; Manon Janssens, exhibition coordinator; Henry Virgin, video installation
Exhibition co-curator: Shino Nomura (Tokyo Opera City Art Gallery)
Exhibits: Moon Soon Furniture—
Satoshi Ohashi, Yang Jingwen, Chu I Iachimoto
Azabu Jyuban and Tomigaya Building Models—
Satoshi Ohashi, Yang Jingwen, Di Ding, Rhina Portillo, Matthias Urschler
National Stadium Model and Renders—
Paulo Flores, Yoshi Uchiyama, Fernando Poucell, Junyi Wang
With the kind support of:
David Gill Galleries, Slamp, United Nude
3D interactive installation: Dassault, sponsored

Credits

―

和訳：

菊池泰子：pp.013-020, p.100, p.173 / 谷理佐：pp.134-140, pp.221-235

原田勝之：p.034, p.039, p.043, p.047, p.048, p.050, p.052, pp.128-129 / 上野黄：p.081, p.089, pp.148-149, p.153, pp.162-163, p.176

林陽一郎：p.007, p.194, p.196, p.198, p.200, p.202, p.204, p.206, p.208, p.210, p.212, p.214, p.216 / 川島奈々未：p.054, p.061, p.075, p.183

編集部：p.032, p.112, p.218

―

Photographs except as noted: GA photographers

p.014, p.017, p.018, p.058, pp.064-067, pp.068-071, pp.074-077, pp.082-084, pp.086-099, p.101, pp.104-111, pp.113-121, pp.136-137, p.139, Yukio Futagawa /

pp.122-124, pp.126-127, pp.130-132, p.174, pp.176-177, Yoshio Futagawa /

pp.150-156 (except 3 images on the left of p.154), pp.158-161, pp.164-167, Katsumasa Tanaka /

p.040, p.041, pp.046-047, p.059, p.157, GA Photographers

–

Renderings and architectural drawings: Zaha Hadid Architects

Interview 1995 (pp.012-020) is reprinted from *GA DOCUMENT EXTRA 03 ZAHA HADID*

Interview 2007 (pp.133-140) is reprinted from *GA DOCUMENT 99*

インタヴュー 1995 (pp.012-020)は『GA DOCUMENT EXTRA 03 ザハ・ハディド』，

インタヴュー 2007 (pp.133-140)は『GA DOCUMENT 99』を再録

ZAHA HADID

ザハ・ハディド

2014年9月25日発行

企画・編集：二川由夫

撮影：GA photographers

デザイン：GA design center

印刷・製本：シナノ印刷株式会社

発行：エーディーエー・エディタ・トーキョー

東京都渋谷区千駄ヶ谷3-12-14

TEL.(03)3403-1581(代)

禁無断転載

ISBN 978-4-87140-688-8 C1052